THE IMPORT OF ESCHATOLOGY
IN JOHN HOWARD YODER'S
CRITIQUE OF CONSTANTINIANISM

Editorial Inquiries:

Mellen Research University Press
534 Pacific Avenue
San Francisco, California 94133

Order Fulfillment:

The Edwin Mellen Press
Box 450
Lewiston, New York 14092

THE IMPORT OF ESCHATOLOGY
IN JOHN HOWARD YODER'S
CRITIQUE OF CONSTANTINIANISM

Philip LeMasters

MELLEN RESEARCH UNIVERSITY PRESS
San Francisco

Library of Congress Cataloging-in-Publication Data

LeMasters, Philip, 1964-
    The import of eschatology in John Howard Yoder's critique of
Constantinianism / Philip LeMasters.
        p.   cm.
    Originally presented as the author's thesis (Ph. D.).
    Includes bibliographical references and index.
    ISBN 0-7734-9807-9
    1. Yoder, John Howard. 2. Eschatology--History of doctrines--20th
century. 3. Christian ethics--History--20th century. 4. Social
ethics--History--20th century. 5. Church and the world--History of
doctrines--20th century. I. Title.
BX8143.Y59L46 1992
241'.0443--dc20   91-44635
                                                     CIP

Printed in the United States of America

To my parents:

Joy and Claude LeMasters

TABLE OF CONTENTS

FOREWORD

The customary expectation of a mentor's modesty in acknowledging the accomplishment of a former student and teaching assistant deserves, now and then, to be renounced; so it is with great pleasure, and not a little pride, that I write this foreword to Professor Philip LeMasters' doctoral dissertation. Early on in its writing, I suggested to the author that this was a publishable project if he persevered in sometimes tedious research, overcame an uncommon set of adverse circumstances, and managed to complete this ambitious project. I think that his study of the import of eschatology in John Howard Yoder's critique of Constantinianism attests to his achievement. This is a mature work of critical theological scholarship, and I am delighted that the editors of the Distinguished Dissertation Series of Mellen Research University Press agree that it is deserving of publication.

Let me say more precisely why this is an important study, and how that is evident in several ways and at different points on the theological compass. First of all, LeMasters has rigorously examined a heretofore largely neglected theme of central importance in Yoder's approach to Christian social ethics. Although some earlier studies have made brief reference to Yoder's eschatology and its relationship to his critique of Constantinianism, no previous investigation has undertaken a thorough, exacting analysis of these themes. The dissertation is particularly helpful in demonstrating how Yoder's eschatology and view of Constantinianism may not be understood well apart from an analysis of their relationships to his views on scripture, christology, ecclesiology, and the moral life. By showing how these several topics are systematically related in Yoder's thought, LeMasters has made a significant contribution to the interpretation of Yoder's entire theological project. To my knowledge, this dissertation provides the most comprehensive analysis of Yoder's work to date.

A second achievement of this dissertation is that it does an outstanding job of evaluating Yoder's project. By treating Yoder within the larger contexts of the history of Christian thought and of Anabaptism, twentieth-century Protestant theology, and contemporary Christian ethics in North America, LeMasters has placed Yoder's contributions in a variety of illuminating contexts; and this, in turn, has permitted some well-warranted judgments about the relative coherence and appropriateness of Yoder's commitments, both methodological and substantive. LeMasters places Yoder under sympathetic yet perceptive scrutiny, noting points of strength and weakness, of coherence and contradiction, of sound reason and theological imprecision. Drawing from his impressive knowledge of Yoder's writings, as well as from an extensive bibliography of secondary sources encompassing a variety of scholarly fields, LeMasters provides an evenhanded yet rigorous assessment of Yoder's work.

I think it worth noting, as a third reason for regarding this an important study, that LeMasters has assembled an impressive bibliography of Yoder's published works to date, together with a thorough listing of important secondary works. Altogether this is a comprehensive catalog of relevant materials which will be of great assistance to other scholars who wish to pursue Yoder studies.

Finally, LeMasters' treatment of Yoder has significant implications not only for Yoder studies and related interests but for a broader range of issues in contemporary discourse on Christian ethics. For example, this is plainly evident in the study's focus on moral reasoning in light of the larger question of the relationship between church and world. Many contemporary voices assert that the church fell from an almost pristine state of grace with the conversion of Constantine, and that the life of the people of God has been woefully distorted since that time by a morally dubious alignment of the church with the corrupt institutions of the world. LeMasters demonstrates that Yoder's argument, which is along these lines, suffers from a lack of historical precision in his view of the pre-Constantinian church, of the life of Constantine, and of the subsequent "Constantinian" history of Christianity.

The dissertation shows that it is not sufficient simply to toss around the descriptive term "Constantinian" without displaying in precise detail how and why such an explicitly historical reference is appropriate to the issue at hand. In light of this critique, LeMasters invites those sympathetic to Yoder's point of view to approach "the Constantinian shift" in a more historically precise and sophisticated way.

Further to that broader range of issues in contemporary discourse on Christian ethics is LeMasters' criticism of Yoder's proposed alternative to Constantinianism, viz., a visible church which is distinct from the world through its faithfulness and obedience to the way of Jesus. Like many others who lament what they see as the continuing influence of Constantine on Christian social ethics, Yoder calls for a communally located ethics of discipleship which is to be a radiant embodiment of God's reign among human beings in a way which is uncorrupted by cooperation with the fallen powers of the world. LeMasters shows that Yoder's ecclesiology displays a lack of historical and sociological precision in his description of this morally rigorous church.

Failing to provide a thick description of when such a church existed in the past, what such a church would look like today, and precisely what sort of practices such a faithful community would require for its maintenance, Yoder does not succeed in identifying a viable historical alternative to the allegedly corrupt church of Constantine. LeMasters' critique argues that theologians who want to describe the church in abstract and ideal terms are obliged to display their alternative ecclesiologies with historical and sociological precision if they wish to be considered real and serious alternatives to the corrupt status quo.

I believe that this work is also instructive for those who, like Yoder, want to use the image of discipleship as the dominant metaphor for the Christian moral life. Yoder suggests that Christians pursue the discipleship of Jesus in a manner uncompromised by concerns for effectiveness in managing the structures and affairs of the world. But LeMasters demonstrates that Yoder's recommendations for Christian political action call for compromising obedience to Jesus -- on Yoder's own terms -- in order to foster worldly involvement and reform. With that account, LeMasters believes that he has identified a major methodological flaw in Yoder's work and a pivotal issue for other Christian ethicists who venture to make discipleship the presiding metaphor for the moral life.

Of course, central to all of this is Yoder's use of scripture. LeMasters' work claims that Yoder's self-espoused hermeneutic of "Biblical Realism" presents an inadequate view of the Bible for constructive theological work. This is the case, in LeMasters' account, largely because of Yoder's failure to provide for a variety of interpretative complexities which are not easily overcome by recourse to a "what the text says" approach to biblical hermeneutics. Readers who are interested in the use of the Bible in Christian ethics will find LeMasters' critique of Yoder on this point interesting and instructive.

As an exercise in theological ethics, and yet another indication of this dissertation's utility for the larger disciplines of Christian ethics, LeMasters' emphasis on the ethical importance of eschatology deserves special notice. Throughout the twentieth century, there has been renewed interest in eschatology and ethics in various forms and contexts; and figures as noteworthy -- and as different as -- Albert Schweitzer, Karl Barth, Oscar Cullmann, Rudolph Bultmann, and Reinhold Niebuhr have given this matter their explicit attention. LeMasters' dissertation examines Yoder's stance on eschatology and ethics in light of his reliance on, and arguments with, such influential scholars as these; and it will engage scholars whose interests embrace the contemporary relevance of debates on eschatology from the earlier decades of this century onwards.

I ought not neglect to say that to my knowledge this is the first major scholarly study to focus exclusively on the ethical project of a contemporary Anabaptist figure in North America. By examining Yoder's work in light of his own denominational tradition, and by bringing him into conversation with scholars from other communions, LeMasters has made a move toward studying Anabaptist ethics within an ecumenical context. Given the often withdrawn image of Anabaptist scholarship, this seems to me a noble and original proposal.

I will be somewhat surprised if LeMasters' dissertation does not become a commended text for future Yoder studies. It is a work of mature theological scholarship which should interest a wide audience in Christian theological and social ethics.

Harmon L. Smith

Professor of Moral Theology
The Divinity School
Duke University
Durham, North Carolina

PREFACE

I begin this preface with a strong word of thanks to several individuals without whose help this project could not have been completed. First on the list is Professor Harmon L. Smith, of Duke University, who supervised my research and writing with both a caring, conscientious spirit and a precise, rigorous frame of mind. Professor Smith has been my advocate, teacher, critic, and friend. On many occasions, he has gone out of his way to be of assistance to me in the production of this manuscript. He has given selflessly of his time, energy, and wisdom on my behalf. Professor Smith is a fine Christian scholar and teacher, and I will always be in his debt for his exemplary performance as my dissertation advisor.

I thank Professors Frederick Herzog, Marshall R. Roderick, Thomas A. Langford, and Geoffrey Wainwright for serving on my dissertation committee. Through their encouragement, advice, and conscientious criticism, they contributed much to the project. I am also grateful to Professor Stanley Hauerwas and Mr. Mark Nation for their bibliographic assistance with this study. They shared generously of their knowledge of Yoder's writings and of the relevant secondary literature, and consequently facilitated my work.

I am especially appreciative of the decision of the editors of Mellen Research University Press to publish this manuscript in the Distinguished Dissertation Series. I am also grateful to the Graduate School, the J. Allen Easley Fund, and the Samuel T. Robinson Fund, all of Wake Forest University, for their generous financial support of this publication project. Professor Fred Horton, also of Wake Forest, likewise deserves credit for his technical help in putting the dissertation into final form.

The author of any work of scholarship owes a large debt to those who have gone before him or her in examining the topic in question. In the research and writing of this manuscript, I have found the previous dissertations written in part on Yoder to be of invaluable assistance. The bibliography of Yoder's published works which was compiled by Professor Gayle Gerber Koontz was especially helpful for my research.

In my estimation, this study of the import of eschatology in Yoder's critique of Constantinianism has scholarly significance at a number of levels. First, it is a clearly original project, as no previous study has analyzed Yoder's eschatology or his critique of Constantinianism in great detail. Indeed, no previous doctoral dissertation has, to my knowledge, focused exclusively on any aspect of Yoder's work. Since Yoder is a major figure in contemporary Christian ethics, a project of this sort is a needed contribution to the analysis of his thought.

Second, the dissertation examines several topics in Yoder's thought which have systematic importance for his views of eschatology and of Constantinianism, ranging from his use of the Bible in ethics to his view of the church. As such, the manuscript is a sound introduction to Yoder's entire project, and provides an evaluation of Yoder on a number of theological and moral issues.

Third, the dissertation provides a comprehensive bibliography of Yoder's publications through 1990, as well as a listing of major secondary sources on Yoder. I certainly hope that the bibliography will be of use to other scholars who wish to pursue Yoder studies.

Fourth, the dissertation focuses on a figure who identifies with a "marginalized" theological and moral tradition, Anabaptism. Yoder's denominational tradition and his intellectual project are sometimes caricatured by scholars in "mainline" traditions who seem to want Anabaptism to function simply as an example of dubious religious thought and practice. This project gives Yoder the respect which his project is due by examining an aspect of his work rigorously and fairly. The conclusions of the study are quite critical of Yoder in many respects. As such, they represent demands for greater intellectual precision in the construction of a Christian social ethic which is strongly informed by Anabaptist tradition.

I am a Baptist whose approach to Christian ethics has been influenced in important ways by Yoder and Anabaptism. Hence, my criticisms of Yoder are likewise intellectual challenges to myself. Though I have not yet begun work on my next book, I am envisioning a study which would outline an ethic of discipleship in a way that avoids the main methodological flaws which the present work finds in Yoder's project.

For example, I criticize Yoder for describing an ethic of discipleship as entailing pure obedience to the way of Jesus without concern for effectiveness in transforming society, while at the same time suggesting that Christians tailor their political action in secular society according to a standard of effectiveness. The crux of the problem is that Yoder criticizes Constantinians for calling the world to embody a moral standard less rigorous than agape, even though his own political strategy lessens the requirements of agape for the sake of communicating effectively with the rulers of society. In this respect, Yoder's project is more concerned with effective political strategizing than he would like to admit. An important task on my agenda is formulating an ethic of discipleship which relaxes this point of tension between obedience and effectiveness in Christian social ethics.

Another of my central criticisms of Yoder concerns his ideal, abstract portrait of the church as a community of faithfulness to Jesus which is uncorrupted by the perverse influences of the world. Yoder contrasts his morally rigorous view of the church with the Constantinian approach to the church as something like the religious branch of the dominant social order which compromises fidelty to the Gospel for the sake of strengthening the larger society. The problem is that Yoder never provides a sufficiently displayed acccount of this rigorous church. Apart from showing in concrete and specific detail how such communities function, and are sustained and reproduced socially, Yoder's ecclesiological discourse seems too ideal to be of much use in describing with precision the moral import of the church in any given time and place in human history. Given the extremely important role of the community of faith for the Christian life in Anabaptist tradition, this is a major shortcoming in Yoder's work.

In this light, another issue which I hope to examine at a later date is precisely this question of the moral significance of the church. I am interested in finding a way to speak of the church as central to the moral life, and distinct from the world, without resorting to illusory and mystifying language about what it means for the church to be faithful to the way of Jesus.

Throughout these, as well as other criticisms of Yoder which I raise in the dissertation, there runs a common thread of tension between his concern for Christian moral reasoning to be faithful to the way of Jesus and capable of addressing social issues in secular society. Yoder seeks to find a way of showing how such political action may be of a piece with Jesus' ministry of God's kingdom, often by suggesting that Christians should call "the powers" of the world to do good and not evil. As the risen Christ is Lord over the rebellious world, Yoder thinks that Christians may call the world to serve its Lord by embodying a realistic level of justice. The ultimate standard of agape is, in his account, too high a goal to be a working norm of moral judgement for the sinful world.

A methodological problem for Yoder is whether his portrait of "the politics of Jesus" has a sufficiently "realistic" orientation to function coherently as a warrant for this sort of worldly political involvement. In other words, it is not clear that Yoder's Christological commitments lend themselves to, or provide coherent support for, the sort of political praxis which he recommends for Christians. Were the political involvement of Christians to be focused on the imitation of Jesus' unambiguous proclamation of the demands of God's reign for human life, which includes non-violence, it would be hard to see how urging the state to abide by just war standards, which Yoder does, would be an appropriate political strategy. Once again, it appears that Yoder is caught between an extremely rigorous style of moral reasoning, which requires pacifism, and the desire to give moral guidance to the state, for which he knows that pacifism is simply not a realistic option.

The tension between the demands of Christianity's high moral ideals and the apparent necessities of pragmatic involvement in the fallen world seems to be one of the characteristics of moral reasoning "between the times" of the inauguration and the consummation of God's reign. It is to Yoder's credit that he has raised such issues so forcefully; it is a weakness of his approach that there exist serious points of tension in his constructive proposals. In large part, this dissertation is an invitation to other scholars to attend with greater precision and exactitude to these very issues of the import of the eschatology for Christian ethics.

Philip LeMasters

Visiting Assistant Professor of
of Religion
Wake Forest University
Winston-Salem, NC

THE IMPORT OF ESCHATOLOGY IN JOHN HOWARD YODER'S CRITIQUE OF CONSTANTINIANISM

CHAPTER 1

INTRODUCTION:

THE PRESENT PROJECT WITHIN THE CONTEXT OF YODER STUDIES

This dissertation analyzes the import of eschatology for John Howard Yoder's critique of Constantinianism. Toward that end, it will describe Yoder's eschatological commitments, together with the hermeneutical assumptions which sustain them. It will demonstrate, moreover, how his eschatology shapes and informs his description and critique of Constantinianism, and it will test his formulation at various points for internal coherence. In an effort to show the practical relevance of Yoder's critique, we will also examine his alternative account of why and how Christians may participate in the affairs of secular society.

Constantinianism is a crucially important metaphor in Yoder's thought for the perversion of Christian ethics, which is symbolized by the conversion of Constantine in the fourth century A. D. and signified by the identification of church and empire. Yoder's rejection of Constantinianism is a prominent theme throughout his writings.[1] This study analyzes how Yoder's eschatology shapes his critique of this approach to Christian ethics.

This chapter introduces the present project by placing it within the larger context of: (1) Yoder's significance in contemporary Christian ethics; (2) Yoder's intellectual biography; (3) the present state of research on Yoder; and (4) a brief justification of the project.

Yoder's Significance in Contemporary Christian Ethics

That Yoder is a significant figure in contemporary Christian ethics is clear from the amount of serious scholarly attention which his work receives.[2]

---

[1]John Howard Yoder, "The Constantinian Sources of Western Social Ethics," The Priestly Kingdom: Social Ethics as Gospel (Notre Dame, Indiana: University of Notre Dame, 1984), 135-147. See also his "The Disavowal of Constantine: An Alternative Perspective on Interfaith Dialogue," Annals 1975/76 (Tantur: Ecumenical Institute for Advanced Theological Studies, 1979): 48ff.; "The Otherness of the Church," The Mennonite Quarterly Review 35 (October 1961): 286-296; Christian Attitudes to War, Peace, and Revolution: A Companion to Bainton (Elkhart, Indiana: Goshen Biblical Seminary, 1982), 37ff.; The Christian Witness to the State (Newton, Kansas: Faith and Life Press, 1964), 55ff.; "If Christ Is Truly Lord," The Original Revolution (Scottdale, Pennsylvania: Herald Press, 1971), 52-84; and "The Christian Case for Democracy," The Priestly Kingdom, 151-171.

[2]See, for example, the discussions of Yoder's work by James Gustafson, Ethics from a Theocentric Perspective, vol. 1 (Chicago: University of Chicago Press, 1981), 74-76; Paul Ramsey, Speak Up for Just War or Pacifism (University Park, Pennsylvania: The Pennsylvania State University Press, 1988), 96-113, 115-122; James McClendon, Jr. Ethics: Systematic Theology, vol. 1 (Nashville: Abingdon Press, 1986), 73-75; Stanley Hauerwas, The Peaceable Kingdom (Notre Dame, Indiana: The University of Notre Dame Press, 1983), 123-127; J. Philip Wogaman, A Christian Method of Moral Judgment (Philadelphia: Westminster Press, 1976), 33ff.; Allen Verhey, The Great Reversal: Ethics and the New Testament (Grand Rapids, Michigan: William B. Eerdmans Publishing Company, 1984), 162, 165; Edward LeRoy Long, A Survey of Recent Christian Ethics (New York: Oxford University Press, 1982), 90-94; Bruce Birch and Larry Rasmussen, Bible and Ethics in the Christian Life (Minneapolis, Minnesota: Augsburg Publishing House, 1976), 17ff. Doctoral dissertations in which Yoder is a major figure include: Michael Cartwright, "Practices, Politics, and Performance: Toward a Communal Hermeneutic for Christian Ethics." (Ph.D. diss., Duke University, 1988); David Michael Hughes, "The Ethical Use of Power: A Discussion with the Christian Perspectives of Reinhold Niebuhr, John Howard Yoder, and Richard J. Barnet." (Ph.D. diss., The Southern Baptist Theological Seminary, 1984); Gayle Gerber Koontz, "Confessional Theology in a Pluralistic Context: A Study of the Theological Ethics of H. Richard Niebuhr and John H. Yoder." (Ph.D. diss., Boston University, 1985); John Erickson McEntyre, "The Increasing Significance of Symbolic Resistance in Selected Fiction from 'War and Peace' to 'Mila 18'." (Ph.D. diss., Graduate Theological

(continued...)

Yoder's work receives such attention, in large part, due to the distinctiveness of his approach. James McClendon comments that Yoder is "the bete noir of contemporary moral theology, especially of mainline Protestant ethics." McClendon describes him in this way because Yoder, in clear contrast to presiding modes of Christian ethics in this century, argues that "the eschatological Jesus" of the New Testament is directly relevant for social ethics.[3]

Yoder's distinctiveness is suggested by his description and critique of "the conventional wisdom" among Christian ethicists about Jesus' significance for the moral life.[4] In the early pages of his The Politics of Jesus: Vicit Agnus Noster, Yoder lists six widely accepted reasons for the common assumption that "Jesus is simply not relevant in any immediate sense to the questions of social

---

[2](...continued)
Union, 1981); Robert M. Parham, III, "An Ethical Analysis of the Christian Social Strategies in the Writings of John C. Bennett, Jacques Ellul, and John H. Yoder." (Ph.D. diss., Baylor University, 1984); Jozef M. L. Van Gerwen, "The Church in the Theological Ethics of Stanley Hauerwas." (Ph.D. diss., Graduate Theological Union, 1984); Milo Dean Van Veldhuizen, "'Philanthropia' in Philo of Alexandria: A Scriptural Perspective." (Ph.D. diss., University of Notre Dame, 1982); Charles Wayne Scriven, "The Transformation of Culture: Christian Social Ethics after H. Richard Niebuhr," (Ph.D. diss., Graduate Theological Union, 1985); Brent Philip Waters, "A Christian Understanding of and Response to Violent Revolution." (D. Min. diss., School of Theology at Claremont, 1984); Joel Andrew Zimbleman, "Theological Ethics and Politics in the Thought of Juan Luis Segundo and John Howard Yoder." (Ph.D. diss., University of Virginia, 1986).

[3]McClendon, Ethics: Systematic Theology, 1:73. See, for example, H. Richard Niebuhr's discussion of the "Christ against Culture" paradigm in his Christ and Culture (New York: Harper & Row Publishers, 1951), 45-82; and Reinhold Niebuhr's treatment of "The Ethic of Jesus" in An Interpretation of Christian Ethics (New York: The Seabury Press, 1979, first published 1935), 22-38. Each portrays an ethic of the discipleship of Jesus in a fashion that makes it an inappropriate model for guiding Christian social involvement. Koontz analyzes the disagreement between Yoder and H. Richard Niebuhr on this point in her "Confessional Theology in Pluralistic Context: A Study of the Theological Ethics of H. Richard Niebuhr and John H. Yoder," 89ff.

[4]See Hughes' treatment of Yoder's significance in this respect in his "The Ethical Significance of Power: A Discussion with the Christian Perspectives of Reinhold Niebuhr, John Howard Yoder, and Richard J. Barnet," 116ff.; as well as Cartwright, "Practices, Politics, and Performance: Toward a Communal Hermeneutic for Christian Ethics," 2ff.

ethics."[5]   First, he notes the "interim ethic" interpretation of Jesus' moral relevance:

> It is possible for the apocalyptic Sermonizer on the Mount to be unconcerned for the survival of the structures of a solid society because he thinks the world is passing away soon. His ethical teachings therefore appropriately pay no attention to society's need for survival and for the patient construction of permanent institutions. The rejection of violence, of self-defense, and of accumulating wealth for the sake of security, and the footlooseness of the prophet of the kingdom are not permanent and generalizable attitudes toward social values, but make sense only if it be assumed that those values are coming to an imminent end. Thus at any point where social ethics must deal with problems of duration, Jesus quite clearly can be of no help.[6]

Yoder suggests that a second common way of establishing Jesus' moral irrelevance is to describe him, "as his Franciscan and Tolstoyan imitators have said," as "a simple rural figure." In this approach, Jesus' "radical personalization of all ethical problems is only possible in a village sociology where knowing everyone and having time to treat everyone as a person is culturally an available possibility." Given this sociological limitation on the relevance of his ethic, Jesus is not directly relevant "to the problems of complex organization, of institutions and offices, cliques and power and crowds."[7]

A third option affirms that, while "Jesus and his early followers lived in a world over which they had no control," Christians, at least in the West, have a responsibility, "inconceivable in Jesus' situation," for the management of

---

[5]Yoder, The Politics of Jesus: Vicit Agnus Noster (Grand Rapids, Michigan: William B. Eerdmans Publishing Company, 1972), 15.

[6]Yoder comments that "The classic American statement of the dependence of Jesus' ethic upon his expectation of an early end to history was Reinhold Niebuhr's Interpretation of Christian Ethics (New York: Harper, 1935)." Yoder, The Politics of Jesus, 16. The notion of an interim ethics was first espoused by Albert Schweitzer, The Quest for the Historical Jesus (New York: MacMillan Company, 1968, first published 1910), 367ff. Paul Ramsey also interprets Jesus' call for non-resistance in this eschatological light in his Basic Christian Ethics (Chicago and London: The University of Chicago Press, 1950), 35.

[7]Yoder, The Politics of Jesus, 16-17.

society. The duty to exercise that responsibility well undercuts the significance of Jesus for social ethics, as it entails that Jesus simply was not concerned with what is now the most important moral task of Christians.[8]

A fourth orientation describes "Jesus' message" as "ahistorical by definition," in the sense that "He dealt with spiritual and not social matters, with the existential and not the concrete." In this approach, Jesus clearly has no direct significance for social ethics.[9]

The fifth common assumption is that Jesus was "a radical monotheist" who taught a "radical discontinuity ...between the world and God" of the sort that relativized all human and social values before the holy otherness of God. As "the practical import of that relativizing, for the substance of ethics, is that these [human] values become autonomous," Jesus' example and teaching do not, in this approach, provide direct guidance for human relations.[10]

The sixth, and final, dominant view is that Jesus' life, death, and resurrection were "a forensic act," the significance of which is the "the work of atonement or the gift of justification." From this perspective, Jesus' task was purely the working of our salvation, "but never shall it be correlated with

---

[8]Yoder, The Politics of Jesus, 17. As examples of this position, he cites Ramsey, Basic Christian Ethics, 167ff. and Ernest C. Colwell, Jesus and the Gospel (New York: Oxford Press, 1963), 47, 60. See also Yoder's critique of the language of responsibility in "Reinhold Niebuhr and Christian Pacifism," The Mennonite Quarterly Review 29 (April 1955): 113.

[9]Yoder, The Politics of Jesus, 17-18. Yoder lists as his example of this orientation Roger Mehl, "The Basis of Christian Social Ethics" in John C. Bennett, ed., Christian Social Ethics in a Changing World (New York: Association, 1966), 44ff.

[10] Yoder, The Politics of Jesus, 18. Yoder comments on this orientation that it "is the central thrust of H. Richard Niebuhr already in his Christ and Culture (New York: Harper, 1951), esp. pp. 234ff, and further in his Radical Monotheism and Western Culture (Harper, 1960), and The Responsible Self (Harper, 1963)." See Yoder's unpublished manuscript, "How Richard Niebuhr Reasons: A Critique of Christ and Culture," for his most detailed analysis of this position.

ethics."[11]

Yoder observes that the common thrust of these several approaches is their claim that Jesus, as portrayed in the New Testament, does not have direct relevance for the moral life. They suggest that

> it cannot have been his [Jesus'] intention...to provide any precise guidance in the field of ethics. His apocalypticism and his radical monotheism may teach us to be modest; his personalism may teach us to cherish the values of face-to-face relationships, but as to the stuff of our decision-making we shall have to have other sources of help.[12]

In opposition to this conclusion, which he suggests is presiding among contemporary Christian ethicists, Yoder argues that "the claims of Jesus are best understood as presenting to men not the avoidance of political options, but one particular social-political-ethical option."[13] For Yoder, this is the option of discipleship, of following Jesus as the basic task of the moral life.[14]

James Gustafson comments that Yoder's work is important precisely because of this stress "on the teachings of Jesus in the gospels, and on the call to discipleship to Jesus." Moreover, he observes that

> What is important to note is that Yoder...is not ashamed to be distinctively Christian, and in effect claims that Christian morality is the morality of Christian persons...Christians have a particular

---

[11]Yoder, The Politics of Jesus, 19. Unlike his discussions of the other presiding views of Christian ethics, Yoder does not cite an example of this purely "forensic" approach. Oliver O'Donovan identifies, and rejects, what appears to be a similarly amoral approach to the Christian life in his critique of "antinomianism...the holding of the Christian faith in a way that expresses disregard, or insufficient regard, for moral questions. [This approach suggests] that morality is not part of the good news that Christians welcome and proclaim." See O'Donovan, Resurrection and Moral Order: An Outline for Evangelical Ethics (Grand Rapids, Michigan: William B. Eerdmans Publishing Company, 1986), 11-12.

[12]Yoder, The Politics of Jesus, 19.

[13]Yoder, The Politics of Jesus, 23.

[14]Yoder suggests that "The real issue is not whether Jesus can make sense in a world far from Galilee, but whether--when he meets us in our world, as he does in fact--we want to follow him." Yoder, "'But We Do See Jesus,'" The Priestly Kingdom, 62.

vocation; they are called to a particular obedience to a particular person who is known through texts written at a particular time long ago....My conviction is that all constructive theology in the Christian tradition needs to be defined to some extent in relation to this radical option...I note Yoder's option here because it is the one most dramatically different from the option that I shall pursue.[15]

Yoder's approach to Christian ethics appears distinctive in comparison with the work of "mainline Protestant" ethicists such as the Niebuhrs, Ramsey, and Gustafson, in large part because of his clear identification with Anabaptism.[16] Indeed, Yoder describes his historic tradition in a fashion that highlights themes which are prominent throughout his publications.

It is one trait of the [Anabaptist emphasis on the] "visibility" of the church that it is not possible to distinguish Christian morality from belief. "Discipleship" was a major dimension of the Anabaptist understanding of what faith means; there is no faith and no church without following Christ in one's life. With a view to the structure of the church, this means that the church is a voluntary community. With regard to the logic of ethical thinking, it means that Christian behavior is Christological, drawing its guidance not from a set of general philosophical principles nor a collection of codified precise obligations, but from the person and the teachings of Jesus.[17]

Yoder is perhaps the first Mennonite ethicist to bring the theological and moral distinctives of his tradition, with its emphases on discipleship and non-violence, into dialogue with the "mainstream" of Christian ethics in North America. Ronald J. Sawatsky comments that

Speaking historically, Yoder is but a sign of the Mennonite recovery from a sectarian retreat to an open witness to the nonresistant Gospel...Yoder has been consciously ecumenical...His

---

[15]Gustafson, Ethics from a Theocentric Perspective, 1: 74-75.

[16]See William F. Storrar's treatment of Yoder as an Anabaptist ethicist in "The State and War in a Nuclear Age," The Scottish Bulletin of Evangelical Theology 3 (Spring 1985): 60ff.

[17]Yoder, "The Recovery of the Anabaptist Vision," Concern Pamphlet #18 (Scottdale, Pennsylvania: Concern, 1971), 14.

is not, however, an ecumenism which weakens the tradition, rather the very opposite is true. It is the imperative to call all Christians to unqualified obedience to Jesus Christ that motivates this ecumenical dialogue.[18]

While Yoder argues for an ethic of discipleship which is clearly shaped by his "'radical reformation' confession," he insists that his view "is founded in Scripture and catholic tradition, and is pertinent today as a call for all Christian believers."[19] A sign of Yoder's competence as a spokesperson for his tradition is that the interpretation of his work is a decisive factor in the disagreement over the appropriateness of Christian pacifism by Methodist theologians Paul Ramsey and Stanley Hauerwas.[20]

In addition to the significance of his arguments for pacifism and an ethic of discipleship, Yoder is noteworthy for his communitarian ecclesiology which envisions a visible church as the social locus of the moral life of the Christian. Again in line with Anabaptism, he notes that "Voluntary commitment to a community distinct from the total society provides resources for practical moral reasoning of a kind which are by definition unthinkable where that option is not offered."[21] Says Yoder,

> The church is herself a society. Her very existence, the fraternal relations of her members, their ways of dealing with their differences and their needs are, or rather should be, a demonstration of what love means in social relations. This demonstration cannot be transposed directly into non-Christian society, for in the church it functions only on the basis of repentance and faith; yet by analogy certain of its aspects may be

---

[18]Rodney J. Sawatsky, "John Howard Yoder," in Non-Violence: Central to Christian Spirituality, ed. Joseph T. Culliton, Toronto Studies in Theology, vol. 8 (New York: The Edwin Mellen Press, 1982), 240. Another sign of Yoder's ecumenicity is his service as president of the Society of Christian ethics in 1988.

[19]Yoder, The Priestly Kingdom, 8.

[20]Ramsey, Speak Up for Just War or Pacifism, 114ff.

[21]Yoder, "The Hermeneutics of Peoplehood," The Priestly Kingdom, 25.

instructive as stimuli to the conscience of society.[22]

As this passage indicates, Yoder's emphasis on the integrity of the church does not rule out interest in extra-ecclesial affairs. Indeed, a good bit of Yoder's work is devoted to conceptual analysis of how Christians may pursue discipleship in the larger society. For example, in The Christian Witness to the State Yoder affirms the use of "middle axioms" to express "with no embarrassment in pagan terms" what God's justice requires of the state.[23] In The Christian and Capital Punishment, Yoder develops a theological argument for the abolition of the death penalty, and supplements that position with a various "practical" points designed to be of use in persuading non-Christian officials.[24] In a move that may seem surprising for a pacifist, Yoder has attended in recent years to the logic of just war theory to argue that the society which espouses it must be held accountable to the presupposition that unjust wars may occur and must be resisted by moral people.[25]

By bringing the distinctives of his Anabaptist tradition "into the open" among the discourse of ethicists from other traditions, Yoder has brought an alternative, and often neglected, perspective into dialogue with dominant construals of Christian social ethics.

Perhaps nowhere does his challenge hit more closely to the heart of the

---

[22]Yoder, The Christian Witness to the State, 17. Yoder's ecclesiology has had a particular influence on Hauerwas' work. "The more I read of Yoder's scattered essays, the more I began to think he represented a fundamental challenge to the way I had been taught to think of 'social ethics.' Surprisingly, Yoder's account of the church fit almost exactly the kind of community I was beginning to think was required by an ethics of virtue." Hauerwas, The Peaceable Kingdom, xxiv.

[23]Yoder, The Christian Witness to the State, 73.

[24]Yoder, The Christian and Capital Punishment (Newton, Kansas: Faith and Life Press, 1961): 4ff., 17ff.

[25]Yoder, When War Is Unjust: Being Honest in Just-War Thinking (Minneapolis: Augsburg Publishing House, 1984), 82. See also Yoder's "Surrender: A Moral Imperative," The Review of Politics 48 (Fall 1986): 576-595; and "A Consistent Alternative View Within The Just War Family," Faith and Philosophy 2 (April 1985): 112-119.

discipline of Christian ethics, in both its theoretical and practical aspects, than in his critique of "The Constantinian Sources of Western Social Ethics." It is Yoder's claim that the dominant "axioms of Western social thought are the product of the deep shift in the relation of church and world for which Constantine...became the symbol."[26] Says Yoder,

> In the tradition of Ernst Troeltsch, Western theological ethics assumes that the choice of options is fixed in logic and for all times and places by the way the Constantinian heritage dealt with the question. Either one accepts, without serious qualification, the responsibility of politics, i. e. of governing, with whatever means that takes, or one chooses a withdrawn position of either personal-monastic-vocational or sectarian character which is "apolitical."....Troeltsch has obtained a wide following in American thought through the brothers Niebuhr; it is very difficult for an American Protestant ethicist even to conceive that questions might be posed in other terms.[27]

Later chapters will examine in detail how Yoder's eschatology shapes his description and critique of Constantinianism and its influence on Christian moral reason. Suffice it to note here that Yoder seeks to demonstrate how Christian social ethics might be conceived differently, how the following of Jesus in "the divine-human society, the church, the body of Christ" might be a viable political option that challenges the pragmatic "realism" of managing the larger society "responsibly" in a fashion for which Jesus' example and teaching are not directly relevant.[28]

In summary, Yoder has attempted to frame discussion of the moral relevance of Jesus, the church, and the involvement of Christians in the larger society in a new light. Ethicists from other Christian traditions have engaged him seriously as a thinker who advocates lucidly a position that often challenges the

---

[26]Yoder, "The Constantinian Sources of Western Social Ethics," The Priestly Kingdom, 135ff.

[27]Yoder, The Politics of Jesus, 110.

[28]Yoder, "Reinhold Niebuhr and Christian Pacifism," 115.

very formulation of the questions which they commonly address.

Intellectual Biography

In order to grasp more fully the significance, context, and structure of Yoder's work, it is helpful to attend to some of the more prominent traditional, academic, and personal factors in the development of his thought. The first, and most obvious, factor is his denominational identity.

Born in 1927, Yoder was reared and educated a Mennonite--he received his B.A. from Goshen College in 1947. He worked for the Mennonite Central Committee in France for five years, served on the Mennonite Board of Missions, and taught at Goshen College Biblical Seminary before receiving his Th.D. from the University of Basel in 1962. From 1965 through 1984, Yoder taught at Goshen Biblical Seminary, and served for a period of time as president of that institution. Since 1976, he has taught theology at the University of Notre Dame.[29] He continues to write for Mennonite denominational agencies, and has been a consulting editor for The Mennonite Quarterly Review.[30]

---

[29]Yoder apparently taught at both institutions from 1976 through 1984.

[30] Parham, "An Ethical Analysis of the Christian Social Strategies in the Writings of John C. Bennett, Jacques Ellul, and John H. Yoder," 142-145. For example, Yoder's Christian Witness to the State and The Christian and Capital Punishment are both part of the "Institute of Mennonite Studies Series." A number of his writings, such as The Original Revolution, Nevertheless, and He Came Preaching Peace, are part of "The Christian Peace Shelf" of Herald Press, the editor of which is appointed by the Mennonite Central Committee to represent the historic pacifism of Mennonites.

While Parham states that Yoder studied with Karl Barth at Basel, Hughes, citing a telephone interview with Yoder in "The Ethical Use of Power: A Discussion with the Christian Perspectives of Reinhold Niebuhr, John Howard Yoder, and Richard J. Barnet," 106, suggests that "Yoder never studied directly under Barth...[but] developed [at Basel] what he calls an 'empathy for the movement that (Barth) represents' and a 'parallel of direction and preoccupation with Barth.'" In the preface to his Karl Barth and the Problem of War (Nashville: Abingdon Press, 1970), 7-8, Yoder refers to Barth as "a teacher who was above the need to want those who learned from him to become his disciples." On page 17, he notes that "earlier drafts of this text were prepared at Basel in the course of my doctoral studies in the faculty of theology. A text substantially similar to this one was read by Professor Barth in the summer of 1957." It is safe to conclude, then, that Yoder, though not primarily responsible in his doctoral work to Barth's guidance, did learn from Barth during his time at Basel.

Yoder is, moreover, steeped in the history of Anabaptism. His doctoral dissertation analyzed disputations between Anabaptist and Reformed Christians in Switzerland between 1523 and 1538;[31] and throughout his academic career, he has continued to write, translate, and edit studies relevant to the history of Anabaptism.[32] He is clearly unique among contemporary Christian ethicists in this regard.

Yoder's identification with Anabaptism, and his extensive knowledge of its history, has a profound influence on his approach to Christian ethics. His essay "Radical Reformation Ethics in Ecumenical Perspective" reflects this influence very clearly, in its basic claim that the

> "radical reformers" carried the initial reformation vision through to reject as well these indices [of the church's union with civil government] of the post-Constantinian synthesis. Thereby they changed not simply the definition of certain ministries or churchly practices, but also the entire understanding of what it means to be Christian, and consequently also of how the body of believers relates to the powers of this world. Obviously this must have profound implications for the structure and content of ethics.[33]

Yoder suggests that the "primary substantial criterion of Christian ethical

---

[31]Yoder, Die Gespraeche zwischen Taeufern und Reformatoren in der Schweiz 1523-1538 (Karlsruhe: H. Schneider, 1962).

[32]See, for example, "The Turning Point in the Zwinglian Reformation," Mennonite Quarterly Review 32 (January 1958): 128-140; "Anabaptists and the Sword Revisited: Systematic Historiography and Undogmatic Nonresistants," Zeitschrift fuer Kirchengeschichte 85 (1974): 270-283; The Legacy of Michael Sattler, ed. and trans. by Yoder (Scottdale, Pennsylvania: Herald Press, 1973); Balthasar Hubmaier: Theologian of Anabaptism, ed. and trans. by Yoder and H. Wayne Pipkin (Scottdale, Pennsylvania: Herald Press, 1989); and "The Hermeneutics of the Anabaptists," Essays on Biblical Interpretation: Anabaptist-Mennonite Perspectives, ed. William M. Swartley (Elkhart, Indiana: Institute of Mennonite Studies, 1984), 11-28.

[33]Yoder, "Radical Reformation Ethics in Ecumenical Perspective, The Priestly Kingdom, 107. See J. Denny Weaver, Becoming Anabaptist (Scottdale, Pennsylvania: Herald Press, 1987), 113ff. for a concise account of Anabaptist faith and practice.

decisions for the radical reformers is the humanity of Jesus of Nazareth."[34] By taking "the story of Jesus as a paradigm" for how humans are to live in a world in which the followers of Jesus are a minority, Christians are to pursue a mode of ethical reasoning that makes other sources of moral guidance "subordinate to the centrality of the guidance of Jesus" in all human affairs.[35]

It is precisely this historic Anabaptist emphasis on discerning what faithfulness to Jesus entails, and holding all other moral norms accountable to that process, which is characteristic of Yoder's project. He seeks to work out the implications for the Christian life of "the politics of Jesus" as a distinct moral option.[36]

That Yoder's ethic is at the same time communitarian reflects another Anabaptist distinctive: "the absolute priority of church over state in the plan of God."[37] Historic Anabaptism affirmed that

> The nature of Christian commitment as a free and uncompelled decision makes practically certain that in any given time and place only a minority of the population will be committed Christian disciples. The Anabaptists saw the transition of the Christian church, especially in the 4th and 5th centuries A. D. to identify with society, as the "Fall of the Church."[38]

Yoder claims, in clear continuity with the Anabaptist tradition, that "Christian ethics is for Christians," within the context of the distinct community called church, which seeks to embody faithfulness to Jesus in a manner distinct from the

---

[34]Yoder, "Radical Reformation Ethics in Ecumenical Perspective," The Priestly Kingdom, 116.

[35]Yoder, "Radical Reformation Ethics in Ecumenical Perspective," The Priestly Kingdom, 118-120.

[36]Yoder, The Politics of Jesus, 23. See also Sawatsky, "John Howard Yoder," Nonviolence: Central to Christian Spirituality, 246ff.

[37]Yoder, The Christian Witness to the State, 17.

[38]Yoder, "The Recovery of the Anabaptist Vision," Concern Pamphlet #18, 16.

world.[39]

It is also important to note, however, that Yoder is a reformer within the Anabaptist tradition due to his repudiation of withdrawal as the dominant strategy for Christians in dealing with the larger society. He resists the "cultural apartness" of "religio-ethnic minority groups like the Mennonites" who have often resigned the larger society to the fruits of its sin.[40] Yoder suggests that the "Traditional Amish-Mennonite" view, which he rejects, makes the error of assuming

> an independent standard of justice [for the larger society], which is thought to be known somehow apart from Christ...This independent standard, which can be both known and attained apart from Christ, is challengeable not only because it raises a claim to be revelation outside of Christ but also because it doubts the biblical affirmation that God in Christ is "Lord" over the world.[41]

Yoder is obviously indebted to Anabaptism; but he is also concerned with moral and political issues facing the world. This is a notable characteristic of his project which appears to have its roots in his openness to the insights of biblical scholars and theologians who are not Anabaptists. Of great importance here is Karl Barth.

Hughes comments that "Even though Yoder never studied directly under Barth, never wrote a paper for Barth, nor even claims to have read Barth thoroughly, he has been profoundly influenced by Barth."[42] Yoder studied at

---

[39]Yoder, "The Otherness of the Church, The Mennonite Quarterly Review 35 (October 1961): 294.

[40]Yoder, The Christian Witness to the State, 88-89. McClendon comments that Yoder "is the scion of old-line Mennonites, and within that community has sometimes been perceived as a troublemaker exactly because he has been so deeply committed to responsible social action." McClendon, Ethics: Systematic Theology, 1:74.

[41]Yoder, The Christian Witness to the State, 71.

[42]Hughes, "The Ethical Use of Power: A Discussion with the Christian Perspectives of Reinhold Niebuhr, John Howard Yoder, and Richard J. Barnet," 106. Yoder succinctly describes

(continued...)

the University of Basel when Barth was a prominent figure on the faculty, and it is interesting to examine Yoder's rejection of a withdrawal ethic in light of Barth's strong insistence on Christ's lordship.

In Karl Barth and the Problem of War, Yoder comments that for Barth

Creation order cannot be affirmed or described apart from Christ; if "preservation" has any place, it is not as the shadow which Creation left behind but as the light which Reconciliation casts before itself.....Barth sees the state as one of the rebellious powers brought into subjection to the lordship of the risen Christ, but not yet totally defeated. This is a new position in contemporary theology in a number of ways:...The attitude to take to the state is then not derived from a reading of its performance, but from the confession of Christ's lordship. That "the powers that be are of God" is not an empirical statement about how well some statesmen are doing; it is a dogmatic statement about the triumph of Christ.[43]

Yoder's own view of Christ's lordship over the state as a basis for the Christian to address government is very close to this formulation. In The Christian and Capital Punishment, he argues that Christ's

lordship does not apply only over the church...If it is Jesus Christ and not some other god or some other lord who rules at the right hand of God, then the purpose, goals, and standards of that rule can be no other than this same Jesus revealed to us while in the flesh, seeking not to destroy, but to save.[44]

Yoder likewise suggests in The Original Revolution that

Christ is not only the Head of the church; He is at the same time

---

[42](...continued)
certain aspects of Barth's project which are congenial to his own in "Karl Barth: How His Mind Kept Changing," How Karl Barth Changed My Mind, ed. Donald K. McKim (Grand Rapids, Michigan: William B. Eerdmans Publishing Company, 1986), 166-171; and "Helpful and Deceptive Dualisms," Horizons in Biblical Theology 10 (December 1988): 76.

[43]Yoder, Karl Barth and the Problem of War (Nashville: Abingdon Press, 1970): 124-125. Yoder is referring here especially to Barth's essays in Community, State, and Church, ed. Will Herberg (Garden City: Doubleday Anchor Books, 1960).

[44]Yoder, The Christian and Capital Punishment, 17-18.

Lord of history, reigning at the right hand of God over the principalities and powers. The old aeon, representative of human history under the mark of sin, has also been brought under the reign of Christ (which is not identical with the consummate kingdom of God. 1 Cor. 15:24). The characteristic of the reign of Christ is that evil, without being blotted out, is channelized by God, in spite of itself, to serve His purposes.[45]

Yoder has obviously engaged Barth seriously, and it is sure that his own formulation of Christ's lordship as a basis for witness to the state has been at least influenced by Barth. This "Barthian link" reflects the fact that Yoder has drawn on theological sources from outside the Anabaptist tradition in a fashion that has enriched his project.

In a similar way, Yoder cites Oscar Cullmann's "D-Day" and "V-Day" analogy, which refers to the Allies' decisive victory over German forces in the Normandy invasion during World War II as the guarantee of the coming Allied victory in the war, as a way of expressing that "Christ has triumphed and is reigning (which is true for the church through the Holy Spirit, and for the world by anticipation) and that the powers of evil are still rampant." Yoder's description of the church as living in a time when "Evil is potentially subdued...but the final triumph of God is yet to come" is a formulation in obvious dependence on Cullmann's exegesis which helps shape Yoder's account of how and why Christians may call upon the state to be just.[46] Yoder argues that,

---

[45]Yoder, "If Christ Is Truly Lord," The Original Revolution, 58-59.

[46]Yoder, The Christian Witness to the State, 9. See also his Preface to Theology: Christology and Theological Method (Elkhart, Indiana: Co-Op Bookstore, 1981), 181ff. For aspects of Cullmann's position which have influenced Yoder see his Christ and Time (Philadelphia: Westminster Press, 1950), 144ff.; The State in the New Testament (New York: Charles Scribner's Sons, 1956), 86-92;and "The Kingship of Christ and the Church in the New Testament," The Early Church: Studies in Early Christian History and Theology ed., A. J. B. Higgins (Philadelphia: Westminster Press, 1956), 105ff. Hughes notes the significance of Cullmann for Yoder in "The Ethical Use of Power: A Discussion with the Christian Perspectives of Reinhold Niebuhr, John Howard Yoder, and Richard J. Barnet," 125-126. Yoder also relies heavily on Hendrik Berkhof's exegesis of the Pauline notion of "the powers" in Christ and the Powers (Scottdale, Pennsylvania: Herald Press, 1962).

because Christ has conquered in principle the rebellious world, Christians are to help order the larger society in a manner consistent with "the ultimate purpose of preserving the fabric of human community as the context within which the church's work can be carried on."[47]

The influence of Barth and Cullmann on Yoder, which later chapters will examine in greater detail, demonstrates that he has drawn from extra-Anabaptist theological sources in ways that have sustained his call for the active involvement of Christians in the larger society. That he has incorporated such sources reflects his openness to other branches of the Christian church.

Yoder's ecumenicity is symbolized, perhaps most powerfully, by his present position as a professor in the University of Notre Dame's Department of Theology. That Yoder teaches and writes from within an institution so clearly affiliated with the Roman Catholic Church reflects his conviction that his project "is pertinent today as a call for all Christian believers" regardless of denominational identification.

While Yoder clearly stands within the historic Anabaptist tradition, he does not want to be ignored on that account by representatives of the more dominant strands of Christianity. He comments that

> If it be the case that Judaism and Christianity by the nature of things cannot be but particular historical communities, it will follow that the specific form of Christian commitment any given author espouses will be best understood by taking into account, rather than abstracting away, the particularity of the author's time and place. In that sense, this text is with no apology the exposition of a "radical reformation" confessional stance...Yet...it would be a serious misunderstanding to cast upon this confessional quality the condescending light which a tolerant democratic pluralism casts on all "sects" and "marginal movements," which at the same time compliments itself for not persecuting them and

---

[47]Yoder, The Christian Witness to the State, 11.

determines not to listen to them.[48]

Throughout his writings, Yoder has helped to ensure that his work would get a hearing by directly addressing issues of great interest to Christians of other confessions. By beginning The Politics of Jesus with his rejection of six common assumptions about Jesus' political irrelevance, Yoder has challenged, in a very clear way, some of the most influential views of Christian ethics in this century.[49] By framing an approach to The Christian Witness to the State, Yoder has directly attacked the Niebuhrian assumption that "a Christian pacifist position rooted...in Christological considerations is thereby irrelevant to the social order."[50]

By testing the practical application of just war theory to determine whether it should "claim its millennial tradition as an intrinsically moral position...[or] is in fact merely a polite camouflage for an ultimate national egotism," Yoder, a pacifist, has provocatively engaged, on its own terms, the view of war which has been dominant in Christianity for centuries.[51] He has brought what has traditionally been understood as a marginal position into the mainstream of discourse by addressing issues of importance to the majority of contemporary Christian ethicists.

In summary, Yoder's intellectual biography is that of a Mennonite theologian who has drawn from, and contributed to, the discourse of other branches of the Christian faith in a truly original way. In light of his tradition's

---

[48]Yoder, The Priestly Kingdom, 8. Dale W. Brown suggests in "Communal Ecclesiology: The Power of the Anabaptist Vision," Theology Today 36 (April 1979):24, that "Anabaptist theology, at its best, offers an ecumenical style which opposes on the one hand any easy amalgamation and acculturation of traditions lest we lose distinctive gifts, while on the other hand the centrality of the great commission calls us from isolationism to dialogue and witness." This is an apt description of Yoder's work.

[49]Yoder, The Politics of Jesus, 15-19.

[50]Yoder, The Christian Witness to the State, 7.

[51]Yoder, "Surrender: A Moral Imperative," 592.

historic emphasis on a communitarian discipleship ethic, he has incorporated, and responded to, various theological and moral discourses in a fashion that has attracted and held the attention of Christians of widespread orientations.[52] By attending to practical matters of casuistry, whether on the death penalty or war, he has sought to engage the worldliest of issues in light of his understanding of the Gospel.

The State of Research on Yoder

While Yoder's work in Christian ethics has received much scholarly attention, there are few studies that analyze his thought rigorously.[53] Other theologians often describe Yoder's method, whether as that of an "evangelical perfectionist" or a "radical Protestant," in order to indicate a path that they will not take, without providing a detailed analysis of his thought.[54]

On the other hand, Bob E. Adams, a sympathetic interpreter of Yoder, very briefly describes Yoder's view of the significance of Scripture for ethics, and "propose[s] Yoder's methodology as an appropriate one for the Christian ethicist." Adam's interest in Yoder appears to be grounded in the latter's success in giving an account of the "actions and words of Jesus..[as] normative in both theology and ethics" through a certain critical use of the findings of biblical scholarship. While Adams engages Yoder as a serious dialogue partner, and

---

[52]That Yoder's work is recognized as a serious alternative even by those who strongly disagree with him demonstrates the cogency of his argument. See, for example, the comments of Gustafson, Ethics from a Theocentric Perspective 1:74-76; and Wogaman, A Christian Method of Moral Judgment, 33ff.

[53]This section of the chapter surveys significant secondary literature on Yoder. As such, its purpose is to observe and briefly describe the sort of attention which his work receives. It will not rigorously engage or evaluate these sources. The final section of the chapter will attend to a number of these studies in greater detail for the purpose of justifying an intensive analysis of Yoder's eschatology in relation to his critique of Constantinianism.

[54]See, for example, Wogaman, A Christian Method of Moral Judgment, 33ff.; Gustafson, Ethics from a Theocentric Perspective, 1:74ff.; and George W. Forell, "A Christian Rationale for Political Engagement Today," Lutheran Theological Seminary Bulletin 68 (Summer 1988): 10ff.

20

believes that he has formulated a sound approach to Christian ethics, Adams' essay sheds little light on Yoder's methodology. He moves quickly from a summary of Yoder's argument in The Politics of Jesus to his own account of the significance of Jesus for the Christian life. Adams does not analyze Yoder's work in an exacting manner.[55]

McClendon, who begins his Ethics: Systematic Theology with the confession that reading The Politics of Jesus "changed my life" by calling him back to "my own profound roots in the Anabaptist...vision," makes constructive and extensive use of Yoder; but like Adams, his primary aim is the formulation of his own position.[56] While McClendon makes a number of telling comments on the nature and structure of Yoder's project, and rightly identifies him as an ethicist for whom Jesus' resurrection as an eschatological event is of great importance, the primary aim of his book is not the explication and analysis of Yoder's work.[57] The same is true of Hauerwas' use of Yoder in The Peaceable Kingdom.[58] Both find discussions of Yoder helpful for the development of their own "narrative ethics."[59]

Yoder's pacifism has been the most widely analyzed aspect of his

---

[55] Bob E. Adams, "Christology and Ethics: A Critical and Personal Essay," Southwestern Journal of Theology 21 (Spring 1979): 62ff. See also Reinhard L. Huetter's comparison of Yoder with Rauschenbusch in "The Church: Midwife of History or Witness of the Eschaton?," Journal of Religious Ethics 18 (Spring 1990): 27-54.

[56] McClendon, Ethics: Systematic Theology, 1: first and unnumbered page of "Preface."

[57] McClendon, Ethics: Systematic Theology, 1: 48, 51, 63, 72-75, 89, 161, 176 ff., 270-272, 296, 301, 306, 318, 320ff., 328.

[58] Hauerwas, The Peaceable Kingdom, 88, 101, 106, 112, 123-127, 131. His "Messianic Pacifism," Worldview 16 (June 1973): 29-33; and "The Nonresistant Church: The Theological Ethics of John Howard Yoder," Vision and Virtue: Essays in Christian Ethical Reflection (Notre Dame, Indiana: Fides Press, Inc. 1974), 197-221, are more focused on the analysis of Yoder's project.

[59] McClendon, Ethics: Systematic Theology, 1: 328; Hauerwas, The Peaceable Kingdom, 123ff.

thought.[60] His use of Scripture for ethics, his communitarian ecclesiology, and his historical research have also received attention.[61] Several dissertations have analyzed various aspects of Yoder's work in recent years, but none has sufficiently attended to his eschatology. John E. McEntyre's "The Increasing Significance of Symbolic Resistance in Selected Fiction from War and Peace to Mila 18" uses Yoder's descriptions of various sorts of pacifism in Nevertheless as "a spectrum of pacifism," in light of which a number of novels which embody "the ethic of symbolic resistance" may be analyzed.[62] While this dissertation

---

[60]Representative discussions of Yoder's pacifism are: Sawatsky, "John Howard Yoder," in Non-Violence--Central to Christian Spirituality, 239-269; Hauerwas, "Messianic Pacifism," 28-33, and "The Nonresistant Church: The Theological Ethics of John Howard Yoder," Vision and Virtue 197-221; Paul Deats, Jr., "Protestant Social Ethics and Pacifism," War or Peace? The Search for New Answers, ed. Thomas Shannon (Maryknoll, New York: Orbis Books, 1980), 75-92; Marlin Vanelderen, "On Studying War--John Howard Yoder," One World 109 (October 1985): 18-19; Ramsey, Speak Up for Just War or Pacifism, 96ff.; Duane K. Friesen, Christian Peacemaking and International Conflict (Scottdale, Pennsylvania: Herald Press, 1986), 88, 154-156; Richard B. Miller, "Christian Pacifism and Just-War Tenets: How Do They Diverge?," Theological Studies 47 (September 1986): 448-472; James W. Skillen, "The Bible, Politics, and Democracy: What Does Biblical Obedience Entail for American Political Thought?," The Bible, Politics, and Democracy, ed. Richard Neuhaus (Grand Rapids, Michigan: William B. Eerdmans Publishing Company, 1987), 70ff.; Rodney Clapp, "Catholics, Anabaptists, and the Bomb," The Christian Century 105 (2 November 1988): 979-981; Ramathate T. H. Dolamo, "Religious Pacifism: A Critical Evaluation of John H. Yoder," (M. Th. thesis, University of South Africa, 1986).

[61]See, for example, Verhey, The Great Reversal: Ethics and the New Testament, 162, 165, 167, 217; Birch and Rasmussen, Bible and Ethics in the Christian Life, 17ff.; Brown, "Communal Ecclesiology: The Power of the Anabaptist Vision," 22-28; Long, A Survey of Recent Christian Ethics, 90-94; William R. Estep, The Anabaptist Story (Grand Rapids, Michigan: William B. Eerdmans Publishing Company, 1975), 18, 49, 50.

Yoder's books are widely reviewed. See, for example, Harlan Beckley, Review of The Priestly Kingdom, Theology Today 42 (October 1985): 371-372; David A. Shank, Review of The Priestly Kingdom, The Mennonite Quarterly Review 60 (April 1986): 215-216; R. S. Powers, Review of What Would You Do?, The Christian Century 101 (17 October 1984): 962-964; N. Elliot, Review of When War Is Unjust, The Princeton Seminary Bulletin 5 (1984): 263-266; John A. Wood, Review of What Would You Do?, Journal of Church and State 27 (Winter 1985): 146-147; Allan M. Parrent, Review of When War Is Unjust 67 (January 1985): 67-92; C. Burchard, Review of Die Politik Jesu: Der Weg des Kreuzes, Theologische Zeitschrift 20 (1984): 87-89.

[62]MacEntyre, "The Increasing Significance of Symbolic Resistance in Selected Fiction from War and Peace to Mila 18," abstract page 1.

does not seek to illumine the workings of Yoder's project, it does demonstrate that Yoder has portrayed the varieties of pacifism in a manner that rings true with the descriptions of the human condition found in certain major works of literature. That MacEntyre uses Yoder for this creative purpose reflects the cogency of Yoder's descriptive work on pacifism.[63]

Milo Dean Van Veldhuizen briefly discusses Yoder's ethical method in his "'Philanthropia' in Philo of Alexandria: A Scriptural Perspective." He uses Yoder as one of several contemporary Christian ethicists with whom he compares Philo, but does not make a significant contribution to the interpretation of Yoder's work. [64]

Robert M. Parham's "An Ethical Analysis of the Christian Social Strategies in the Writings of John C. Bennett, Jacques Ellul, and John Howard Yoder" contributes to research on Yoder by providing both a concise, lucid description of his project and a sustained comparison of his view of Christian social involvement with two ethicists of notably different orientations. Parham's dissertation is particularly helpful in its demonstration of the significance of ecclesiology and Christology for shaping Yoder's ethical method.[65]

David Michael Hughes' "The Ethical Use of Power: A Discussion with the Christian Perspectives of Reinhold Niebuhr, John Howard Yoder, and Richard J. Barnet" is similar to Parham's in bringing Yoder into dialogue with major ethicists of different Christian traditions. Hughes' study is distinctive in its focus on power within Christian ethics, and provides an insightful description and critique of Yoder's approach to this issue. Also like Parham, he makes a nice

---

[63]McEntyre, "The Increasing Significance of Symbolic Resistance in Selected Fiction from War and Peace to Mila 18," 28, 183, 222.

[64]Milo Dean Van Veldhuizen, "'Philanthropia' in Philo of Alexandria: A Scriptural Perspective," 6-8, 131-132.

[65]Parham, "An Ethical Analysis of the Christian Social Strategies of John C. Bennett, Jacques Ellul, and John Howard Yoder," 148ff., 177-199, 200ff.

summary of Yoder's view of the Christian life.[66]

Jozef M. L. Van Gerwen's dissertation, "The Church in the Theological Ethics of Stanley Hauerwas," provides a brief, but insightful, account of Yoder's ecclesiology as a challenge to "the monopoly of [Troeltschian] church-type projects on the American theology scene," a challenge which has influenced Hauerwas. He rightly notes that Yoder advocates "the critical witness" of Christians to the larger society in a way that is distinct from the "sectarian" stereotype of a withdrawal ethic.[67]

Brent Philip Waters' "A Christian Understanding of and Response to Violent Revolution" discusses Yoder as the proponent of "a nonviolent but radically revolutionary ethic" that interprets Jesus' example, teaching, and proclamation of God's eschatological reign as crucial and distinctive sources of moral wisdom. While his treatment of Yoder is brief and his research less than thorough, he portrays the gist of Yoder's "politics of Jesus" orientation to the moral life.[68]

Gayle Gerber Koontz' "Confessional Theology in Pluralistic Context: A Study of the Theological Ethics of H. Richard Niebuhr and John H. Yoder" goes beyond previous work on Yoder to compare him, in a very thorough manner, as a confessional Christian theologian with so important a figure as H. Richard Niebuhr. Koontz contrasts Niebuhr's theocentricity with Yoder's Christocentric orientation in a fashion that displays well both the theological presuppositions and implications of their respective options. By attending to their hermeneutical orientations, epistemological assumptions, views of Scripture, and

---

[66]Hughes, "The Ethical Use of Power: A Discussion with the Christian Perspectives of Reinhold Niebuhr, John Howard Yoder, and Richard J. Barnet," 126ff.

[67]Van Gerwen, "The Church in the Theological Ethics of Stanley Hauerwas," 129-142.

[68]Waters, "A Christian Understanding of and Response to Violent Revolution," 107-116.

ecclesiologies, she gives a truly insightful account of Yoder's project.[69]

Charles Wayne Scriven's "The Transformation of Culture: Christian Social Ethics after H. Richard Niebuhr" likewise illumines Yoder's project by bringing him into conversation with the influential author of Christ and Culture.[70] Scriven advances the thesis that an Anabaptist approach to the transformation of culture is more adequate theologically than Niebuhr's Augustinian-Calvinist project. Drawing from sources of the historic Anabaptist tradition and engaging several contemporary theologians, he incorporates a number of distinctive aspects of Yoder's thought in formulating his alternative to Niebuhr.[71]

Joel Andrew Zimbleman's "Theological Ethics and Politics in the Thought of Juan Luis Segundo and John Howard Yoder" compares the work of these two theologians. By demonstrating how the respective theological orientations of Segundo and Yoder shape their understandings of proper Christian involvement in society, and comparing their projects, Zimbleman makes lucid what is at stake in the divergent options of the two figures. He competently describes and evaluates Yoder's theologically informed view of political involvement.[72]

Michael Cartwright, in his "Practices, Politics, and Performance: Toward a Communal Hermeneutic for Christian Ethics," seriously engages Yoder as a dialogue partner in his effort to construct a "communal hermeneutic" of

---

[69]Koontz, "Confessional Theology in Pluralistic Context: A Study of the Theological Ethics of H. Richard Niebuhr and John H. Yoder," 67ff., 234ff.

[70]Scriven's dissertation has been published as The Transformation of Culture: Christian Social Ethics after H. Richard Niebuhr (Scottdale, Pennsylvania: Herald Press, 1988).

[71]Scriven, The Transformation of Culture: Christian Social Ethics after H. Richard Niebuhr, 17ff., 146-158, 159ff.

[72]Zimbleman, "Theological Ethics and Politics in the Thought of Juan Luis Segundo and John Howard Yoder," 191ff., 253ff., 323ff.

Scripture. Cartwright describes Yoder as one of the first among contemporary Christian ethicists to attend to the "politics of interpretation" and notes his indebtedness to "biblical realism" and historic Anabaptism.[73]

In summarizing this survey of secondary literature on Yoder, it is clear that his work has received attention ranging in intensity from the brief comments of book reviews to the laborious analysis of doctoral dissertations. Particular methodological aspects of his project have been incorporated by sympathetic interpreters and severely criticized by others. Commentators of various points of view have engaged seriously Yoder's pacifism and analysis of just war theory. Dissertations, with varying points of emphasis, have compared his project with figures of such stature as the Niebuhrs, Bennett, and Segundo. The larger focus and structure of his thought are widely expounded in the secondary literature.[74]

Justification of the Present Project

In all of these commentaries, a particular aspect of Yoder's thought which has not received sustained scholarly analysis is his eschatology. Parham notes, for example, that a limitation of his analysis of Yoder is his failure to attend to eschatology.[75] Hughes comments that "eschatology is vital to Yoder," but does not examine the theme rigorously.[76] Likewise, Koontz does not develop this aspect of Yoder's work in her comparison of him with H. Richard

---

[73]Cartwright, "Practices, Politics, and Performance: Toward a Communal Hermeneutic for Christian Ethics," 9ff., 374ff.

[74]See this volume's bibliography for a listing of significant published secondary literature on Yoder.

[75]Parham, "An Ethical Analysis of the Christian Social Strategies in the Writings of John C. Bennett, Jacques Ellul, and John Howard Yoder," 238.

[76]Hughes, "The Ethical Use of Power: A Discussion with the Christian Perspectives of Reinhold Niebuhr, John Howard Yoder, and Richard J. Barnet," 124-126.

Niebuhr.[77]

Zimbleman acknowledges that Yoder "transforms the Christian theology of history into a theology of Christian eschatology," but an exacting analysis of Yoder's eschatology is not a major focus of his study.[78] Van Veldhuizen, Van Gerwen, and Waters refer, in various ways, to the significance of eschatology for Yoder; but none of them examines the issue in detail.[79] Similarly, Beckley observes that Yoder has "a biblical eschatology" that shapes his approach to ethics, but he does not develop the point.[80] Hauerwas refers to the "eschatological context" of Yoder's work, but he does not go beyond a surface analysis.[81]

McClendon attends to Yoder's eschatology in a more explicit, but insufficient, fashion. He notes that, for Yoder,

> The real Jesus was the eschatological Jesus. His mission was the inauguration of a new social order not comprehended by the old aeon; his message was "the kingdom coming"; his method was--the way of the cross, for his followers and for himself. Thus the ethics of Jesus was grounded and founded in eschatology, but that made him, not irrelevant, but immediately relevant to the prevailing social structures of his own day and equally relevant to those of our own....Yoder's view is deeply influenced by his eschatology--by a doctrine of two aeons, the old and the new, and by the idea of Messianic community, the believers' church, that

---

[77]Koontz, "Confessional Theology in a Pluralistic Context: A Study of the Theological Ethics of H. Richard Niebuhr and John H. Yoder," 37.

[78]Zimbleman, "Theological Ethics and Politics in the Thought of Juan Luis Segundo and John Howard Yoder," 215ff.

[79]Van Veldhuizen, "'Philanthropia in Philo of Alexandria: An Ethical Perspective," 8; Van Gerwen, "The Church in the Theological Ethics of Stanley Hauerwas," 136; Waters, "A Christian Understanding of and Response to Violent Revolution," 113ff.

[80]Harlan Beckley, "A Christian Affirmation of Rawls's Idea of Justice as Fairness," Journal of Religious Ethics 14 (Fall 1986): 232.

[81]Hauerwas, "The Nonresistant Church: The Theological Ethics of John Howard Yoder," 207ff.

inhabits the new aeon while still confronting the old.[82]

He observes further that for Yoder "eschatology and our attitude to peacemaking are two sides of a single coin." Yoder's eschatological commitments enable the description of

> the world of power struggles and decisions, of self-made selves and of the powers that be... [as] the shabby and pretentious cosmos that it is, while our eyes instead grow accustomed to the light of a new aeon, pupils adjusting to the dawning of the coming age in which Christ alone is Lord and we servants of his lordship and thus of one another.[83]

McClendon's comments raise the issue of the significance of eschatology for Yoder's view of the Christian life. By observing that Yoder's understandings of Jesus, the church, the world, and discipleship are informed by his view of a new aeon of history, McClendon identifies an aspect of Yoder's work which appears to be important for the interpretation of his entire project: the significance of Yoder's eschatology for his view of Christian ethics.

Zimbleman confirms the shaping influence of eschatology for Yoder's moral analysis, especially with reference to the formulation of his critique of "Constantinianism."

> Yoder rejects all visions of history that lack a proper eschatological vision....The attack against "heretical" theologies of eschatology is expressed most systematically in Yoder's opposition to "Constantinianism." While the term at times denotes a substantive position associated with the Church contemporary with the restructuring of the Roman Empire around the faith (A.D. 313), it more often is employed by Yoder to identify the general tendency growing out of the alliance of Church and state that rejects several fundamental elements of a proper eschatology. "Constantinianism" is a generic term applied to all Christian theological visions which exhibit 1) a misunderstanding of the

---

[82]McClendon, Ethics: Systematic Theology, 1:73-74. See also Huetter's brief treatment of Yoder's eschatology in "The Church: Midwife of History or Witness of the Eschaton?," 39ff.

[83]McClendon, Ethics: Systematic Theology, 1:318-321.

proper minoritarian posture of the Church in the world, and 2) the correlative conception of the relationship of Church witness to the world that is demanded by this posture, including a specific formulation of the Christian's use of and dependency on coercion, power, force, and violence to accomplish specific ends.[84]

While Zimbleman does not pursue the issue in great detail, his observation on the importance of eschatology for Yoder's critique of Constantinianism raises a provocative issue that strikes at the heart of Yoder's project.[85] Given Yoder's identification with historic Anabaptism, a critique of the "established church" that identifies too closely with the power structures of the larger society, or that is Constantinian, is a theme throughout his work.[86] As this issue of the relationship between the church and the world bears directly upon the sort of moral reasoning appropriate to disciples of Jesus, indeed to the interpretation of the "particular social-political-ethical option" of Jesus that is at the center of Yoder's writings, it is clearly an area of great importance for the interpretation of Yoder's entire project.[87]

The present study will focus on the significance of Yoder's eschatology for his critique of Constantinianism. By rigorously examining the relationship between these two themes in Yoder's work, it will take an original approach by displaying in detail how the assumptions and rationale of his eschatology inform and shape a dominant motif of his work in Christian ethics. The study will both

---

[84]Zimbleman, "Theological Ethics and Politics in the Thought of Juan Luis Segundo and John Howard Yoder," 218-219.

[85]Zimbleman, "Theological Ethics and Politics in the Thought of Juan Luis Segundo and John Howard Yoder," 218ff; see also Hughes, "The Ethical Use of Power: A Discussion with the Christian Perspectives of Reinhold Niebuhr, John Howard Yoder, and Richard J. Barnet," 133.

[86]See, for example, Yoder, "The Disavowal of Constantine: An Alternative Perspective on Interfaith Dialogue," 48ff.; "The Otherness of the Church," 286-296; Christian Attitudes to War, Peace, and Revolution: A Companion to Bainton, 37ff.; "The Constantinian Sources of Western Social Ethics," The Priestly Kingdom, 135ff.; The Christian Witness to the State, 55ff.

[87]Yoder, The Politics of Jesus, 23.

analyze this aspect of Yoder's thought and evaluate his approach in terms of its internal coherence. As such, the project seeks to make a constructive contribution to Yoder studies by displaying the significance of his eschatology as a major aspect of his moral project.

CHAPTER 2

SALIENT ASPECTS OF YODER'S ESCHATOLOGY

This chapter furthers the analysis of the import of eschatology for
Yoder's critique of Constantinianism by examining in detail Yoder's
eschatological commitments. In this way, it lays an important part of the
groundwork for the explicit discussion of Yoder's view of Constantinianism in
following chapters. Its analysis divides into five sections: (1) Yoder's basic
eschatological orientation; (2) his use and interpretation of Scripture; (3) the
relationship of eschatology to Christology; (4) the relationship of eschatology to
ecclesiology; and (5) the basic significance of his eschatology for the moral life.
Throughout these sections, the chapter displays and evaluates the rationale of
Yoder's eschatology and its basic significance for his larger approach to Christian
ethics.

Basic Orientation

The basic orientation of Yoder's eschatology is that of an "already but not yet" view of the fulfillment of God's kingdom.[1] Foundational for his formulation of eschatology is the claim that

> The New Testament sees our present age--the age of the church, extending from Pentecost to the Parousia--as a period of the overlapping of two aeons. These aeons are not distinct periods of time, for they exist simultaneously. They differ rather in nature or in direction; one points backwards to human history outside of (before) Christ; the other points forward to the fullness of the kingdom of God, of which it is a foretaste. Each aeon has a social manifestation: the former in the "world," the latter in the church or body of Christ.[2]

The new age or aeon "came into history in a decisive way with the incarnation and the entire work of Christ." Jesus embodied "self-giving, nonresistant love" which challenged the coercive violence of the political and social orders of his day. Jesus' crucifixion demonstrates "how God deals with evil" through agape that "seeks neither effectiveness nor justice, and is willing to suffer any loss or seeming defeat for the sake of obedience." Jesus' death on the cross was not, however, a defeat; for "Christ's obedience unto death was crowned by the miracle of the resurrection and the exaltation at the right hand of God."[3]

Yoder suggests that the chief characteristic of the new age begun in

---

[1]Yoder suggests that "The reign of the Father remains identified with the not-yet-arrived end of the age (1 Cor. 15:24)." Before that time, Christ reigns over "the kingdom of the Son." It is in this sense that God's reign is present but not yet consummated. Yoder, The Christian Witness to the State, 10. See Hughes, "The Ethical Use of Power: A Discussion with the Christian Perspectives of Reinhold Niebuhr, John Howard Yoder, and Richard J. Barnet," 124-126; Zimbleman, "The Theological Ethics and Politics in the Thought of Juan Luis Segundo and John Howard Yoder," 215-225; and McClendon, Ethics: Systematic Theology, 1:73-75, 318ff.

The purpose of this section of the chapter is to display in broad outline the shape of Yoder's eschatology. Explicit evaluation and criticism of Yoder's position will come in later sections of the chapter.

[2]Yoder, "If Christ Is Truly Lord," The Original Revolution, 55.

[3]Yoder, "If Christ is Truly Lord," The Original Revolution, 55-56.

Jesus is that

> Christ is not only the Head of the church; He is at the same time
> Lord of history, reigning at the right hand of God over the
> principalities and powers. The old aeon, representative of human
> history under the mark of sin, has also been brought under the
> reign of Christ (which is not identical with the consummate
> kingdom of God. 1 Cor. 15:24). The characteristic of the reign
> of Christ is that evil, without being blotted out, is channelized by
> God, in spite of itself, to serve His purposes.[4]

Yoder cites Oscar Cullmann's "D-Day" and "V-Day" analogy as a way
of expressing that "Christ has triumphed and is reigning (which is true for the
church through the Holy Spirit, and for the world by anticipation) and that the
powers of evil are still rampant."[5] Indeed,

> The present aeon is characterized by sin and centered on man; the
> coming aeon is the redemptive reality which entered history in an
> ultimate way in Christ. The present age, by rejecting obedience,
> has rejected the only possible ground for man's own well-being;
> the coming age is characterized by God's will being done. The
> seal of the possibility of His will's being done is the presence of
> the Holy Spirit, given to the church as a foretaste of the eventual
> consummation of God's kingdom. Thus, although the new aeon
> is described as coming, it is not only a future quantity. The old
> has already begun to be superseded by the new, and the focus of
> that victory is the body of Christ, first the man Christ Jesus, and
> then derivatively the fellowship of obedient believers.[6]

As this passage indicates, the church is an eschatological reality for
Yoder.

> This new body, the church, as aftertaste of God's loving triumph
> on the cross and foretaste of His ultimate loving triumph in His

---

[4]Yoder, "If Christ Is Truly Lord," The Original Revolution, 58-59. See also his The Christian and Capital Punishment, 15.

[5]Yoder, The Christian Witness to the State, 9; "If Christ Is Truly Lord," The Original Revolution, 60.

[6]Yoder, The Christian Witness to the State, 9.

kingdom, has a task within history. History is the framework in which the church evangelizes, so that the true meaning of history is the fact that God has chosen to use it for such a "scaffolding" service.[7]

Indeed, the "church is called to be now what the world is called to be ultimately."[8] It is to be a foretaste and sign of God's reign through the power of the Spirit. Yoder suggests that "the ultimate meaning of history will not be found in the course of earthly empires or the development of proud cultures, but in the calling together of the 'chosen race, royal priesthood, holy nation,' which is the church of Christ."[9]

Yoder suggests that an important characteristic of the church is its eschatological patience, its faithful waiting for God to fulfill history on God's terms. In light of the vision of Revelation 4-5, and the affirmation that "The lamb that was slain is worthy to receive power!," Christians know that "the cross and not the sword, suffering and not brute power determines the meaning of history. The key to the obedience of God's people is not their effectiveness but their patience."[10] This patience is modeled on that displayed by Jesus of Nazareth, the crucified and now risen Lord: "[H]e is to be looked at as a mover of history and as the standard by which Christians must learn how they are to look at the moving of history."[11]

History is moved, however, by a Lord who chose the cross over

---

[7]Yoder, The Christian Witness to the State, 10-11.

[8]Yoder, "The Kingdom as Social Ethic," The Priestly Kingdom, 92.

[9]Yoder, The Christian Witness to the State, 13. See also his "The Otherness of the Church," The Mennonite Quarterly Review, 287ff.; Preface to Theology, 177ff.;and He Came Preaching Peace, 24.

[10]Yoder, The Politics of Jesus, 238. See also his "The Spirit of God and the Politics of Men," Journal of Theology for Southern Africa 29 (December 1979): 71; "Armaments and Eschatology," Studies in Christian Ethics (1988): 53; and "To Serve Our God and to Rule the World," The Annual of the Society of Christian Ethics (1988): 3ff.

[11]Yoder, The Politics of Jesus, 239.

conventional standards of "effectiveness" in history. Thereby,

> Christ renounced the claim to govern history....His emptying of
> himself, his accepting the form of servanthood and obedience unto
> death is precisely his renunciation of lordship, his apparent
> abandonment of any obligation to be effective in making history
> move down the right track.[12]

It is God's action of vindicating the dead and humiliated Jesus which establishes the ultimate power of weakness in the new age.

> The key to the ultimate relevance and to the triumph of the good
> is not any calculation at all, paradoxical or otherwise, of efficacy,
> but rather simple obedience...The cross is not a recipe for
> resurrection. Suffering is not a tool to make people come around,
> nor a good in itself. But the kind of faithfulness that is willing to
> accept evident defeat rather than complicity with evil is, by virtue
> of its conformity with what happens to God when he works among
> men, aligned with the ultimate triumph of the Lamb.[13]

During the present overlapping of the two ages, and before the final triumph of the Lamb, Christ reigns over the rebellious "powers" and orders them to serve God's designs. Christians, in light of their eschatological hope, are to accept the suffering heaped upon them by a rebellious world.[14] Says Yoder,

> [B]ecause he is Lord over those who persecute us, we can remain
> faithful in our suffering. Those who persecute us are somehow
> permitted to do so by Christ because his purposes include that.
> Therefore we can accept our martyrdom as the way to serve him,
> knowing our obedience will ultimately be vindicated. We can be
> faithful in persecution because we know it is not the last word.[15]

The last word, which has yet to come, is that "the way of the Lamb is

---

[12]Yoder, The Politics of Jesus, 240-242.

[13]Yoder, The Politics of Jesus, 244-245.

[14]Yoder relies here upon Hendrik Berkhof's analysis of "the powers" in Christ and the Powers (Scottdale, Pennsylvania: Herald Press, 1962). The next section of the chapter will examine Yoder's use of this concept in detail.

[15]Yoder, Preface to Theology, 177.

36

what will finally conquer."[16] God's reign will someday find consummation when "he has put all enemies under his feet" (1 Cor. 15:25). Until that time, Christians live between the times of Pentecost and Parousia, before God's final and complete triumph over evil.[17] The church is the unique foretaste of God's age through the power of the Spirit which seeks to embody presently, and in opposition to the world, obedience to the way of the crucified and risen Lord.[18]

Yoder's Use and Interpretation of Scripture

In order to grasp more fully the nature and function of Yoder's eschatological commitments, it is helpful to examine his use and interpretation of Scripture. As Yoder understands himself to be articulating a biblical eschatology, it is important to determine precisely how he formulates his position in relation to the Bible.

Yoder comments in the "Preface" to The Politics of Jesus that the volume

> represents an exercise in fundamental philosophical hermeneutics, trying to apply in the area of the life of the Christian community the insights with regard to the distinct biblical world view which have previously been promoted under the name of "biblical realism." Since the pioneer statements of Hendrik Kraemer, Otto Piper, Paul Minear, Markus Barth, and Claude Tresmontant, it has become thinkable that there might be about the biblical vision of reality certain dimensions which refuse to be pushed into the mold of any one contemporary world view, but which stand in creative tension with the cultural functions of our age or perhaps of any age...What the present volume offers is a late ripening, in the field of ethics, of the same biblical realist revolution in which precisely ecclesiology and eschatology come to have a new import

---

[16]Yoder, "If Christ Is Truly Lord," The Original Revolution, 72.

[17]Yoder describes the Christian life in an explicitly eschatological context in, for example, "To Serve our God and to Rule the World," 3ff.; and "Armaments and Eschatology," 43ff.

[18]Yoder, The Christian Witness to the State, 9ff. See also his "If Christ Is Truly Lord," The Original Revolution, 57.

for the substance of ethics.[19]

In following the lead of that "revolution" in biblical interpretation, Yoder's chief hermeneutical concern is whether "where it is clear what it [Scripture] says, we are going to let that testimony count rather than subjecting it to the superior authority of our own contemporary hermeneutic framework."[20] The assumptions of biblical realism enable Yoder to attempt to interpret reality in light of the world view espoused by Scripture. Says Yoder of this orientation,

[Biblical realism] is not a discipline but a particular set of convictions. It begins by criticizing unbiblical views such as the platonic, dualistic view of things in favor of trying to think the way the Bible itself thinks...[I]t opens one's mind to take seriously the elements that have been forgotten over the centuries, such as the place of the demonic in the biblical view of man in society. It enables people to be open to the possibilities that the Bible might think with a different logic than we think with...[21]

Yoder notes that biblical realism arose as a "post-critical reorientation" in response to both "the waning power...of the Scholastic Protestant Orthodox" view of the Bible and the emergence of "the [modern] doubters and...critics" of

---

[19]Yoder, The Politics of Jesus, 5-6. Representative works of "biblical realism" are Hendrikus Berkhof, Christ and the Powers; Paul Minear, Eyes of Faith: A Study of the Biblical Point of View (Philadelphia: Westminister Press, 1946); and Markus Barth, Conversation with the Bible (New York: Holt, Rinehart, and Winston, 1964). Cartwright discusses this movement's influence on Yoder in "Practices, Politics, and Performance: Toward a Communal Hermeneutic for Christian Ethics," 379ff. Hughes also analyzes it in "The Ethical Use of Power: A Discussion with the Christian Perspectives of Reinhold Niebuhr, John Howard Yoder, and Richard J. Barnet," 109-116.

[20]Yoder, "The Use of the Bible in Theology," The Use of the Bible in Theology/Evangelical Options, ed. Robert K. Johnston (Atlanta: John Knox Press, 1985), 116; See also his "But We Do See Jesus," The Priestly Kingdom, 49; "Jesus and Power," On Earth Peace, ed. Donald F. Durnbaugh (Elgin, Illinois: Brethren Press 1978): 370-372; and "The Biblical Mandate," The Chicago Declaration, ed. Ronald J. Sider (Carol Stream, Illinois: Creation House, 1974), 91ff.

[21]Yoder, Preface to Theology, 297. See also Yoder's comments on biblical realism in Christian Attitudes to War, Peace, and Revolution, 425, 438, and "The Authority of the Canon," Essays on Biblical Interpretation: Anabaptist/Mennonite Perspectives, 271ff..

38

biblical authority.[22] He affirms this orientation as a "post-modern acceptance of the particularity of the Christian story" which makes intelligible the claim that "the people of God in present history live from and toward the promise of the whole world's salvation" as that is portrayed in Scripture.[23] He understands the Bible to present one way, among many other historically contingent options, of viewing the world.[24]

In this light, the hermeneutical task for Yoder is basically to interpret reality, including human history, our world, and ourselves, in light of the world view of the Bible. This orientation has the moral significance of encouraging

> us to expect that the issues of power, community, and violence are appropriate issues to which to expect the Scriptures to speak, saying things that we might not have heard before with the same clarity. It disconnects our search for those answers from some of the traditionally polarized "evangelical" debates about inerrancy or about the choice between social action and evangelism. As those dead debates are set aside, the capacity of the text to speak on topics of war, peace, and revolution is qualitatively increased. That would make no difference if the texts were of a kind which in matter of fact were interested in other-worldly concerns alone, or were intrinsically in favor of supporting oppressive social systems. It does happen, however, that the texts are actually dealing with matters of justice and liberation, once the dualistic screen which kept them from being read that way has been pulled aside.[25]

---

[22]Yoder, Christian Attitudes to War, Peace, and Revolution, 425. See his discussion of Protestant scholasticism in relation to Tridentine Catholicism and modernism's approaches to the Bible in "The Authority of the Canon," Essays on Biblical Interpretation: Anabaptist/Mennonite Perspectives, 266ff.

[23]Yoder, "Introduction," The Priestly Kingdom, 9, 12.

[24]Yoder, "But We Do See Jesus," The Priestly Kingdom, 61-62.

[25]Yoder, The Christian Attitudes to War, Peace, and Revolution, 426. See also his "Biblical Roots of Liberation Theology," Grail 1 (September 1985): 55ff.; "The Spirit of God and the Politics of Men," 62ff.; "La politica de Jesus: su etica pacifista," Cuadernos de teologia 7 (1986): 263ff.; and "Civil Religion in America," The Priestly Kingdom, 179ff. for discussions of the Bible's political agenda.

It is precisely Yoder's aim, for example, in The Politics of Jesus to challenge assumptions about Jesus' relevance for the moral life that do not square with "biblical truth."[26] Yoder seeks to establish this truth by attending, in this instance, to the narrative of Luke's gospel. Through a reading of that story, and a dialogue with contemporary biblical scholarship, he concludes that

> Jesus was not just a moralist whose teachings had some political implications; he was not primarily a teacher of spirituality whose public ministry unfortunately was seen in a political light; he was not just a sacrificial lamb preparing for his immolation, or a God-Man whose divine status calls us to disregard his humanity. Jesus was, in his divinely mandated (i. e. promised, anointed, messianic) prophethood, priesthood, and kingship, the bearer of a new possibility of human, social, and therefore political relationships.[27]

Yoder's basic hermeneutical move here is to interpret what is possible in the world in light of his understanding of biblical truth. Rather than holding the New Testament portraits of Jesus' call to discipleship accountable to what he considers the conventional moral wisdom that managing society effectively is the ultimate goal of social ethics, and hence making Jesus' call morally irrelevant because it does not serve that goal, Yoder seeks to hold the social and political realities of life accountable to the particular new possibility or way of life demanded by the Jesus of the New Testament.[28] Yoder understands Christians to be called to the realistic imitation of Jesus especially as regards his crucifixion.

> The cross of Christ was the price of his obedience to God amidst a rebellious world; it was suffering for having done right, for loving where others hated, for representing in the flesh the forgiveness and the righteousness of God among men both less forgiving and less righteous. The cross of Christ was God's

---

[26]Yoder, The Politics of Jesus, 12, 15-19.

[27]Yoder, The Politics of Jesus, 63.

[28]Yoder, The Politics of Jesus, 23. See also his "But We Do See Jesus," The Priestly Kingdom, 62.

method of overcoming evil with good. The cross of the Christian
is not different. It is the price of one's obedience to God's love
toward all people in a world ruled by hate. Such unflinching love
for friend and foe alike will mean hostility and suffering for us,
as it did for him.[29]

Yoder's point is clear: Christians are to interpret their lives, and place
in the world, in light of the life and teachings of Christ as portrayed in Scripture.
The Bible represents his way, which culminated in crucifixion, as a distinct
social, political, and moral option, and Christians are to follow him. This,
according to Yoder, is the heart of the biblical world view.[30]

Yoder makes a similar move in calling for the eschatological
interpretation of history in light of Christ's triumph over "the powers."[31] He
follows Hendrik Berkhof's treatment of passages, such as Romans 8:38; 1
Corinthians 2:8, 15:24-26; and Colossians 1:16, 2:15, that refer to "powers,"
"rulers," and "principalities" as structures created by God which have rebelled
against God's purposes.[32]

As Berkhof comments,

The powers are no longer instruments, linkages between God's
love, as revealed in Christ, and the visible world of creation. In
fact, they have become gods (Galatians 4:8), behaving as though
they were the ultimate ground of being, and demanding from men
an appropriate worship. This is the demonic reversal which has
taken place on the invisible side of creation. No longer do the
Powers bind man and God together; they separate them. They
stand as a roadblock between the Creator and His creation.[33]

---

[29]Yoder, He Came Preaching Peace, 19.

[30]Of course, Yoder's formulation reflects his reliance upon the findings of certain biblical
scholars, as well as on particular theological commitments which are characteristic of his
Anabaptist position. This section of the chapter will conclude with an explicit evaluation of
Yoder's use of Scripture and biblical scholarship.

[31]Yoder, The Politics of Jesus, 135ff. See also his The Christian Witness to the State, 8.

[32]Yoder, The Politics of Jesus, 144.

[33]Berkhof, Christ and the Powers, 30.

But through his death and resurrection,

> Christ has "triumphed over them" [the powers]...The resurrection manifests what was already accomplished at the cross: that in Christ God has challenged the Powers, has penetrated into their territory, and has displayed that He is stronger than they....In principle the victory is certain; yet the battle continues until the triumph will have become effective on all fronts and visible to all.[34]

For Berkhof, the powers will be fully subordinated to God only in the eschaton. Presently, "they follow the triumph-wagon of the conquering Christ as slaves," being used by God, despite their rebellion, to serve the divine purpose of ordering society in a fashion that allows the work of the church to proceed.[35]

Following Berkhof's treatment of the powers, Yoder comments on the authority of the state as a power in Romans 13 that

> God is not said to create or institute or ordain the [particular] powers that be, but only to order them, to put them in order, sovereignly to tell them where they belong, what is their place...God does not take responsibility for the existence of the rebellious "powers that be" or for their shape or identity; they already are. What the text says is that he orders them, brings them into line, that by his permissive government he lines them up with his purpose.[36]

The state is for Yoder simply "a fact" of life in a fallen world.[37] The new age begun in Jesus Christ "means for the state the obligation to serve God by encouraging the good and restraining evil, i. e., to serve peace, to preserve the social cohesion in which the leaven of the gospel can build the church, and also render the old aeon more tolerable."[38] The state is a power to be ordered

---

[34]Berkhof, Christ and the Powers, 39-40.

[35]Berkhof, Christ and the Powers, 41, 46.

[36]Yoder, The Politics of Jesus, 203.

[37]Yoder, The Christian and Capital Punishment, 12.

[38]Yoder, "If Christ Is Truly Lord," The Original Revolution, 73.

by God in light of Christ's lordship over the world. On the nature of this lordship over the state, Yoder comments that

> The time between the ascension of Christ and the defeat of the last enemy, when the kingdom of the Son will give place to the consummated kingdom of the Father, is thus characterized by the ways in which the reign of Christ channels violence, turning it against itself, so as to preserve as much as possible of the order (taxis) which is the pre-condition of human society and thereby also a vehicle for the work of the church.[39]

Yoder's use of Berkhof's work on "the powers" demonstrates clearly his hermeneutical method. He establishes, through reliance on exegetical scholarship, what he thinks is "the biblical perspective" and seeks to interpret present reality in that light. Yoder moves from Berkhof's exegetical work to an account of the state's proper function. By locating the state within the larger perspective of powers which have been in principle conquered by the lordship of Christ in a new age of God's salvation, but whose perfect submission is reserved for the future consummation of God's reign, he attempts to interpret the worldliest of matters in light of what he thinks is the biblical world view.

In addition to the influence of Berkhof upon Yoder, it is clear that Oscar Cullmann's exegetical and theological scholarship has profoundly shaped his eschatology.[40] Yoder makes reference to Cullmann's "D-Day" and "V-Day" analogy in a number of central passages.[41]

An important aspect of Cullmann's project is to show that "redemptive history" is a crucial part of New Testament proclamation, that a view of God's salvific involvement in history is not a dispensable husk to be removed from the

---

[39]Yoder, The Christian Witness to the State, 12.

[40]Berkhof notes his indebtedness to Cullmann in Christ and the Powers, 74.

[41]Yoder, "If Christ Is Truly Lord," in The Original Revolution, 60. See also The Christian Witness to the State, 9; Yoder, Preface to Theology, 181ff. Yoder cites Cullmann on the authority of Scripture in "The Authority of the Canon," Essays on Biblical Interpretation: Anabaptist/Mennonite Perspectives, 274, 283.

kernel of the Gospel.[42]   The "mid-point" of history for Cullmann is the resurrection of Jesus: "the mid-point of the process has already been reached."[43] The decisive victory of God in history has already been won. Says Cullmann,

> The decisive battle in a war may already have occurred in a relatively early stage of the war, and yet the war still continues...Precisely this is the situation of which the New Testament is conscious...the revelation consists precisely in the fact of the proclamation that that event on the cross, together with the resurrection which followed, was the already concluded decisive battle.[44]

Despite that victory, there exists in the present time tension between "'this age' and 'the coming age'" inaugurated in Jesus Christ.[45] This tension is reflected by Cullmann's understanding of the Regnum Christi as the present era of salvation history which still awaits the coming fulfillment of God's kingdom.[46] Cullmann notes that the church finds its identity precisely from its foreshadowing of the coming age in the present order.

> The relation of tension between mid-point and end, which is so characteristic of the present intermediate period, is manifested in the Church in a manner that exactly corresponds to the Lordship of Christ, since Church and Kingdom of Christ coincide in time. The Church is the earthly center from which the full Lordship of Christ becomes visible. It is the Body of Christ as the Crucified but also Risen One. It is the "spiritual body" of Christ, and through participation in it in worthy enjoyment of the Lord's Supper the believer already appropriates the fruits of the Holy

---

[42]Cullmann, Christ and Time, 27.

[43]Cullmann, Christ and Time, 82.

[44]Cullmann, Christ and Time, 84. See Eldon J. Epp's discussion of Cullmann's eschatology in his "Mediating Approaches to the Kingdom: Werner Georg Kuemmel and George Eldon Ladd," The Kingdom of God in 20th-Century Interpretation, ed. Wendell Willis (Peabody, Massachusetts: Hendrickson Publishers, 1987), 35ff.

[45]Cullmann, Christ and Time, 145.

[46]Cullmann, "The Kingship of Christ and the Church in the New Testament," The Early Church: Studies in Early Christian History and Theology, 109ff.

Spirit, even in the area of his earthly life (1 Cor. 11:30). The Church is the place where the Spirit, this feature of the eschatological period, is already at work as "earnest," as "firstfruits."[47]

Cullmann also describes the state in eschatological perspective. As he sees tension between the "'already fulfilled' and 'not yet completed'" aspects of God's reign, he insists that Christians recognize both the necessity and the limitations of the state. The state is neither the kingdom of God nor God's chief agent in history, but it has a place "in God's economy of salvation" for the ordering of human existence in between the times of Pentecost and Parousia.[48]

Cullmann appears to be significant for Yoder in two ways. First, Cullmann's hermeneutical method of describing history, the church, and the state in light of "the biblical point of view" is very much like what Yoder calls the interpretative strategy of biblical realism. Given Yoder's citation of Cullmann at various points, it is a safe assumption that Yoder has developed his hermeneutical orientation through reliance, at least in part, on Cullmann.

Second, Cullmann's work on the eschatology of the New Testament has had a clear influence Yoder. He follows Cullmann in describing present history as realistically located between Pentecost and Parousia, in a segment of time over which Christ is lord, but which is not yet God's fulfilled kingdom. The church finds itself, in this view, as a foretaste of God's fulfilled reign in the midst of a world that embodies the old aeon. That Yoder employs the "D-Day" and "V-Day" analogy (which Cullmann uses to make an exegetical point), in order to interpret and describe history in a realistic fashion, is a lucid sign of the basic

---

[47]Cullmann, Christ and Time, 154-155.

[48]Cullmann, The State in the New Testament (New York: Charles Scribner's Sons, 1956), 87-90. See also his "The Kingship of Christ and the Church in the New Testament," The Early Church: Studies in Early Christian History and Theology, 105ff., which Yoder cites in The Christian Witness to the State, 9.

hermeneutical orientation that profoundly shapes his eschatology.[49]

In order to display briefly Yoder's actual use of Scripture, it is helpful to attend to some of the more important exegetical choices that he makes in formulating his eschatology. He uses 1 Corinthians 15:20-28 to display the present state of Christ's lordship in contrast to the future consummated reign of God.[50] He interprets the vision of Revelation 4-5 to indicate that the risen Lord is the key to the fulfillment of history.[51] Through reliance on such passages that are oriented toward the future of the kingdom, Yoder emphasizes that God's reign is not yet consummated.

There is also in his work, however, a strong emphasis on the present nature of God's kingdom: "The New Testament says more than the traditional eschatological debate does about the dimension of partial fulfillment now."[52] In light of his reading of Luke's gospel as a narrative which emphasizes the presence of the kingdom in Jesus' ministry, Yoder comments that

> The kingdom of God is a social order and not a hidden one. It is not a universal catastrophe independent of the will of men; it is that concrete jubilary obedience, in pardon and repentance, the possibility of which is proclaimed beginning right now, opening up the real accessibility of a new order in which grace and justice are linked, which men have only to accept. It does not assume time will end tomorrow; it reveals why it is meaningful that history should go on at all [emphasis mine].[53]

---

[49]Yoder, The Christian Witness to the State, 9.

[50]Yoder, The Christian Witness to the State, 9-10; See also his "If Christ Is Truly Lord," in The Original Revolution, 58; and Preface to Theology, 176.

[51]Yoder, The Politics of Jesus, 237ff. See also his "Armaments and Eschatology," 53; He Came Preaching Peace, 29; and "To Serve Our God and to Rule the World," 3ff.

[52]Yoder, Preface to Theology, 203.

[53]Yoder, The Politics of Jesus, 26ff., 108. We have emphasized Yoder's claim about the meaning of history in anticipation of a rigorous analysis, which will come in the following two chapters, of Yoder's view of God's governance of history during the present age. The crux of
(continued...)

Yoder reads various prophetic passages in the Old Testament as referring to, and being fulfilled in, Jesus' ministry.[54] He cites Matthew 4:17, 23-25 as indications that "Jesus began His own personal ministry by announcing the beginning of this [new and long awaited] age."[55] Comments Yoder,

> The new aeon came into history in a decisive way with the incarnation and the entire work of Christ. Christ had been awaited eagerly by Judaism for centuries; but when He came He was rejected, for the new aeon He revealed was not what men wanted. The Jews were awaiting a new age, a bringing to fulfillment of God's plan; but they expected it to confirm and to vindicate all their national hopes, prides, and solidarities. Thus Christ's claim and His kingdom were to them scandalous.[56]

This brief glance at Yoder's exegetical choices reveals that he interprets passages which emphasize both the "already" and "not yet" aspects of God's reign in a way that holds them in creative and mutually conditioned tension. Recognizing the existence of both sorts of passages in the New Testament, he sees God's reign as present but not yet fulfilled. In order to appreciate more fully the import of this aspect of Yoder's reading of Scripture, it is useful to place his formulation within the context of twentieth century biblical scholarship on the eschatology of the New Testament.

In this context, it is clear that Yoder's formulation is opposed to that of Albert Schweitzer, who described Jesus' message as a "thorough-going eschatology" in which the kingdom is entirely future. For Schweitzer, Jesus'

---

[53](...continued)
the issue is the extent to which God's purposes in history are knowable, and whether Yoder has attended to this issue, in both his critique of Constantinianism and his proposed alternative view of Christian social action, in a coherent fashion.

[54]Yoder, He Came Preaching Peace, 96ff.

[55]Yoder, "If Christ Is Truly Lord," in The Original Revolution, 37. See also his discussion of the Sermon on the Mount in relation to the kingdom in "Jesus' Life-Style Sermon and Prayer," Social Themes of the Christian Year: A Commentary on the Lectionary, ed. Dieter T. Hessel (Philadelphia: Geneva Press, 1983), 87ff.

[56]Yoder, "If Christ Is Truly Lord," in The Original Revolution, 55.

preaching called for present repentance in expectation of the kingdom's coming, and embraced the famous notion of an "interim ethics" appropriate for the brief time between Jesus' ministry and the coming of the new age. According to Schweitzer, when the kingdom did not come during the disciples' preaching mission, Jesus tried to force the hand of God for its manifestation by his own death. These hopes, however, went unfulfilled and the future kingdom expected by Jesus did not arrive.[57]

In response to Schweitzer, C. H. Dodd attempted to put a more congenial face on Jesus' ministry with his project of "realized eschatology." Dodd suggested that in Jesus' ministry God's kingdom and the fulfillment of its blessings were already present.[58] He thought that the kingdom had remained present since Jesus' time, and sought to display how synoptic texts that referred to the kingdom as present could be read as a key for interpreting references to the kingdom as future.

Dodd argued for realized eschatology in his 1935 Shaffer Lectures, later published as The Parables of the Kingdom. From Matthew 12:28 and Luke 11:20, he gathered that Jesus' exorcisms meant that "the sovereign power of God has come into effective operation." He reads Mark 1:14-15 and Luke 10:9-11 in light of those passages to conclude that Jesus thought the kingdom "a matter of present experience" rather than "something to come in the near future."[59] In The Apostolic Preaching and Its Developments, Dodd suggested that elements of

---

[57]Albert Schweitzer, The Quest for the Historical Jesus, 380ff. Yoder challenges Schweitzer's view implicitly in The Politics of Jesus, 16. See Willis' account of Schweitzer's significance in "The Discovery of the Eschatological Kingdom: Johannes Weiss and Albert Schweitzer," The Kingdom of God in 20th-Century Interpretation, 1-14.

[58]C. H. Dodd, The Parables of the Kingdom (New York: Charles Scribner's Sons, 1961), 82. For a helpful discussion of Dodd and Bultmann as post-Schweitzer exegetes, see Richard H. Hiers, Jr., "Pivotal Reactions to the Eschatological Interpretations: Rudolf Bultmann and C. H. Dodd," The Kingdom of God in 20th-Century Interpretation, 15-23.

[59]Dodd, The Parables of the Kingdom, 28-31.

futuristic eschatology in the gospels are the work of later church formulation, as the earliest tradition of Jesus' preaching is precisely that of realized eschatology.[60]

Rudolf Bultmann responded to the eschatological challenge raised by Schweitzer differently. In Jesus and Mythology, he agreed with Schweitzer that

[T]he kingdom of God is not immanent in the world and does not grow as part of the world's history, but is rather eschatological, i. e., the kingdom of God transcends the historical order...God will suddenly put an end to the world and to its history and He will bring in a new world, the world of eternal blessedness.[61]

Bultmann rejected Dodd's realized eschatology as unjustified "escape reasoning," and proposed instead that "Jesus clearly expected the irruption of God's Reign as a miraculous, world-transforming event" in the near future.[62]

In a way distinct from both Schweitzer and Dodd, Bultmann set out to "demythologize" Jesus' eschatological preaching in order to display the timeless understanding of existence and morality present in it. Says Bultmann,

The one concern in his teaching was that man should conceive his immediate concrete situation as the decision to which he is constrained, and should decide in this moment for God and surrender his natural will. Just this is what we found to be the final significance of the eschatological message, that man now stands under the necessity of decision, that his "Now" is always...the last hour, in which his decision against the world and for God is demanded, in which every claim of his own is to be

---

[60]Dodd, The Apostolic Preaching and Its Developments (London: Hodder and Stoughton, 1936), 21ff.

[61]Rudolf Bultmann, Jesus Christ and Mythology (New York: Charles Scribner's Sons, 1951), 12. See Raul Gabas Pallas' Escatologia protestante in la actualidad (Victoriensa: Publicationes del Seminario de Vitoria, 1964) 20: 201-229 for a concise, lucid description of Bultmann's eschatology within the context of his larger theological project.

[62]Bultmann, Jesus Christ and Mythology, 22.

silenced.[63]

In contrast to both the entirely future views of God's kingdom espoused by Schweitzer and Bultmann and the "realized" view of Dodd, we have noted above how Cullmann finds elements of "the already" and "the not yet" in Jesus' preaching and the apostolic witness. He suggests that God's reign has already begun in Jesus, but that it has not yet been fulfilled. Far from an interim period between Jesus' proclamation and the beginning of the kingdom, the church stands "in a segment of time...between Christ's ascension and his Parousia," between "D-Day" and "V-Day" as points of the inauguration and consummation of the kingdom. [64] Cullmann thinks that we live in the time of the "Regnum Christi" which will one day be fulfilled in the consummated Kingdom of God.[65]

Norman Perrin's doctoral dissertation, The Kingdom of God in the Teaching of Jesus, documents and evaluates much of the debate among biblical scholars on Jesus as an eschatological figure up through the mid-twentieth century. He notes that positions like Cullmann's have won a consensus among students of the New Testament.

> [The debate has] established that the Kingdom is both present and future in the teaching of Jesus. The discussion has reached this point; Weiss and Schweitzer were not able to convince the world of scholarship that it was wholly future. Dodd was not able to maintain his original [realized] view...and Bultmann's wholly futuristic interpretation was modified [by his students].[66]

Yoder, as is clear in light of his reliance on Cullmann, has constructed

---

[63]Bultmann, Jesus and the Word (New York: Charles Scribner's Sons, 1958), 131. See Yoder's critique of Bultmann's approach to ethics in "The Hermeneutics of Peoplehood," The Priestly Kingdom, 18-19.

[64]Cullmann, Christ and Time, 150.

[65]Cullmann, "The Kingship of Christ and the Church in the New Testament," The Early Church: Studies in Early Christian History and Theology, 110.

[66]Norman Perrin, The Kingdom of God in the Teaching of Jesus (London: SCM Press, 1963), 159.

50

his eschatology in light of that consensus among biblical scholars. He sees Jesus as the inaugurator of God's reign who now as the risen Lord "rules at the right hand of God" in anticipation of the fulfillment of the kingdom.[67] Yoder affirms the kingdom's presence in Jesus' ministry (Luke 4:21) and awaits its fulfillment when "he delivers up the kingdom to the God and Father, when he has abolished all rule and all authority and power. For he must reign until he has put all enemies under his feet" (1 Cor. 15:24-25).

Yoder "sees our present age--the age of the church, extending from Pentecost to Parousia--as a period of the overlapping of two aeons." The final consummation of the kingdom will be the ultimate victory of the new aeon over the old.[68]

In analyzing Yoder's use of the Bible, Cartwright notes a tension in his thought between an emphasis on the meaning of the "text itself" or the "biblical point of view" and the role of the "hermeneutic community" in interpreting Scripture.[69] It is clear that two characteristics of Yoder's method--that Scripture is to be read Christologically and communally--do not appear to be of a piece with the "what the text says" approach of biblical realism. Yoder suggests that, within the context of "an open process" which looks for the guidance of the Spirit, the community of faith reads Scripture in light of its confession that "the

---

[67]Yoder, The Christian and Capital Punishment, 15.

[68]Yoder, "If Christ Is Truly Lord," The Original Revolution, 55. Yoder appears to agree with Cullmann's formulation in "The Kingship of Christ and the Church in the New Testament," The Early Church: Studies in Early Christian History and Theology, 109, that "the Regnum Christi and the Church of Christ coincide with a chronologically limited phase of this time, namely the phase which has already begun and in which we are living, the beginning of which is behind and the end of which is before us..."

[69]Cartwright, "Practices, Politics, and Performance: Toward a Communal Hermeneutic for Christian Ethics," 386ff.

man Jesus" whom it portrays is "Lord and Christ."[70]

Yoder is obviously aware of various ways in which his Anabaptism has shaped his interpretation of Scripture.[71] Yet he does not think that the recognition of a "hermeneutical matrix" of tradition, which is brought to biblical interpretation, disqualifies his appeal to biblical authority. Says Yoder,

> To recognize that there is no reading of Scripture without an interpreting frame does not set aside the canonical witness as a baseline and a critical instance, or make it only one of "two sources" [the other being post-canonical tradition]. One's "hermeneutical matrix" is like the microscope in microbiology. You cannot see the tiny organisms without the microscope, but the microscope never becomes the microbe. The use of the microscope might impose upon the microbe certain very severe conditions before it can be seen...but even here the electron which the microscope uses to see with is not the molecule. It is, in other words, thoroughly possible to distinguish in principle between the object of knowledge and the way of knowing it, and to affirm the priority of the former. In a similar sense, Protestant biblicists do not deny that they use language and logic, but they need not grant that that makes their reading hopelessly subjective. They can grant that the Scripture was produced by churches out of traditions that were not "Scripture" until long after they were edited and recorded, and that contemporary interpretation is moved by contemporary priorities and challenges, without thereby conceding as desirable or even as possible that all of that process be controlled by a particular agent in the teaching of the church.[72]

It is interesting to note, in this light, that Yoder makes clear appeals to

---

[70]Yoder, "The Hermeneutics of Peoplehood," in The Priestly Kingdom, 22, 37, 43. He describes these points of emphasis in historical perspective in "The Hermeneutics of the Anabaptists," in Essays on Biblical Interpretation: Anabaptist/Mennonite Perspectives, 11-28.

[71]He comments, for example, in "The Hermeneutics of Peoplehood," The Priestly Kingdom, 37, that "For the radical Protestant there will always be a canon within the canon: namely, that recorded experience of practical moral reasoning in genuine human form that bears the name of Jesus."

[72]Yoder, "The Authority of Tradition," The Priestly Kingdom, 66-67.

52

Scripture as a source of authority throughout his intentionally "Protestant" essay on the church as a hermeneutical community.[73] Indeed, he seeks to justify his communal and Christological reading of Scripture precisely on biblical terms. He believes that such a hermeneutical method is demanded by Scripture.[74] Moreover, Yoder is not primarily concerned with arguing, on every theological point, in terms of Scripture versus tradition, but rather in opposing what "is counter to the Scriptures...The issue is (as Jesus said it) the traditions of men versus the commandment of God," and not simply whether one makes explicit appeal to the words of the Bible.[75]

It may be most helpful, then, to suggest that Yoder's hermeneutical orientation seeks to be faithful to "the biblical point of view" by interpreting the Bible in the fashion which he believes that the Bible itself demands: in the church and in light of the confession that Jesus is Lord. The key implication of biblical realism is, for Yoder, that Christians adopt the world view of the Bible as their own.[76] Yoder is well aware that his approach is one of many historically contingent options, and that others may and do read the Bible differently. His claim is that he stands within a tradition which, through its Christocentric and communal reading, is being faithful to the message of the Bible. Thereby, his tradition participates in

> a process of reaching back again to the origins, to the earliest memories of the event itself, confident that the testimony,

---

[73]Yoder, "The Hermeneutics of Peoplehood: A Protestant Perspective," The Priestly Kingdom, 22, 26, 29ff.

[74]Yoder, "A People in the World: Theological Interpretation," The Concept of the Believers' Church, ed. James Leo Garrett (Scottdale, Pennsylvania: Herald Press, 1969), 19; "But We Do See Jesus," The Priestly Kingdom, 49-54.

[75]Yoder, "The Authority of Tradition," The Priestly Kingdom, 76.

[76]This hermeneutical strategy underwrites, for example, Yoder's call to make the social ethic espoused by the New Testament, and especially by its portrayals of Jesus, the "one particular social-political-ethical option" which is normative for the Christian life. Yoder, The Politics of Jesus, 22-23.

however intimately integrated with the belief of the witnesses, is not a wax nose, and will serve to illuminate and sometimes adjudicate our present path.[77]

As this formulation indicates, Yoder stands within a tradition that seeks to employ Scripture as the ultimately authoritative resource for theology and ethics, which requires interpretation in the community of faith and in light of the confession that Jesus is the Christ.

This conclusion confirms Cartwright's doubt that Yoder's simple reference to "the biblical vision of reality," which biblical realism aims to display and hold in tension with modernity, is an adequate statement of Yoder's hermeneutical orientation.[78] It is a problematic formulation because it appears to claim that Scripture is self-interpreting in a fashion that does not acknowledge the fact that interpreters are influenced by traditions and communities which inform their views of "the biblical vision of reality." It also appears to claim a unity for the "world view" of the Bible which does not take into account its diverse authorship and forms of literature. Neither does it allow for various levels of meaning which readers may discover in the text.[79]

As Yoder recognizes that traditions, such as Anabaptism, shape one's reading of the Bible, he would do well to qualify his references to biblical realism in a way that displays more clearly how the theological tradition of the interpreter shapes his or her account of "the biblical point of view." While Yoder has clearly grappled with these issues, he does not appear to have reformulated his

---

[77]Yoder, "The Authority of Tradition," The Priestly Kingdom, 70.

[78]Yoder, The Politics of Jesus, 5.

[79]See David C. Steinmetz, "The Superiority of Pre-Critical Exegesis," Theology Today 37 (April 1980): 27-38, for a brief discussion of various levels of meaning which Christians have found in biblical texts.

biblical realism explicitly in this light.[80] Hence, his continued use of the term is troubling.

Another problematic aspect of Yoder's hermeneutical strategy is his reliance on biblical scholarship for the construction of "the biblical point of view." The problem is that Yoder does not make clear by what standard he affirms certain findings of biblical studies to be appropriate portraits of the world view of the Bible. In this regard, it is interesting to note that he cites most often the findings of historical-critical research done between 1940 and 1970.[81] Yoder does not appear to take account of more recent studies, whether those of the historical-critical mode or of the schools of literary criticism, which might be pertinent to his project.[82]

As Yoder does not seem to have addressed the issue of how he discriminates among various contruals of "what the text says," he is open to a critique of arbitrariness in his use of biblical scholarship. Indeed, a project which purports to be shaped decisively by the world view of the Bible, and which relies at a crucial points on the findings of exegetes, would need to employ clear and rigorous criteria for the determination of precisely which exegetical findings are

---

[80]While Yoder's "The Authority of Tradition," The Priestly Kingdom, 63-79, reflects concern for this issue, it does not address critically the language of biblical realism in light of the influence of theological tradition on interpreters of Scripture.

[81]See, for example, his many references to biblical scholars of that period in The Politics of Jesus, as well as in his list of suggested readings on New Testament studies in his more recent Preface to Theology, 14-15. We have noted above Yoder's reliance on the findings of Cullmann and Berkhof, both of whom wrote during this time period.

[82]There are many relatively recent works in New Testament studies, which he has not apparently engaged, that would seem to be relevant for Yoder's pursuit for "the world view of the Bible." These include, but are by no means limited to: Amos Wilder, Early Christian Rhetoric: The Language of the Gospel (Cambridge, Massachusetts: Harvard University Press, 1971); Norman Perrin, Jesus and the Language of the Kingdom (Philadelphia: Fortress Press, 1976); R. Alan Culpepper, Anatomy of the Fourth Gospel: A Study in Literary Design (Philadelphia: Fortress Press, 1983); and Gerhard Lohfink, Jesus and Community: The Social Dimension of Christian Faith (Philadelphia: Fortress Press, 1984).

appropriate resources for theological construction. Apart from the use of such criteria, there would seem to be the danger that only those findings of biblical scholarship which support the present commitments of the theologian would be cited as sources. In such a situation, it would not be clear what role biblical scholarship would play other than that of "proof texting" preconceived theological commitments.

That sort of uncritical support for privileged theological discourse would indicate the collapse of biblical realism as a hermeneutical orientation capable of critically informing constructive theological work by holding it accountable to the best available account of "the biblical point of view." As Yoder has not demonstrated how his use of a certain segment of the biblical scholarship of a generation ago, as well as his lack of reference to more recent studies, is methodologically warranted, it is by no means clear that his project is able to distinguish a finely honed account of "the world view of the Bible" from a less precise one. As such, it is not evident that Yoder's methodology is appropriate to the rhetoric of biblical realism.[83] This criticism raises once again the ambiguous nature of the relationship between Yoder's appeals to both modern biblical criticism and the interpretative authority of the community of faith.

Another puzzling aspect of Yoder's reliance on biblical scholarship is raised by his claim in The Politics of Jesus, which is filled with references to New Testament exegesis, that

> it is safer for the life of the church to have the whole people of God reading the whole body of canonical Scripture than to trust for her enlightenment only to certain of the filtering processes through which the learned men of a given age would insist all the

---

[83]It is noteworthy that this difficulty in Yoder's use of Scripture is not identified in Birch and Rasmussen's discussion of Yoder in Bible and Ethics and the Christian Life, 18ff. Neither does Hughes raise the issue in his discussion of Yoder's biblical realism in "The Ethical Use of Power: A Discussion with the Christian Perspectives of Reinhold Niebuhr, John Howard Yoder, and Richard J. Barnet," 109-116.

truth must pass.[84]

That Yoder begins a book, in which he draws heavily from New Testament scholarship, with the claim that the community of faith's reading of Scripture is in someways privileged over the findings of critical biblical studies, affirms Cartwright's criticism that there is an unresolved tension in Yoder's thought between the "what the text says" approach of biblical realism, which establishes the meaning of the text through the tools of modern biblical scholarship, and a communal hermeneutic for the interpretation of Scripture.[85]

While Yoder suggests that biblical realism is, in large part, a theologically motivated hermeneutical strategy which seeks to display "the wholeness" of the Bible by making clear "what the author of the text means to say," he does not appear to recognize certain points of tension raised by the affirmation of both modern critical biblical studies and "my post-modern acceptance of the particularity of the Christian story without subjecting it...to...some specific 'scientific method.'"[86] For example, one could ask how

---

[84]Yoder, The Politics of Jesus, 14.

[85]Cartwright, "Practices, Politics and Performance: Toward a Communal Hermeneutic for Christian Ethics," 386ff.

[86]Yoder, "Introduction," The Priestly Kingdom, 9. In "The Authority of the Canon," Essays on Biblical Interpretation: Anabaptist-Mennonite Perspectives, 273ff., Yoder emphasizes the importance of redaction criticism for ensuring that the canonical text's portrayal of "the full meaning of Jesus" is displayed with historical integrity. But he also argues, in "The Use of the Bible in Theology," The Use of the Bible in Theology/Evangelical Options, 116, that his "biblical realist position is only possible as a post-critical phenomenon. It is scholastic orthodoxy which is naively pre-critical when it assumes that the scriptural text standing there alone can be interpreted faithfully and can be equated with our systematic restructuring of its contents. What is at stake is not whether the Bible can be interpreted at this great distance without linguistic and hermeneutical tools but whether, at those points where it is clear what it says, we are going to let that testimony count rather than subjecting it to the superior authority of our own contemporary hermeneutic framework."

Yoder apparently wants the community of faith to profit from the insights of modern biblical criticism. It is not clear in his formulation, however, whether the findings of historical criticism or the traditioned claims of the church are to have the upper hand in determining the meaning of a text. Yoder affirms the necessity of critical biblical studies for the historically precise determination of "what the text says," but at the same time calls for a post-critical reading

(continued...)

the community of faith may go about appropriating the findings of biblical studies. How would they discriminate among various construals of "what the text says"? By what standard or authority would they challenge a particular critical claim about Scripture as inappropriate for acceptance by the church? How might they avoid affirming only those findings which supported their preconceived convictions?

These are but a few examples of questions, raised by Yoder's espoused hermeneutical strategy, which he does not answer. As such, we may tentatively conclude that there are significant points of tension in Yoder's use of Scripture, which call into question the adequacy of his claim to be analyzing the Christian life from the perspective of "the world view of the Bible." These criticisms point to difficulties in Yoder's treatment of the major sources of knowledge which he claims for his project, the Bible and the traditionally located discernment of the community of faith.

Such epistemological inadequacies may prove quite troubling for Yoder's entire project, as they cast doubt on his ability to give a coherent account of the validity of key theological and moral claims. As the analysis of Yoder's work develops throughout the dissertation, we will, at various points, test the epistemological basis of his treatment of certain substantive themes.

The Relationship of Eschatology to Christology

That Christology is an important theological theme for Yoder is obvious from a glance at the titles of a few of his books: Preface to Theology: Christology and Theological Method, The Politics of Jesus, and He Came Preaching Peace. Within the context of his espoused biblical realism, Yoder approaches Christology as the subject matter of the most distinctive message

---

[86](...continued)
of Scripture in light of the community's discernment. Yoder does not display with precision how the interaction of biblical scholarship and communal interpretation is to take place. This is a significant point of tension in his use of Scripture.

proclaimed by the New Testament: that Jesus is Lord.[87] Its authors were making known the particular truth of the Gospel in a world that was not looking for a lord like Jesus. Yoder comments on the authors of the New Testament:

A handful of messianic Jews, moving beyond the defense of their somewhat separate society to attack the intellectual bastions of majority culture, refused to contextualize their message by clothing it in the categories the world held ready. Instead, they seized the categories, hammered them into other shapes, and turned the cosmology on its head, with Jesus both at the bottom, crucified as a common criminal, and at the top, preexistent Son and creator, and the church his instrument in today's battle.[88]

In discussing the particularity of the New Testament's claims about Jesus, Yoder uses terms with eschatological significance.

[T]he messianic Jewish witnesses also affirmed that under his lordship that cosmos will find its true coherence and meaning. To use the example of Colossians, the powers are not merely defeated in their claim to sovereignty, and humbled; they are also reenlisted in the original creative purpose of the service of humanity and God. Or in John, the logos/sophia vision of the rationality of the universe and of history is not only dethroned but also put to work illuminating everyone who comes into the world, and empowering sons and daughters. To know that the Lamb who was slain was worthy to receive power not only enables his disciples to face martyrdom when they must; it also encourages them to go about their daily crafts...without being driven by cosmic doubt. Even before the broken world can be made whole by the Second Coming, the witnesses to the first coming--through the very fact that they proclaim Christ above the powers, the Son above the angels--are enabled to go on proleptically in the

---

[87]Yoder, "But We Do See Jesus," The Priestly Kingdom, 49. For discussions of Yoder's Christology, see Parham, "An Ethical Analysis of the Christian Social Strategies in the Writings of John C. Bennet, Jacques Ellul, and John Howard Yoder," 183ff.; Hughes, "The Ethical Use of Power: A Discussion with the Christian Perspectives of Reinhold Niebuhr, John Howard Yoder, and Richard J. Barnet," 116ff.; and Zimbleman, "Theological Ethics and Politics in the Thought of Juan Luis Segundo and John Howard Yoder," 191ff.

[88]Yoder, "But We Do See Jesus," The Priestly Kingdom, 54. For a discussion of Yoder's emphasis on the particularity of the good news about Jesus, see Koontz, "Confessional Theology in a Pluralistic Context: A Study of the Theological Ethics of H. Richard Niebuhr and John H. Yoder," 34ff.

redemption of creation. Only this evangelical Christology can found a truly transformationist approach to culture.[89]

In this passage, Yoder suggests essentially that the identification of Jesus as Lord is an eschatological claim: he has conquered the powers and will one day consummate the redemption of all creation.[90] Yoder suggests elsewhere that "the concrete meaning of the term Lord" is precisely that "by His cross, resurrection, ascension, and the pouring out of His spirit, [Jesus] has triumphed over the powers."[91]

Yoder understands Jesus to have triumphed over the powers through his obedience to God.

> The work of Christ is, at its center, obedience (Phil. 2 et al). Christ was exactly what God meant man to be; man in free communion with God, obeying God and loving mankind, even his enemies with God's love.[92]

Jesus embodied God's agape toward sinners through "non-resistance, bearing the other's sinfulness, bearing, literally, his sins." It was only non-resistance that would respect the freedom of humanity to reject him and fulfill God's salvific intention.[93]

The obedience of Jesus to this way of non-resistant love culminated in the cross. For Yoder,

> The sinlessness of Christ is thus not (as for Anselm) a purely legal formality or, as some understand the OT sacrifices, a matter merely of ritual cleanness; His sinlessness is rather the whole

---

[89]Yoder, "But We Do See Jesus," The Priestly Kingdom, 61.

[90]Yoder suggests that the coming fullness of God's redemption will be God's final victory over evil in the eschaton in which God will be the active agent.

[91]Yoder, The Christian Witness to the State, 9.

[92]Yoder, Preface to Theology, 229. In "Christ, the Light of the World," The Original Revolution, 129, Yoder comments that "the humanity of Jesus is a revelation of the purpose of God for a man who wills to do his will."

[93]Yoder, Preface to Theology, 229.

60

point of His life and His obedience-offering. His sinlessness, His obedience, is what He offered to God, and that sinlessness, utter faithfulness to love, cost His life in a world of sinners.[94]

The resurrection is the vindication of Jesus' obedience to the point of death at the hands of sinners.

Ontologically, it is a simple necessity; "Death couldn't hold Him down" (Acts 2:24). Psychologically, the Resurrection is fundamental for discipleship, as it vindicates the rightness, the possibility, the effectiveness of the way of the cross....The resurrection proves that, even when man does his worst, turns the farthest from God's communion, so far as to kill God, he cannot destroy that love. Man has done his worst, and the love of God is still stronger.[95]

The entire life and ministry of Jesus is for Yoder one of obedience to God in the midst of a sinful world. In order for God's salvation to come, the sovereignty of the powers had to be broken.

This is what Jesus did, concretely and historically, by living among men in a genuinely free and human existence. This life brought him, as any genuinely human existence will bring any man, to the cross. In his death the Powers--in this case the most worthy, weighty representatives of Jewish religion and Roman politics--acted in collusion....His very obedience unto death is in itself not only the sign but also the first fruits of an authentic restored humanity...Thus it is his death that provides his victory: "Wherefore God has exalted him highly, and given him the name which is above every name...that every tongue might confess that Jesus Christ is Lord."[96]

It is through the obedience of his life and death that a new age of God's rule has begun. "The new aeon came into history in a decisive way with the

---

[94]Yoder, Preface to Theology, 230.

[95]Yoder, Preface to Theology, 230.

[96]Yoder, The Politics of Jesus, 147-148.

incarnation and the entire work of Christ."[97] Yoder suggests that

> Jesus [in his ministry] is bringing to pass... the newness of the
> age in which God's righteousness is operative among those who
> hear it proclaimed. This reversal of values is not first of all new
> information...it is first of all a whole new world...the kingdom is
> upon us.[98]

The characteristic of Christ's work which is normative for his disciples
is the culmination of his obedience in the crucifixion. Jesus models for his
followers "a substantial, binding, costly social stance" of non-resistant love in the
face of evil.[99] Indeed,

> The cross of Christ was not an inexplicable or chance event,
> which happened to strike him, like illness or accident. To accept
> the cross was his destiny, to move toward it and even to provoke
> it, when he well could have done otherwise...it was the political,
> legally to be expected result of a moral clash with the powers
> ruling his society.[100]

Disciples of Jesus are to follow him in the ministry of God's new age precisely
by living cruciform lives of non-resistant obedience.

> There is thus but one realm in which the concept of imitation
> holds...this is at the point of the concrete social meaning of the
> cross in its relation to enmity and power. Servanthood replaces
> dominion, forgiveness absorbs hostility. Thus--and only thus--are
> we bound by New Testament thought to "be like Jesus."[101]

---

[97]Yoder, "If Christ Is Truly Lord," The Original Revolution, 55. Hauerwas comments in
"The Nonresistant Church: The Theological Ethics of John Howard Yoder," Vision and Virtue,
201, that "By Christ's coming and action a new kingdom has been established as God declares his
Lordship by reclaiming his creation and subduing the powers to his will."

[98]Yoder, "Jesus' Life-Style Sermon and Prayer," Social Themes of the Christian Year, 89.
See also his "Jesus and Power," Ecumenical Review 25 (October 1973): 450.

[99]Yoder, The Politics of Jesus, 130-131.

[100]Yoder, The Politics of Jesus, 132. See also He Came Preaching Peace, 17-21.

[101]Yoder, The Politics of Jesus, 134. See also "Living the Disarmed Life: Christ's Strategy
for Peace," Waging Peace, ed. Jim Wallis (San Francisco: Harper & Row Publishers, 1982),
127. An important task of the fourth chapter will be to determine whether Yoder's proposed
method of Christian social action is consistent with this formulation of the crux of discipleship.

In summary, Yoder's Jesus is an eschatological Jesus. In his construal, the claim that Jesus is the Christ is dependent upon his entire life's work of conquering the powers through his obedience, which has begun a new aeon. Jesus' obedience and defeat of the powers enables humans to confess and follow him as Lord, for the sovereignty of the rebellious powers over us has been broken by him. Because of his resurrection, humanity is in principle free to follow him in discipleship. Hence, we live in a new, but not yet consummated age, that has been inaugurated through his obedience to the Father.[102]

This eschatological Christology has the moral relevance of modeling the sort of non-resistant love required of Christians in the new age. Christians are to follow Jesus in costly obedience.

> The cross of the Christian is no different. It is the price of one's obedience to God's love toward all people in a world ruled by hate. Such unflinching love for friend and foe alike will mean hostility and suffering for us, as it did for him.[103]

The way of the cross is incumbent on those who undertake "the politics of Jesus" in a world over which God's reign is not yet complete.

In making a brief evaluation of Yoder's Christology, it is apparent that there is a general coherence between his eschatology and view of Jesus Christ, in that Jesus is understood as the one who has inaugurated the new age of God's reign which will find fulfillment in the eschaton. As with explicitly eschatological questions, Yoder seeks to portray Jesus in light of the interpretative strategy of biblical realism. While, as we noted earlier, Yoder's use of biblical realism is problematic, it is clear that he is at least consistent in attempting to view Jesus Christ in light of "the biblical point of view."

One advantage to Yoder's method is his insistence that Christological

---

[102]Parham summarizes succinctly Jesus' eschatological significance for Yoder in "An Ethical Analysis of the Christian Social Strategies in the Writings of John C. Bennett, Jacques Ellul, and John Howard Yoder," 186-188.

[103]Yoder, He Came Preaching Peace, 19.

construction be held accountable to New Testament portraits of Jesus.[104] Jon Sobrino points to the importance of such an orientation:

> There is an important epistemological implication in the fact that we make the historical Jesus the starting point of Christology. It is Jesus himself, in his own historical life, who raises the whole question of his own person. We are forced into a very different position. Instead of asking questions, we ourselves are now called into question by Jesus. Thus it is the historical Jesus who brings Christology into crisis, effecting the epistemological break that is necessary if Christology is not to be simply the outcome of the natural person's inertial wishes and projections....If a Christology disregards the historical Jesus, it turns into an abstract Christology that is historically alienating and open to manipulation.[105]

While Yoder does not frame his Christology in a way that distinguishes explicitly between discourse concerning "the historical Jesus" and "the Christ of faith," he does assume that the New Testament's portrayals of Jesus are historically accurate in their identifications of Jesus of Nazareth as the Christ. Indeed, he insists that theological descriptions of the Christ be held accountable to the life in human history of the Incarnate Word.[106] Yoder welcomes critical efforts which seek to portray with historical accuracy the life of Jesus, largely because he suspects that they will challenge "the traditional dogmatic picture of

---

[104]Yoder, "The Hermeneutics of Peoplehood," The Priestly Kingdom, 37. The Politics of Jesus is, of course, largely an attempt to construct a view of Jesus in light of the New Testament witness.

[105]Jon Sobrino, Christology at the Crossroads (Maryknoll, New York: Orbis Books, 1978), 353.

[106]Sawatsky comments that "Yoder's Christology is fully orthodox if Nicaea is considered normative. Jesus is understood as both God and man not merely for the sake of orthodoxy, but for the sake of Christian ethics. In his death Jesus revealed how God responds to evil, namely, by coming among men, labeling sins and injustices, taking upon himself the suffering men inflict upon one another, and doing all this nonresistantly to the point of his own death. In his humanity Jesus prescribed God's purposes for man. The unity of Jesus with his father is correctly understood, not in terms of substance, but rather of will and deed, that is, of perfect obedience to the will of the father. For example, in siding with the poor and rejecting the sword and the throne, Jesus reveals the will of God." Sawatsky, "John Howard Yoder," Non-violence: Central to Christian Spirituality, 246.

64

the apolitical Jesus."[107]

Yoder's approach is advantageous because it seeks to hold Christological construction accountable to New Testament portayals of Jesus Christ; and, hence, tends to resist the temptation to interpret Jesus "in our own image," to domesticate him into a compliant Lord who does not call us, or our world, into serious question. As Wolfhart Pannenberg comments, it is a crucial task of Christology to make sure "that we do not speak unknowingly of something quite different under the name of Jesus."[108] As Yoder's criticism of portraits of Jesus which obscure our Lord's moral relevance indicate, it is clear that Yoder seeks to keep Jesus of Nazareth, as portrayed in the New Testament, at the heart of Christology.[109]

It is fitting, then, to ask whether Yoder's account of the Jesus of the New Testament is formulated adequately. The question arises in light of Yoder's emphasis on the synoptic gospels' portraits of Jesus. Yoder focuses especially on Luke's gospel, given its emphasis on certain social aspects of Jesus' ministry.[110] This emphasis on the synoptics leads Ramsey to describe Yoder's Christology as "Jesucentric," oriented on the person of Jesus of Nazareth apparently without sufficient awareness of the richness of Christological options which focus on the

---

[107]Yoder, The Politics of Jesus, 24-25. For Sobrino's account of "the Jesus of history" as opposed to "the Christ of Faith," see Christology at the Crossroads, 273ff. As noted in the second section of this chapter, Yoder does not display lucidly the dynamics of the church's use of such modern biblical scholarship.

[108]Wolfhart Pannenberg, Jesus--God and Man (Philadelphia: Westminster Press, 1977), 365.

[109]Yoder, The Politics of Jesus, 15-25.

[110]The Politics of Jesus places more emphasis on Luke than on any of the other gospels. Throughout his writings, Yoder tends to frame the Christian life within the context of discipleship in a fashion that draws most heavily on the synoptics. See, for example, "The Political Axioms of the Sermon on the Mount," The Original Revolution, 34-51.

pre-existent Logos, the glory of the risen Christ, and other theological themes.[111]

It appears, however, that Yoder does not neglect "the cosmic Christ" of certain portions of the Pauline and Johannine literature. Especially in his appropriation of Cullmann and Berkhof's exegetical work, Yoder addresses the moral relevance of the risen Christ who will redeem history.[112] He likewise incorporates the "logos Christology" of the prologue to John's gospel with his claim that

> what is known in Jesus is precisely the same, in authority and in meaning, as what underlies creation. When he says "there was nothing of what came to be that did not come to be through him," John is not propounding a new theory about creation. He is simply repeating the Genesis report, which shows God creating by his Word. But from that report he draws a negation. God has not revealed himself otherwise. He has not revealed a different purpose or character through creation than what we now encounter with Jesus.[113]

It is to Yoder's credit that he has drawn from the variety of Christological themes

---

[111]Ramsey, Speak Up for Just War or Pacifism, 111ff. It is noteworthy that there is little well developed analysis of Yoder's Christology in the secondary literature. Ramsey's treatment of the theme is quite brief, as is Zimbleman's discussion in "Theological Ethics and Politics in the Thought of Juan Luis Segundo and John Howard Yoder," 191ff. The same is true, for example, of Parham, "An Ethical Analysis of the Christian Social Strategies in the Writings of John C. Bennett, Jacques Ellul, and John Howard Yoder," 183-189; Hughes, "The Ethical Use of Power: A Discussion with the Christian Perspectives of Reinhold Niebuhr, John Howard Yoder, and Richard J. Barnet," 116-122; and Adams, "Christology and Ethics: A Critical and Personal Essay," 55-69.

[112]See, for example, The Christian Witness to the State, 8ff.; "But We Do See Jesus," The Priestly Kingdom, 50ff.; The Politics of Jesus, 135ff., 233ff.; "Glory in a Tent," He Came Preaching Peace, 69ff.; and Preface to Theology, 172ff.

[113]Yoder, "Glory in a Tent," He Came Preaching Peace, 82. Yoder also refers to the prologue in "But We Do See Jesus," The Priestly Kingdom, 50-51. In the next section of the chapter, as well as in coming chapters, we will examine critically the role which creation plays for Yoder in moral discernment.

66

in the New Testament. In this light, Ramsey's criticism seems unwarranted.[114]

In keeping with the epistemological questions raised in the previous section about points of tension in Yoder's affirmation of both the findings of critical biblical scholarship and the traditioned wisdom of the community of faith as sources for theological construction, it is interesting to ask by what methodological standards Yoder has selected both the passages of Scripture and the biblical scholarship in light of which he formulates his Christology. Yoder's emphasis on "the synoptic Jesus" seems to reflect Anabaptism's traditional stress on the following of the Jesus who called disciples and required of them a life characterized by the singleminded pursuit of the ministry of God's reign.[115]

As noted above, Yoder's Christology does not focus exclusively on this portrait of Jesus of Nazareth, as it also takes account of New Testament passages which portray the Christ as Logos and risen Lord. For the exegetical analysis of such texts, Yoder appears to rely most strongly on the findings of scholars such as Cullmann and Berkhof. It is from them, for example, that Yoder gets his account of the risen Christ's victory over the powers as an event which guarantees the coming fullness of God's reign.[116]

It is safe to conclude, then, that Yoder's choice of central passages for Christological construction is strongly influenced by his Anabaptist tradition. It is less clear, however, by what standard Yoder has chosen the biblical scholarship on which he relies for interpreting these and other New Testament texts. Yoder might respond that he chose the studies which were generally thought by scholars

---

[114]Of course, Ramsey is correct in his claim that Christians may formulate coherent Christologies which are substantially different from that of Yoder. His charge of a problematically onesided "Jesucentrism" which neglects the full range of the New Testament's Christological themes, however, reflects an inadequate grasp of Yoder's project. Ramsey, Speak Up for Just War or Pacifism, 112ff.

[115]See Weaver, Becoming Anabaptist, 120ff.

[116]See, for example, Yoder, The Christian Witness to the State, 8ff.

to be the best at the time at which he used them.[117] It is not evident, however, what authority the consensus of biblical scholars should play for Yoder's theological construction, given his emphasis on a communally located, Christologically centered interpretation of Scripture.

What precise dynamics of interaction, for example, are appropriate for the community's appropriation of a given critical account of the New Testament's portrayal of Jesus Christ? How much trust, or conversely how much suspicion, should the community of faith bring to its reading of biblical scholarship which may underwrite an historicist account of the meaning of a text which could severely limit the range of the community's interpretation of given passages? Especially in light of Yoder's claim that "The church precedes the world epistemologically. We know more fully from Jesus Christ and in the context of the confessed faith than we know in other ways," it seems quite important for Yoder to provide a lucid account of how theologians are to discriminate among various accounts of biblical scholarship.[118]

This criticism does not, however, directly challenge on substantive grounds the adequacy of Yoder's Christology. Rather, it identifies a troubling point of ambiguity in the epistemological basis of his formulation. This point of difficulty, then, should be held in tension with our earlier more appreciative remarks on Yoder's Christology.

---

[117]That would seem to be an implication of the stress which Yoder places on the importance of critical biblical studies in The Politics of Jesus, 24-25; and "The Authority of the Canon," Essays on Biblical Interpretation/Anabaptist-Mennonite Perspectives, 273ff.

[118]In light of the diverse renderings of Scripture provided by various contemporary biblical scholars, it would seem important for Yoder to attend to these issues in order for him to sustain his project of biblical realism with a high degree of methodological precision. Given the widely differing interpretations of the Bible which are available today, including, for example, the liberationist projects of Jose Miranda, Marx and the Bible (Maryknoll, New York: Orbis Books, 1974) and J. Severino Croatto, Biblical Hermeneutics: Toward a Theory of Reading as the Production of Meaning (Maryknoll, New York: Orbis Books, 1987), issues of how theologians will discriminate among works of biblical studies are extremely pertinent.

The Significance of Eschatology for Ecclesiology

Yoder understands the church to be an eschatological community, the "aftertaste of God's loving triumph on the cross and foretaste of His ultimate loving triumph in His kingdom."[119] The new aeon begun in Jesus "has a social manifestation...[in] the church or the body of Christ."[120] It is in the church that Christ's victory over the powers, and action in history, is most directly evident.

> In spite of the present visible dominion of the "powers" of "this present evil age," the triumph of Christ has already guaranteed that the ultimate meaning of history will not be found in the course of earthly empires or the development of proud cultures, but in the calling together of the "chosen race, royal priesthood, holy nation," which is the church of Christ. The church is not fundamentally a source of moral stimulus to encourage the development of a better society--though a faithful church should also have this effect--it is for the sake of the church's own work that society continues to function. The meaning of history...lies in the creation and work of the church.[121]

An essential characteristic of the church for Yoder is "her own obedience to the standards of discipleship." The church is to engage in

> evangelistic activity (in the traditional, restricted sense of that term...), but just as fundamentally in the service of the needy, and equally in her refusal to use means unfitting of her ends....The church is herself a society. Her very existence, the fraternal relations of her members, their ways of dealing with their differences and their needs are, or rather should be, a demonstration of what love means in social relations.[122]

Through its faithfulness and obedience to Christ, the church is to foreshadow the perfect submission to God that the consummated kingdom will

---

[119]Yoder, The Christian Witness to the State, 10.

[120]Yoder, "If Christ Is Truly Lord," The Original Revolution, 55.

[121]Yoder, The Christian Witness to the State, 13.

[122]Yoder, The Christian Witness to the State, 17.

bring.[123] In this sense, the church

> discharges a modeling mission. The church is called to be now what the world is called to be ultimately. To describe their own community Jews and Christians have classically used terms like those claimed by the structures of the wider world: "people," "nation," "kingdom," even "army." These are not simply poetic figures of speech. They imply the calling to see oneself as doing already on behalf of the wider world what the world is destined for in God's creative purpose.[124]

In light of this foreshadowing mission of the church, Yoder attends in detail in "The Hermeneutics of Peoplehood" to the sort of order and discernment which are appropriate to the church's eschatological identity. In particular, he notes the importance of procedures for reconciliation within the community. In light of Matthew 18:15-18, he suggests that

> A transcendent moral ratification is claimed for the decisions made in the conversation of two or three or more, in a context of forgiveness and in the juridical form of listening to the several witnesses.[125]

The text presents "a kind of situation ethics, i. e., a procedure for doing practical moral reasoning, in a context of conflict, right in the situation where divergent views are being lived out in such a way as to cause offense." The procedure is contextualized by its eschatological location: members prod one another in a forgiving fashion to live faithfully as disciples in the new aeon.

Yoder thinks that to display more fully how the practical moral reasoning of the church works "we need to ask not how ideas work but how the

---

[123]Yoder, "The Original Revolution," The Original Revolution, 30-31.

[124]Yoder, "The Kingdom as Social Ethic," The Priestly KIngdom, 92.

[125]Yoder, "The Hermeneutics of Peoplehood," The Priestly Kingdom, 27. See Yoder's "Binding and Loosing" in John White and Ken Blue, Healing the Wounded: The Costly Love of Church Discipline (Downers Grove, Illinois: InterVarsity Press, 1985), 211-234, for a more detailed account of his view of reconciliation in the church.

community works."[126]   While every member of the community has a distinctive place in its life, he identifies a few necessary agents.

First, he notes "Agents of Direction" who speak prophetically to provide "a vision of the place of the believing community in history, which vision locates moral reasoning" (1 Cor. 14:3, 29). The validity of such speech is judged by the community under the guidance of the Spirit.[127]   Also, there are "Agents of Memory" who speak as servants of the community and its shared memory. "Scripture is the collective scribal memory," the primary substance of the memory to be tapped for guidance in the present.[128]   "Agents of Linguistic Self-Consciousness" will "watch out for the sophomoric temptation of verbal distinctions without substantial necessity, and of purely verbal solutions to substantial problems." This agent will be a teacher of the community in matters of faithfulness.[129]   "Agents of Order and Due Process" will ensure that "everyone else is heard, and that the conclusions reached are genuinely consensual" in the community.[130]

As this essay indicates, a crucial factor for Yoder is "the communal context" in terms of which various forms of moral reasoning will be pursued. He wants to "attend more carefully to the agencies of a shared discerning process" than to decisionist sensibilities that reflect for him the inadequacies of individualistic accounts of the moral life.[131]   Rather than focusing on metaethical distinctions, "the task of the teacher will rather be...to contribute to

---

[126]Yoder, "The Hermeneutics of Peoplehood," The Priestly Kingdom, 27-28.

[127]Yoder, "The Hermeneutics of Peoplehood," The Priestly Kingdom, 29.

[128]Yoder, "The Hermeneutics of Peoplehood," The Priestly Kingdom, 31.

[129]Yoder, "The Hermeneutics of Peoplehood," The Priestly Kingdom, 32-33.

[130]Yoder, "The Hermeneutics of Peoplehood," The Priestly Kingdom, 33.

[131]Yoder, "The Hermeneutics of Peoplehood," The Priestly Kingdom, 34-35.

the community's awareness that every decision includes elements of principle, elements of character and due process, and elements of utility." The guiding moral norm of discernment is "that recorded experience of practical moral reasoning in genuine human form that bears that name Jesus." Variety of ethical theory is acceptable, so long as diverse construals display the requirements of discipleship in particular instances.[132]

Yoder's description of procedures that sustain communal faithfulness ends with the provocative remark that "The only way to see how this will work will be to see how it will work."[133] By that claim, he seeks to avoid the temptation of articulating a sophisticated theory of discipleship that would take precedence over the embodied experience and practical wisdom of communities that strive to live under the guidance of the Spirit as a foretaste of God's kingdom.[134]

That Yoder attends with such care to the procedures of moral reason and discernment in the community of faith is an indication of the unique importance that the church has for him in eschatological perspective. We live in

> the age of the church....The same life of the new aeon which was revealed in Christ is also the possession of the church, since Pentecost answered the Old Testament's longings for a "pouring out of the Spirit on all flesh" and a "law written in the heart." The Holy Spirit is the "down payment" on the coming glory and

---

[132]Yoder, "The Hermeneutics of Peoplehood," The Priestly Kingdom, 36-37.

[133]Yoder, "The Hermeneutics of Peoplehood," The Priestly Kingdom, 45.

[134]It is important to note here that Yoder is not advocating a "situation ethics" of the sort espoused by Joseph Fletcher in Situation Ethics: The New Morality (Philadelphia: The Westminster Press, 1966). An important aspect of Fletcher's project, as stated on p. 145, is the claim that "love's decisions are made situationally, not prescriptively." Fletcher suggests that agents may perform actions which embody love through a radically situational mode of discernment which recognizes no abiding standards, procedures, or norms for determining what love requires across situations. In contrast to Fletcher, Yoder places great emphasis on abiding procedures and norms, which are socially located in the community of faith and which will guide discernment across situations. See Ramsey, Deeds and Rules in Christian Ethics (Lanham, Maryland: University Press of America, 1983) for an detailed analysis of Fletcher's position.

the new life of the resurrection is the path of the Christian now.[135]

Indeed, the church is "the miracle of the new humanity" in its actual demonstration of an alternative social order to the fallen, divisive ways of the world. The existence of this sort of community is vital for the very proclamation of the Gospel, for "there can be no evangelistic call addressed to a person inviting him to enter a new kind of fellowship and learning if there is not such a body of persons..." This social body is also "a discerning community," the communal structure necessary for describing well God's action and requirements in history. Says Yoder,

> The promise of the presence of the Holy Spirit is clearly correlated in the New Testament with the need for the church prophetically to discern right and wrong in the events of the age. Not all visible events are God at work, not all "action" is divine, not every spirit is of Christ...The church is qualified to be such an agent of discernment... because she has in her allegiance to Jesus Christ criteria of good and evil which are significantly different from those which prevail in even the most respectable segments of the larger society.[136]

In emphasizing the necessity of the church for God's salvific work, Yoder argues that

> The creation of the one new humanity [in the church] by breaking down the wall between the two kinds of people of whom the world is made, Jews and Gentiles, is not simply the result of reconciliation of individuals with God...This creation of the one new humanity is itself the purpose which God had in all ages, is itself the "mystery," the gospel to be proclaimed. In every direction we might follow this exposition, the distinctiveness of the church of believers is prerequisite to the meaningfulness of the

---

[135]Yoder, "If Christ Is Truly Lord," The Original Revolution, 5, 57.

[136]Yoder, "A People in the World: Theological Interpretation," The Concept of the Believers' Church, 259, 276-277. See also his "Helpful and Deceptive Dualisms," 80.

gospel message.[137]

Yoder's view of the church as a visible body comprised of believers who join voluntarily to pursue together discipleship in a manner distinct from the ways of the larger society is characteristic of his Anabaptist tradition.[138]   He advocates an ecclesiology that, in clear disagreement with the "church" and "sect" typology of Ernst Troeltsch, sees the Christian life as the necessarily social and political, and practically inevitably minoritarian, pursuit of the discipleship of Jesus in the ministry of the kingdom which he inaugurated.[139]

The church is, in Yoder's thought, the community through which God trains, forms, and guides disciples.[140]   It is the hermeneutic community in

---

[137]Yoder, "A People in the World: Theological Interpretation," The Concept of the Believers' Church, 259. See also his "The Apostle's Apology Revisited," The New Way of Jesus, ed. William Klassen (Newton, Kansas: Faith and Life Press, 1980), 133.

[138]Yoder, "The Otherness of the Church," 287ff.; See also his "The Recovery of the Anabaptist Vision," Concern Pamphlet #18, 14ff.; and "Radical Reformation Ethics in Ecumenical Perspective," The Priestly Kingdom, 105ff.;   Important secondary sources on the Anabaptist nature of his ecclesiology include Brown, "Communal Ecclesiology: The Power of the Anabaptist Vision," Theology Today 36 (April 1979): 25; Sawatsky, "John Howard Yoder," Non-Violence: Central to Christian Spirituality, 242ff; Koontz, "Confessional Theology in Pluralistic Context: A Study of the Theological Ethics of H. Richard Niebuhr and John H. Yoder," 148ff.; Jozef M. L. Van Gerwen, "The Church in the Theological Ethics of Stanley Hauerwas," 129-142; Weaver, Becoming Anabaptist: The Origin and Significance of Sixteenth-Century Anabaptism, 113ff.

[139]Yoder provides an alternative to Troeltsch's typology in "A People in the World," The Concept of the Believers' Church, 256ff.   He argues against Troeltsch, for example, in The Politics of Jesus, 189-191, on the relevance of Jesus for social ethics.

The basic question of social ethics for Troeltsch was "How can the church harmonize with these main forces [state and society] in such a way that together they will form a unity of civilization?" He found that only the church type has resources for meeting that challenge, as the sect combines Jesus' radical ethic with an absolute view of natural law which together are so rigorous and unrealistic in their expectations for human behavior that withdrawal from the relativities and complexities of culture is their only alternative. Troeltsch's classic statements on "church" versus "sect" are found in his The Social Teachings of the Christian Church (New York: The MacMillan Company, 1931), 32, 379-80, 1000, 1011. See Duane Friesen, "Normative Factors in Troeltsch's Typology of Religious Association," Journal of Religious Ethics 3 (Fall 1975): 271-283 for an analysis of the theological assumptions that inform Troeltsch's project.

[140]Yoder, "The Recovery of the Anabaptist Vision," Concern Pamphlet #18, 17, 20. See also "The Hermeneutics of Peoplehood," The Priestly Kingdom, 26ff.

which Scripture is interpreted for practical guidance.[141] It is the faithful community that follows Jesus in non-resistant love in the midst of a sinful world. It is the sign of Christ's victory over the powers in its socially embodied demonstration of what the kingdom requires for human relations.[142] It is the manifestation of "the politics of men (and women) under the teaching and empowerment of God's spirit."[143] As the foretaste of God's kingdom, it is the chief instrument of God in the new aeon during the time between Pentecost and Parousia.[144] It is an eschatological community.

In evaluating Yoder's ecclesiology, it is apparent that there is a general coherence between his eschatology and view of the church, as the church is identified as a foretaste of the new age of God's reign which was begun in Jesus Christ. His treatment of the church is of a piece with his eschatology. Despite the difficulties with Yoder's hermeneutical strategy of biblical realism, it is also clear that he at least attempts to formulate his view of the church in light of what he takes to be "the biblical point of view." Hence, Yoder is consistent in his treatment of eschatology, Christology, and ecclesiology, as he seeks to treat each theme in light of "the world view of the Bible." Of course, Yoder's view of what the Bible requires for each theme bears strong similarity to Anabaptism.[145]

---

[141]Yoder, "The Hermeneutics of the Anabaptists," Essays on Biblical Interpretation/Anabaptist-Mennonite Perspectives, 21ff. See also his "The Hermeneutics of Peoplehood," The Priestly Kingdom, 37.

[142]Yoder, The Christian Witness to the State, 9.

[143]Yoder, "The Spirit of God and the Politics of Men," 66.

[144]Yoder, "Reinhold Niebuhr and Christian Pacifism," 115. See also his "Discerning the Kingdom of God in the Struggles of the World," International Review of Mission 68 (October 1979): 368.

[145]This point indicates, as noted above, a significant point of tension in Yoder's thought. He speaks of "the biblical point of view" in a way that does not explicitly display a critical awareness of the influence of his theological tradition upon his reading of Scripture and appropriation of biblical scholarship. As Yoder appears to be cognizant of various ways in which denominational

(continued...)

Wogaman identifies a problematic element of Yoder's ecclesiology in his description of Yoder as an "evangelical perfectionist" who does not allow for compromise of the norm of nonresistant love in the Christian life.[146] Throughout Yoder's discourse on the church, one gets a strong sense that he is describing a perfectly sanctified community the common life of which unambiguously manifests the glory of God's reign.[147] For Yoder, the church is to embody Christ's victory over the rebellious powers, and is, thereby, to present a stark alternative of socially realized love to the corrupted ways of the world.[148]

Given Yoder's high moral vision of the life of the church, it is hard to know precisely of whom or what Yoder is speaking when he writes of this sanctified alternative community. While he makes references, at various points in his writings on the Christian life, to the church before the conversion of Constantine, certain Reformation groups, and more modern Christian movements as paradigms for the community of faith, he nowhere demonstrates in concrete historical detail how and why he identifies them as paradigmatic examples of faithfulness.[149]

---

[145](...continued) traditions shape interpretations of Scripture, he would do well to reformulate his allegiance to biblical realism in that light. See Yoder, "The Authority of Tradition," The Priestly Kingdom, 66ff.

[146]Wogaman, A Christian Method of Moral Judgment, 32-35.

[147]See, for example, Yoder's comment on the "modeling mission" of the church in "The Kingdom as Social Ethic," The Priestly Kingdom, 92.

[148]Yoder, The Christian Witness to the State, 8ff.

[149]See, for example, "The Hermeneutics of Peoplehood," The Priestly Kingdom, 22f; "The Constantinian Sources of Western Social Ethics, The Priestly Kingdom, 135ff; "If Christ Is Truly Lord," The Original Revolution, 55ff; and Christian Attitudes To War, Peace, and Revolution, 23ff.

While Yoder has published a number of historical studies on Anabaptism, he has not displayed in concrete detail how Anabaptists have lived up to his high ecclesiological standards (continued...)

While Yoder does provide a rationale for his admiration of certain groups, usually making reference to their pacifism and ethic of discipleship in resistance to corrupting cultural influences, he does not display the particulars of their historical and cultural situations in a fashion that would make clear precisely how they embodied a foretaste of God's reign. As, on Yoder's terms, the church must constantly discern its path of faithfulness admist the myriad particulars of life, it would seem necessary for an exacting portrayal of a rightly faithful church to display in great detail how its members went about manifesting God's reign in their particular situation. Apart from a such a forthcoming examination of an actual group of Christians who embody God's kingdom in their common life, it is not clear that Yoder's discourse on the church is descriptive of any socially realized group in human history.[150]

It is, likewise, hard to know where Yoder would draw the boundaries

---

[149](...continued)
relative to their particular historical, cultural settings. Neither has Yoder expounded his view of the Christian life through explicit, exacting references to certain historical groups in a way that illuminates, in light of their example, precisely what the church must do and be in the contemporary setting in order to manifest God's reign. See, for example, Yoder's "Recovery of the Anabaptist Vision," Concern Pamphlet #18, 5ff. and "The Hermeneutics of the Anabaptist," Essays on Biblical Interpretation/Anabaptist-Mennonite Perspectives, 11ff.

[150]The thrust of this criticism is that Yoder's discourse on the church does not appear to take sufficient account of the fact that notions of discipleship or pacifism must be incarnated in given social situations in order for them to be more than rhetorical devices. As Yoder suggests that the church must incarnate these norms well in order for it to manifest God's reign, he needs to attend to aspects of the complexity and ambiguity of discipleship in particular situations in the world. For example, while it is clear that Yoder finds racism to be inconsistent with the life of discipleship, it is not apparent precisely how he thinks that the church may discern the presence of, and resist, racism in its midst. What would it mean, in concrete detail, to be vigilant against a given manifestation of racism in a certain historical situation which is characterized by determinate social conditions? It would seem that the church, for Yoder, would need to be able to perform such discernment in order for it to manifest God's reign. To the extent that he does not describe in concrete detail a community's resistance of racism, or any other worldly corruption, it is not clear precisely why Yoder has identified any group of Christians as the church. Apart from an exacting analysis of what discipleship requires admist the myriad particulars of life, it is impossible to determine who is being the church--especially when the church is described in terms of moral perfection. See James Cone, God of the Oppressed (New York: Seabury Press, 1975), 2-3, for a brief description of how racism corrupts the church in the American South.

of the church. Given that the community of faith is to manifest faithfulness to the way of Jesus in whatever social setting it finds itself, a number of discriminating judgments would seem to be in order for the determination of who is being church at any given time. It would appear, for example, that the particular demands of discipleship in the racist, slaveholding American South in 1850 would be distinct from those appropriate to Christians in the Roman Empire in the second century A. D. As near perfection in the following of Jesus appears to be a necessary condition for the church on Yoder's terms, he would do well to provide a much more detailed analysis of what it would mean to be the church, and how that would be ascertained, in a variety of given historical settings. Granted, that is a strong demand to make of a theologian, as it would require a fairly high level of historical and sociological acumen in order to describe such settings well. But, given the extremely rigorous language which Yoder uses to describe the church, it seems appropriate to demand of him as clear an account as possible of how ecclesial identity would be determined in given situations. Apart from such an account, Yoder's treatment of the church seems, at most, to be a rhetorical call for the faithfulness of Christians which is unable to portray with clarity both what such faithfulness required in the past and how the demands of discipleship are to be met, as well as discerned, in contemporary situations. While Yoder points to examples of the ecclesial pattern of which he speaks, he fails to develop these examples in a way that makes lucid what the church, as an eschatological community, must do and be in order to manifest a foretaste of God's reign.[151]

---

[151]There is, consequently, an epistemological difficulty in Yoder's account of the church. While he has identified particular biblical themes, theological notions, and examples in the history of Christian faith as sources for the church's knowledge of what it means to be the church today, Yoder has failed to display precisely how these sources interact to provide appropriate guidance to the community of faith. While Yoder also places great emphasis on the discernment of the community in determining the particular requirements of discipleship in given circumstances, he has not described with clarity how the church is to appropriate its knowledge of the cultural setting in which it finds itself. How, for example, is the church to determine which given account of its

(continued...)

The Basic Significance of Eschatology for the Moral Life

Yoder's eschatology has an important shaping role for his view of Christian ethics. A first aspect of this influence, which an earlier section of the chapter treated in part, is that Jesus, as the inaugurator of God's new age, is the model of obedience before God whom Christians are to imitate in non-resistant love.

The claim that the Jesus portrayed in Scripture is Lord, which is for Yoder an eschatological claim designating his dominion over the rebellious powers, "is the center which must guide critical value choices, so that we may be called to subordinate or even to reject those values which contradict Jesus."[152] For Yoder, "that recorded experience of practical moral reasoning in genuine human form that bears the name Jesus" is the ultimate norm of Christian ethics.[153] As it is through Jesus' obedience unto death and God's vindication of that obedience through resurrection that God has defeated the rebellious powers in principle and has begun a new aeon, Christians are to imitate Jesus' "substantial, binding, costly social stance" of non-resistant love which led to crucifixion.[154] The way of Jesus must be our way of living in the new age.[155]

---

[151](...continued)
cultural location is most appropriate for its use? What particular procedures or standards should the church use in processing such information for the sake of getting a clear picture of what it means to be the church in that situation? To the extent that Yoder has not indicated with clarity how the church will know how these various sources of knowledge should interact in particular historical situations, his account of the church's life is epistemologically inadequate.

[152]Yoder, "Introduction," The Priestly Kingdom, 11.

[153]Yoder, "The Hermeneutics of Peoplehood," The Priestly Kingdom, 37.

[154]Yoder, The Politics of Jesus, 130-131.

[155]Yoder, "Christ, the Light of the World," The Original Revolution, 129. Ramsey criticizes Yoder on this point in Speak Up for Just War or Pacifism, 113-114:

(continued...)

A second implication of Yoder's eschatology for his view of Christian ethics is, as described in the preceding section, his account of the church as a foretaste of the new age which sustains the pursuit of discipleship. Because of the gift of the Spirit to the church as the power and sign of God's reign, Christian ethics is "ecclesiocentric" for Yoder.[156] The church embodies the resources and structures necessary for sustaining Christian moral discernment. The church has this important role precisely because it is the locus of God's salvific activity in the new age.[157]

But perhaps the most fundamental implication of eschatology for ethics in Yoder's thought is its justification of an ethic of <u>obedience</u> to the non-resistant way of Jesus in a fashion that is critical of <u>consequentialist</u> moral reasoning.[158] This ethic of obedience is an important aspect of his view of the moral relevance

---

[155](...continued)
"We are told that the politics of Jesus should be our politics; his nonresistance of evil, our nonresisting love even of enemy-neighbors; his way of doing his Father's reconciliation, our reconciling spirit. The disciple is not greater than his master. This states that Jesus is THE pattern, THE example.

Yet, on other views of the person and work of Jesus Christ, the foregoing does not follow. One thing, at least, we do not imitate in Jesus Christ, namely, the fact that he had no Jesus Christ to imitate. He had no savior made flesh. He prayed that "all may be one; as thou, Father, are in me, and I in thee, that they also may be one in us" (John 17:21). His incarnation, his life as the God-man among us, his suffering, his death, his resurrection were unique, never to be repeated. Certainly not by us. He was THE Pattern, so as at any moment to assume an accusative role of Judge. He is Pattern, yet also Savior. We are neither co-Creators nor co-Saviors. Hence, as the Reformers knew, we are to follow him--from a distance. We are not to take up <u>his</u> cross, but <u>our</u> cross to follow him. This is a sufficient sketch of some possible alternative Christologies--some, I say, and only possible--in which are rooted the different discipleships of Christian pacifists and justified-war Christians."

[156]Yoder, "Discerning the Kingdom of God in the Struggles of the World," 368.

[157]Yoder, The Christian Witness to the State, 9.

[158]Yoder uses terms such as "utilitarian," "cost-benefit calculation," "pragmatism," and "consequential" interchangeably to speak of modes of moral reason that operate primarily in terms of the intended result. Yoder, "The Constantinian Basis of Western Social Ethics," The Priestly Kingdom, 140, 211. He does not distinguish between various sorts of teleological moral theories in the way that an analytic moral philosopher like William Frankena does in Ethics (Englewood Cliffs, New Jersey: Prentice-Hall, Inc., 1972), 14-16, 34ff.

of both Christology and ecclesiology. Jesus is an example of obedience to be imitated. The church is a community that seeks to embody and sustain obedience to his example.

Yoder believes that Jesus' obedience to God's agapic will culminated in his death and resurrection as the victory of God over the rebellious powers. This victory has begun a new age which will one day consummate in God's fulfilled reign. The vision of Revelation 4-5 that this crucified Lord is the key to history's meaning and redemption establishes for Yoder his way of "simple obedience...reflecting the character of the love of God" as being "aligned with the ultimate triumph of the Lamb."[159] Through confessing the crucified and risen Lord's coming triumph, Christians should see that "the calculating link between our obedience and ultimate efficacy has been broken, since the triumph of God comes through resurrection and not through effective sovereignty or assured survival."[160]

Yoder suggests that Christians, in this eschatological context, are to pursue an ethic of obedience

> Because that is the shape of the work of Christ. The relation between our obedience and the achievement of God's purposes stands in analogy to the hidden lordship of Him who was crucified and raised.[161]

Indeed,

> Those for whom Jesus Christ is the hope of the world will...not measure their contemporary social involvement by its efficacy for tomorrow nor by its success in providing work, or freedom, or food or in building new social structures, but by identifying with the Lord in whom they have placed their trust. This is why it is sure to succeed. The certainty of effect is founded not in our capacity to construct a mechanical model of the connection from

---

[159]Yoder, The Politics of Jesus, 245.

[160]Yoder, The Politics of Jesus, 246.

[161]Yoder, "Christ, the Hope of the World," The Original Revolution, 155.

here to there, to "sight down the line of our obedience" to His triumph; but rather in the confession itself.[162]

This passage, with its references to success and efficacy, reflects a point of subtlety in Yoder's argument. Namely, he does not make a thoroughgoing rejection of effectiveness as a point of consideration in moral reasoning. In fact, he suggests elsewhere that the confession of Jesus as the redeemer of history entails the claim that "obedience to his rule cannot be dysfunctional. Principled or virtuous behavior cannot be imprudent generally, though it may well appear so punctually."[163]

Indeed, Yoder notes that he is "increasingly convinced that the debate between the effectiveness ethic and the principle ethic is a false debate." What is really at stake is "this goal versus that goal" or "this principle versus that principle" within a larger interpretative framework that makes one more attractive than the other. To say, for example, "'let righteousness be done even if the heavens fall'" is to assume

> a conviction about Providence, trusting that if the heavens fall God has another better set of heavens ready, which is part of the process, so even that is not thumbing your nose at results. It's trusting God who gave us the rules to know more about the results than we know...[Ultimately the issue here [is] who wants to be in charge [of interpreting the meaning of history]. By then it is clear that it is not after all a clean philosophical issue between two kinds of ethical reasoning.[164]

The sort of consequentialist moral reasoning that Yoder wants to reject is that which describes what it would mean to be effective, and what ends to pursue, in a fashion that is not shaped by the confession that Jesus is the Lord and Redeemer of history. Put another way, it seeks "to govern history....to be effective in making history move down the right track" according to its own

---

[162]Yoder, "Christ, the Hope of the World," The Original Revolution, 160.

[163]Yoder, "The Hermeneutics of Peoplehood," The Priestly Kingdom, 37.

[164]Yoder, Christian Attitudes to War, Peace, and Revolution, 436-437.

standards, rather than seeking obedience to history's savior.[165] Yoder rejects that sort of Promethean moral "engineering."[166]

A philosophical way of grasping the rationale of Yoder's eschatologically informed position is to attend to Alasdair MacIntyre's view of the description of human behavior within a narrative context.[167] Says MacIntyre on the question of how observers describe action,

> We place the agent's intentions...with reference to their role in the history of the setting or settings to which they belong...Narrative history of a certain kind turns out to be the basic and essential genre for the characterization of human actions.[168]

MacIntyre provides an example to display how intelligible action requires location within a narrative. He asks us to imagine someone saying to him, "The name of the common wild duck is Histrionicus histrionicus histrionicus." In order to provide an account of what the person was doing in uttering those words, MacIntyre suggests that he would have to locate the statement within one of several possible narrative construals. For example, the speaker might have mistaken MacIntyre for someone who had earlier asked him the Latin name for the common wild duck, might be saying whatever came to mind as a therapeutic exercise to overcome shyness, or might be a spy attempting to identify himself to his contact. "In each case the act of utterance become [sic] intelligible by finding its place in a narrative."[169]

---

[165]Yoder, The Politics of Jesus, 241-242.

[166]Yoder, personal correspondence with Stanley Hauerwas, 7 November 1972. See also his "Armaments and Eschatology," 55; "To Serve Our God and to Rule the World," 3ff.; and Christian Attitudes to War, Peace, and Revolution, 437.

[167]Yoder does not rely on MacIntyre for his account of eschatology's moral relevance. I am using MacIntyre's analysis simply as a way of illuminating the theological workings of Yoder's project.

[168]Alasdair MacIntyre, After Virtue (Notre Dame, Indiana: The University of Notre Dame Press, 1984), 208.

[169]MacIntyre, After Virtue, 210.

Not only conversation, but "all human transactions in general" have a narrative quality for MacIntyre. The thrust of his point appears to be that actions require a setting, a context, a location within a set of shared expectations for their intelligibility, their meaningful description. Says he, "If in the middle of my lecture on Kant's ethics I suddenly broke six eggs into a bowl and added flour and sugar, proceeding all the while with my Kantian exegesis, I have not...performed an intelligible action."[170]

Since moral judgments are statements about intelligible action, for to make a moral evaluation requires that the speaker has made sense of what he or she is evaluating, it is possible to use MacIntyre's narrative analysis in a way that will illumine how Yoder's eschatology shapes his evaluation of moral norms such as obedience and effectiveness. Yoder's "biblical realism," in terms of which he sees the world as between God's decisive and ultimate victory, enables him to describe morality in light of "the Christian story" that Jesus has inaugurated a new age which will consummate one day in God's fulfilled reign, that the church lives eschatologically between the times of Pentecost and Parousia. Interpreting the significance of human action within the context of this story or narrative, Yoder suggests that humans should pursue faithfulness to the obedient way of Jesus, which way has been uniquely vindicated through the resurrection as the beginning of the fulfillment of history, of the end of the narrative.

This story entails that obedience to the non-resistant way of Jesus succeeds ultimately and eschatologically. The story of Jesus' life, death, and resurrection guarantees the coming completion and full redemption of history. Jesus models the true way of living in God's universe. What is ultimately effective, what is aligned with history coming out right, may not for Yoder be determined apart from obedience to the Lord of history.

For Yoder, this claim "is basically a dogmatic proclamation: if Christ

---

[170]MacIntyre, After Virtue, 209-211.

84

is Lord, then the Lamb that was slain is worthy to receive power; then crucifixion is ultimately in phase with victory."[171] It is therefore illegitimate to describe prudence or effectiveness in a manner that is not consistent with what God's ultimate victory will entail. While an action of disobedience to God may achieve the intended result of the actor, it is ultimately a dysfunctional, unsuccessful action because it is of the old aeon which is passing away, which has already been defeated.

On Yoder's terms, "If Jesus Christ is Lord, [dis]obedience to his rule...[is] dysfunctional. [Un]principled or [un]virtuous behavior...[is] imprudent generally, though it may well [not] appear to be so punctually."[172] When seen in the context of the eschatological narrative of Christ's victory over the powers, only obedience to his way is the proper mode of the moral life.

As a nuance of his position, Yoder apparently thinks that, within the shaping context of this eschatological narrative, it is appropriate to speak of ways in which obedience is effective punctually without making effectiveness an autonomous moral norm. That God's redemptive action is the basis of the validity of obedience radically contextualizes for him notions of effectiveness.

Those notions are ultimately dependent upon God's victory, not our calculation, for their legitimacy and effect. Says Yoder,

> If we claim to justify the actions we take by the effects they promise, we shall be led to pride in the abuse of power in those cases when it seems that we can reach our goals by the means at our disposal...[W]e are drawn away from the faithfulness of service and singleness of a disciple's mind. We are drawn into the twofold pride of thinking that we, more than others, see things are they really are, and of claiming the duty and the power to move history aright. If our faithfulness is to be guided by the kind of man Jesus was, it must cease to be guided by the quest to

---

[171]Yoder, personal correspondence to Stanley Hauerwas, 7 November 1972.

[172]Yoder, "The Hermeneutics of Peoplehood," The Priestly Kingdom, 37.

have dominion over the course of events.[173]

While moral discernment should not focus on how to control history as though the risen Christ were not its and our Lord, Christians may find their obedience to be effective in, for example, "the unmasking of idols" in society or the pursuing of "pioneer" ministries to meet unaddressed needs. Yoder also comments that "deeds of Christian obedience" may be effective in unforseen ways.

> [T]hey contribute to the building up of pressure, creating a subterranean reservoir of saving and invigorating power which can be tapped at the point where men are most thirsty. Sociologists may speak of it as the creation of custom, the development of public opinion, or the raising of the general level of capacity for generous conduct. All of these are simply other ways of affirming that the relationship between my obedience and the accomplishment of the purposes of God must include my losing track of my own effectiveness in the great reservoir of the pressure of love.[174]

It is most helpful to see Yoder's critique of consequentialist moral reasoning, then, as an insistence that obedience to the non-resistant way of Jesus be made a controlling norm over notions of effectiveness. Within the context of an obedience that recognizes Christ's lordship over history, the Christian may observe present results that are consistent with the lordship of Christ. Those results are for Yoder signs of Christ's present, though as yet unconsummated, rule over history. They are the fruits of obedience sought by the Christian because obedience demands them, not because they appear immediately effective to the moral agent. The basis for determining what is ultimately effective is the eschatological victory of God, not our consequentialist calculation. Says Yoder of the moral life,

---

[173]Yoder, "Christ, the Hope of the World," The Original Revolution, 154.

[174]Yoder, "Christ, the Hope of the World," The Original Revolution, 157-158. He also attends to the effectiveness of obedience in "The Kingdom As Social Ethic," The Priestly Kingdom, 96-101.

86

We are not marching to Zion because we think that by our own momentum we can get there. But that is still where we are going. We are marching to Zion because, when God lets down from heaven the new Jerusalem prepared for us, we want to be the kind of persons and the kind of community that will not feel strange there. In such ways there is a link between our obedience and the accomplishments of God's purposes. We see it when we find life by way of the cross, power by means of weakness, wisdom by means of foolishness...This is the evangelical norm of social efficacy.[175]

In summary, Yoder's eschatology strongly shapes and informs his view of the moral life. It identifies Jesus as victor over the powers, as a Lord to be imitated in obedience to God. It locates the church as a community which sustains this obedience as a foretaste of the new age. It makes intelligible an ethic of obedience which radically contextualizes consequentialist moral reasoning within the eschatological narrative of the victory of the Lamb. Obedience alone is ultimately effective because of the coming, final victory of the risen Lord.

There is little explicit criticism of Yoder's eschatologically shaped ethic of obedience in the secondary literature.[176] In evaluating his formulation, it is interesting to note that a "between the times" eschatology of the sort espoused by Yoder may be, and often has been, interpreted in a fashion which limits the direct relevance of Jesus' example as a norm for discerning what obedience to God entails. For example, Ramsey suggests that Jesus' teaching of non-resistance, which was shaped decisively by his mistaken apocalyptic expectation for the imminent fulfillment of God's reign, is not directly binding upon Christians who continue to await the Parousia.[177] Comments Ramsey,

In face of the inbreaking kingdom, moral decision was stripped of

---

[175]Yoder, "Christ, the Hope of the World," The Original Revolution, 159.

[176]See, for example, Wogaman's general comments on Yoder's rejection of an ethic of compromise for the sake of effectiveness in A Christian Method of Moral Judgement, 187-191.

[177]Ramsey, Basic Christian Ethics, 33-35.

all prudential considerations, all calculation of what is right in terms of consequences which in this present age normally follow certain lines of action. Not only all prudential calculation of consequences likely to fall upon the agent himself, but likewise all sober regard for the future performance of his responsibility for family or friends, duties to oneself and fixed duties to others, both alike were jettisoned from view. Preferential loves, even those justifiable in normal times, were supplanted by entirely non-preferential regard for whomever happened to be standing by, friend or enemy, bullying sergeant or indigent beggar. All that mattered was perfect obedience to God. All that mattered was complete readiness for the kingdom to come. All that mattered was the single individual a man happened to confront. All that mattered was unhesitating, total love.[178]

Ramsey suggests that the abiding essence of Jesus' teaching, for life in a world which has not yet come under the full reign of God, is the requirement for disinterested love of the neighbor.[179] In a not yet fully redeemed world, Ramsey suggests that Christians often have more than one neighbor at a time, and that the protection of one neighbor from unjustified attack by another may very well require the use of deadly force. Such violent resistance, claims Ramsey, is an act of love, in obedience to Jesus' command and example, in a manner appropriate to the conditions of life in a world "between the times."[180]

In light of his eschatological commitments and rejection of Jesus' apocalypticism, Ramsey formulates an ethic of obedience which differs from Yoder's in at least one obvious respect: Ramsey's legitimation of the use of deadly force by Christians. From Ramsey's perspective, his disagreement with Yoder is not primarily about competition between norms of obedience and efficacy.

> The future is radically unpredictable, for both pacifist and just warrior alike. We need to withdraw Niebuhr's somewhat

---

[178]Ramsey, Basic Christian Ethics, 39.

[179]Ramsey, Basic Christian Ethics, 92.

[180]Ramsey, Basic Christian Ethics, 171ff.

88

condescending tribute to the peace churches. We need to affirm
the coeval, equally worthy, irreducible parting of the ways of
Christian pacifists and justified-war Christians. Neither is able to
depend on the consequences in the whole of their activities. All
this can be said, I believe, while holding that in the divine
economy for this world just war is the meaning of statecraft, and
that pacifism cannot be addressed to states. Still, these are
equally Christian discipleships. And the freedom of state action
trammels up but little that destiny has in store.
The intermingling of the Two Cities is through the heart of every
just-war Christian...We belong to this temporal city and are
engaged in the continuance of it, yet our citizenship is also in
another City, not made with hands, whose builder and maker is
God and his Christ.[181]

Suffice it to note that Yoder's position is not the only approach to Christian ethics

which, in light of an "already but not yet" eschatology, emphasizes the

importance of obedience over effectiveness in moral reasoning.[182]

It is interesting, in this light, to note that Ramsey and Yoder share a

"between the times" eschatology which appears to have a similar metaethical

significance for both of them. Eschatology provides a temporal background

which locates the Christian life in a segment of history in which moral action may

not be described properly apart from obedience to the God incarnate in Jesus.

While Ramsey and Yoder often make clearly different normative judgments,

especially on the use of deadly force by Christians, they appear to share a

common eschatological outlook which informs their respective accounts of the

nature and task of Christian ethics.

It is also important to note that there is a general coherence to the

relationship between Yoder's eschatology and view of Christian ethics. He

describes moral agents as standing within a narrative, a temporal sequence of

---

[181]Ramsey, Speak Up for Just War or Pacifism, 123.

[182]An important conceptual base of Ramsey's entire project is his commitment to the
disinterested love of neighbor as the key obligation of the Christian life. Christians are to obey
God by loving in this way. See Ramsey, Basic Christian Ethics, 23ff; 367-388.

events which will culminate in the final vindication of the crucified and risen Lord over all creation. Within the context of this scheme of expectation, Christians are to serve God by following the example of Jesus' obedience even to the point of death. As Jesus' way of obedience has been uniquely vindicated by resurrection as a guarantee of the kingdom's future consummation, Yoder seems correct in his claim that Christians may not view notions of success or effectiveness as though the slain Lamb were not the Victor.[183]

This chapter has indicated points of both weakness and strength in Yoder's method. Particularly troubling aspects of his work include the unresolved tension between his reliance on biblical realism and his communal method of interpreting Scripture, and his unclear and ideal descriptions of the moral life of the church. These are quite important critical points, as Yoder seeks to expound a view of Christian ethics which is decisively shaped by both "the biblical point of view" and the church's moral discernment. As such, significant points of tension concerning Scripture and the church threaten both the methodological adequacy and the epistemological basis of his project. The following chapters will determine the severity of these threats.

A postive aspect of Yoder's work is that he attempts to interpret eschatology in a consistent manner throughout his project. From the perspective of his reading of Scripture, he identifies a basic eschatological orientation which he brings to his analysis of Christology, ecclesiology, and view of the moral life. His Christology is well informed by a variety of the New Testament portraits of Jesus. Yoder approaches the moral life in a way that is generally consistent with his eschatological commitments.

The following chapter, by attending explicitly to his critique of

---

[183]Yoder's disagreement with Ramsey is about what obedience to Christ requires in the present age. In this regard, Ramsey appears correct in his claim, in Speak Up for Just War or Pacifism, 112-114, that important Christological issues are at stake in the debate between just warriors and pacifists. The fourth chapter will evaluate Yoder's pacifism in light of Ramsey's critique, and examine the role of consequential reasoning in Yoder's approach to Christian social action.

Constantinianism, will display further the significance of eschatology for Yoder's project. Through its focus on Yoder's treatment of this particular, and quite involved, question of social ethics, it will enable a more detailed and substantive evaluation of his position.

CHAPTER 3

YODER'S CRITIQUE OF CONSTANTINIANISM

This chapter examines explicitly, and in detail, the rationale of Yoder's critique of Constantinianism. It divides into four sections: (1) an analysis of what Yoder means by "Constantinianism"; (2) a discussion of Constantinianism's eschatological assumptions; (3) an examination of the significance of Constantinianism for the relationship between church and world; and (4) an analysis of Yoder's view of the significance of Constantinianism for moral reason.

What Does Yoder Mean by "Constantinianism"?

"Constantinianism" is, in Yoder's thought, a crucially important metaphor for the perversion of Christian ethics wrought by the identification of church and empire and symbolized by the conversion of Constantine. Yoder is not particularly interested in the faith of the man Constantine, nor in the date of

92

his conversion as the punctual downfall of the church.[1] Instead, he notes that Constantine "stands for a new era in the history of Christianity." This new era, and its new mode of moral reason, is displayed for Yoder most graphically in the fact that

> the pre-Constantinian Christians had been pacifists, rejecting the violence of army and empire not only because they had no share of power, but because they considered it morally wrong; the post-Constantinian Christians considered imperial violence to be not only morally tolerable but a positive good and a Christian duty.[2]

Yoder suggests that "the most pertinent fact" about the Constantinian era

---

[1]Given Yoder's lack of interest in the precise historical events surrounding Constantine, it is puzzling that he has chosen "Constantinianism" as an important theme of his project. Later sections of the chapter will provide an explicit evaluation of Yoder's use of the term.

[2]Yoder, "The Constantinian Sources of Western Social Ethics," The Priestly Kingdom, 135. Yoder discusses the significance of pacifism for the Christian life in, for example, The Politics of Jesus, 130-134; "The Original Revolution," The Original Revolution, 23ff.; and Nevertheless, 122-127.

Yoder's claim for the pacifism of Christians who lived before Constantine is challenged by the findings of John Helgeland, Robert J. Daly, and J. Patout Burns in Christians and the Military: The Early Experience (Philadelphia: Fortress Press, 1985), 87-93. In addition to suggesting that Christians participated in the military at least by the middle of the third century A. D., they note that the Constantinian synthesis was not a matter of "the church suddenly selling its soul." Rather, the union of church and empire was "a fairly natural and logical development from the kind of experience Christians were having and the kind of reflection they were engaging in throughout the previous century. Origen, as we pointed out, presented what comes closest to a theory of Christian pacifism in the pre-Constantinian church. But, as we also pointed out, the very logic of his argument against Celsus in A. D. 248 drove Christians, in a changed situation, toward the kind of accomodation and cooperation we see beginning to take place under Constantine."

See Hughes, "The Ethical Use of Power: A Discussion with the Christian Perspectives of Reinhold Niebuhr, John Howard Yoder, and Richard J. Barnet," 133ff.; Parham, "An Ethical Analysis of the Christian Social Strategies in the Writings of John C. Bennett, Jacques Ellul, and John Howard Yoder," 149ff.; Koontz, "Confessional Theology in a Pluralistic Context: A Study of the Theological Ethics of H. Richard Niebuhr and John H. Yoder," 214; and Zimbleman, "Theological Ethics and Politics in the Thought of Juan Luis Segundo and John Howard Yoder," 217ff. for discussions of Yoder's view of Constantinianism. None of these sources engage this aspect of Yoder's thought rigorously or in detail.

While Yoder does not attend to Constantine's reign primarily as an object for historical analysis, but more as a metaphor that embodies ethical perversion, his account of Constantinianism warrants some historical scrutiny to determine whether this metaphor is informed by accurate historiography. Toward that end, this section concludes with a brief discussion of historical research on Constantine and his reign.

"is that the two visible realities, Church and world, were fused. There is no longer anything to call 'world'; State, economy, art, rhetoric, superstition and war have all been baptized."[3] In this way, the entire social order was declared "Christian" in a fashion which severely compromised the integrity of the church as a visible, distinct community of faith. Yoder thinks that this shift had decisive consequences for Christian faith and practice.

> The practical outworkings of this reversal were unavoidable. Since the Church has been filled with people in whom repentance and faith, the presuppositions of discipleship are absent, the ethical requirements set by the Church must be adapted to the achievement level of respectable unbelief...The statesman, who a century earlier would have been proud to declare that his profession was unchristian by nature, now wants to be told the opposite...[S]ince there are no more confessing heathen,...every profession must be declared Christian...The autonomy of the State and of the other realms of culture is not brought concretely under the lordship of Christ, with the total revision of form and content which that would involve; it has been baptized while retaining its former content.[4]

Moreover, Yoder suggests that Christian eschatology undergoes a major revision with this alliance of church and empire.

> [W]ith the age of Constantine, Providence no longer needed to be an object of faith, for God's governance of history had become empirically evident in the person of the Christian ruler of the

---

[3]Yoder, "The Otherness of the Church," 288. See also his "If Christ Is Truly Lord," The Original Revolution, 65ff. It is noteworthy that Yoder suggests that, with the union of church and empire, "There is no longer anything to call 'world.'" Apparently, he thinks that there was still something to call "church." But given Yoder's rigorous moral view of the church, as described in the previous chapter, it is not clear how or why he should identify such an allegedly corrupt institution as the church. This point again raises the questions: Whom is Yoder describing when he speaks of the church? What are the boundaries or markers of the church? That, as noted above, there are historians who deny that pre-Constantinian Christianity was uniformly pacifist and rigidly separated from the world calls into question Yoder's strategy of pointing to the pre-Constantinian church as a model of faithfulness to Jesus Christ.

[4]Yoder, "The Otherness of the Church," 289. See also "The Constantinian Sources of Western Social Ethics," The Priestly Kingdom, 137; and "The Disavowal of Constantine: An Alternative Perspective on Interfaith Dialogue," 50ff.

world. The concept of millennium was soon pulled back from the future (whether distant or imminent) into the present. All that God can possibly have in store for a future victory is more of what has already been won....Before Constantine, one knew as a fact of everyday experience that there was a believing Christian community but one had to "take it on faith" that God was governing history. After Constantine, one had to believe without seeing that there was a community of believers, within the nominally Christian mass, but one knew for a fact that God was in control of history [through the dominion of the empire].[5]

Given this redescription of church and Providence, which saw the larger social order as the present embodiment of God's reign, the determining norm of Christian moral reason became the "strengthening [of] the regime." The sustenance of the dominant cultural order became the highest good of moral analysis. Yoder suggests that this orientation led logically to the Crusade ethic in which the enemy of the empire

has become the "infidel," the incarnation of anti-faith. To destroy him, or to give one's life in the attempt, has become a positively virtuous undertaking...Our world has a divinely imparted duty to destroy or to rule over their world.[6]

Now it is assumed "that civil government is the main bearer of historical movement." This assumption has significance for both the reading of history and moral reason, as

History is [now] told as the story of dynasties, their conflicts and alliances. The ruler, not the average person or the weak person, is the model for ethical deliberations. A moral statement on the rightness of truth-telling or the wrongness of killing is tested first by whether a ruler can meet such standards. "Social ethics" means not what everyone should think and do about social questions, but

---

[5]Yoder, "The Constantinian Sources of Western Social Ethics," in The Priestly Kingdom, 136-137. See also his "The Disavowal of Constantine: An Alternative Perspective on Interfaith Dialogue," 52; and "If Christ Is Truly Lord," The Original Revolution, 64ff.

[6]Yoder, "The Constantinian Sources of Western Social Ethics," The Priestly Kingdom, 137-138. See also "Armaments and Eschatology," 49, where he refers to the "immanentized hope" of Christendom which "robbed us of the capacity to discern bad news or to bring good" by absolutizing the present order.

what people in power should be told to do with their power. The place of the church or of persons speaking for Christian morality (including academic theologians) is that of "chaplaincy," i. e., a part of the power structure itself. The content of ethical guidance is not the teaching of Jesus but the duties of "station" or "office" or "vocation."[7]

Presuming the demise of a Christian ethic that is distinct from that of the larger society, Yoder notes that because "Christianity is dominant, the bearer of history is Everyman--baptized but not necessarily thereby possessed of the resources of faith." Moral reason must now meet two additional standards.

First, "Can you ask such behavior of everyone?" Given the practical necessity of sustaining a social order, "pressure builds rapidly for a duality in ethics" that will allow the vast majority to live according the exigencies of supporting the empire, while a small minority will seek obedience to the way of Jesus.[8] Comments Yoder, "Then the Reformation polemic against works righteousness and monasticism removed the upper, more demanding, level."

The second question is "What would happen if everyone did it?" That is, if everyone pursued the higher level of obedience. Yoder comments that

here our only point is to observe that such reasoning would have been preposterous in the early church and remains ludicrous wherever committed Christians accept realistically their minority status. For more fitting than "What if everybody did it" would be its inverse, "What if nobody else acted like a Christian, but we did?"[9]

---

[7]Yoder, "The Constantinian Sources of Western Social Ethics," The Priestly Kingdom, 138. See also "Reinhold Niebuhr and Christian Pacifism," 115.

[8]The following chapter will determine to what extent Yoder's "non-Constantinian" project of Christian social involvement is of a piece with this "duality in ethics."

[9]Yoder, "The Constantinian Sources of Western Social Ethics," The Priestly Kingdom, 139. See also "Christ, the Hope of the World," The Original Revolution, 174ff.; and The Christian and Capital Punishment, 11. Of course, Yoder's way of putting it avoids directly answering the question of what the results would be if everyone pursued discipleship faithfully. As Yoder suggests that Christians should conform their political action to a standard of obedience rather than of effectiveness, he is not primarily concerned with displaying the positive social results of the
(continued...)

A further implication of Constantinianism is "the transformation of moral deliberation into utilitarianism." Given that "the evident course of history is held to be empirically discernible" in the dominant social order, and "the prosperity of our regime is the measure of good, all morality boils down to efficacy. Right action is what works" in supporting the empire. "[W]hat does not promise results can hardly be right." Yoder suggests that

> the [current] dominance of the engineering approach to ethics, reducing all values to the calculation of pressures promising to bring about imperative results, is itself a long-range echo of the Constantinian wedding of piety with power; it is an approach foreign to the biblical thought world and makes no sense in a missionary situation where believers are few and powerless.[10]

Another "more doctrinal implication" is "the victory of metaphysical dualism." As with Constantine "The church we see is not the believing community," but simply an organizational branch of the empire, there is a "visible/ invisible duality" with implications throughout the Christian life. Given the contrast between the pragmatic necessities of the empire and Jesus's call for obedience,

> What could be easier than to reserve the ethics of love for the inward or for the personal, while the ethics of power are for the outward world of structures? Interiorization and individualization, like the developments of the special worlds of cult and mediation, were not purely philosophical invasions which took over because they were intellectually convincing. They did so because they were functional. They explained and justified the growing distance from Jesus and his replacement by other authorities and another

---

[9](...continued)
Christian life. As well, Yoder believes that the rigorous way of discipleship has been, and will likely continue to be, an inevitably minoritarian and unpopular way of life. It is useful, in many respects, to see his project as an answer to the question: "What if nobody else acted like a Christian, but we did?"

[10]Yoder, "The Constantinian Sources of Western Social Ethics," The Priestly Kingdom, 140. See also his "Armaments and Eschatology," 53-58; and "Christ, the Hope of the World," The Original Revolution, 151ff.

political vision than that of the Kingdom of God.[11]

Yoder argues, moreover, that the Constantinian shift continues to have a direct, shaping impact on Christian moral reason in an age in which there is no longer a "Christian" empire. With the modern rise of nationalism, the state has replaced "'Christendom' as the definition of cultural identity and historical meaning." Under this arrangement, "One can now have wars, even holy wars, against other Christian nations."[12] With this development, "The basic Constantinian vision remains, only on a much smaller, provincial scale. Let us call this 'neo-Constantinianism.'"

Even with the rise of the institutional separation of church and state, he thinks that the state often retains the moral blessing of the church through the church's moral identification with the state. Comments Yoder,

> Once the separation of church and state is seen as theologically desirable, a society where this separation is achieved is not a pagan society but a nation structured according to the will of God. American patriotism remains highly religious...Moral identification of church with nation remains despite institutional separation...Let us call this arrangement "neo-neo-Constantinian."[13]

Even within nations that are officially anti-Christian, such as some Marxist states, Yoder notes that "Christians remain patriotic...[to the point of] claiming that their faith does not make them disloyal to the nation." Churches in such settings may actually be "financed by a Marxist regime," and often espouse the political views of their government in ecumenical meetings.

---

[11]Yoder, "The Constantinian Sources of Western Social Ethics," The Priestly Kingdom, 141. See also his Christian Attitudes to War, Peace, and Revolution, 43ff.; and "The Experiential Etiology of Evangelical Dualism," Missiology: An International Review XI (October 1983): 449ff.

[12]Yoder, "The Constantinian Sources of Western Social Ethics," The Priestly Kingdom, 141. See also his "Christ the Hope of the World," The Original Revolution, 148ff.

[13]Yoder, "The Constantinian Sources of Western Social Ethics," The Priestly Kingdom, 142. Also see Yoder's discussions of the role of Christianity in western democratic societies in "The Christian Case for Democracy," and "Civil Religion in America," The Priestly Kingdom, 151ff., 172ff.

98

Comments Yoder,

> This continuing moral identification despite mutual ideological
> disavowal might be called "neo-neo-neo-Constantinian." The
> social arrangement has been changed sweepingly. Civil authorities
> profess the intention that the church shall wither away, yet for the
> time being they support it from the resources of the socialist
> economy. Churchmen are outspokenly loyal not only to their
> people and their culture but even to their regime's current
> policies.[14]

Yet another possible permutation of Constantinian moral reason is that of identifying "God's cause and Christians' loyalty with a regime which is future rather than present: with a 'revolution' or 'liberation' which, being morally imperative, is sure to come." This approach sees God's providential rule of history manifest in "a better power system yet to come, with which Christians should proleptically identify." Yoder calls this approach "'neo-neo-neo-neo-Constantinianism'" for its vision of a coming "partnership with power."[15]

The common "basic structural error" shared by these paradigms is "the identification of a civil authority as the bearer of God's cause."[16] An implication of this error, which is present in various ways in each approach, is "the sacrifice of catholicity" as Christianity is identified with a particular political order. Yoder points out that

> Constantine did not really rule the whole world. To link the
> church with Rome and Byzantium meant writing off the known
> neighbors to the north, east, and south, some Christian, to say

---

[14]Yoder, "The Constantinian Sources of Western Social Ethics," The Priestly Kingdom, 142-143.

[15]Yoder, "The Constantinian Sources of Western Social Ethics," The Priestly Kingdom, 143. See Yoder's critique, but not thoroughgoing rejection, of liberation theology on these grounds in his "Biblical Roots of Liberation Theology," Grail 1 (September 1985): 72-73; and his Christian Attitudes to War, Peace and Revolution, 511ff.

[16]An important task of the following chapter will be to determine to what extent Yoder's project of Christian social involvement shares this "basic structural error."

nothing of the rest of the globe.[17]

This fragmentation was compounded when "the empire was reduced from the whole Mediterranean world to Charlemagne's Europe, and then to the nation." Thereby, various social orders claimed unique identification with the Gospel. The present situation of moral discourse, in Yoder's thought, reflects a long tradition of such divisiveness.

> That churchmen should see the poor or the proletariat or the party as the churches' allies in moving the world is meaningful only when Marxist construals of history are appealing. Long before, however, the same moves were made when it was the nobility, or the bourgeoisie, who seemed to be the bearers of liberation.[18]

In addition to the progressive loss of catholicity,[19] "the church's capacity to be critical" of the dominant social order has decreased with the rise of the various "neo-Constantinianisms." Of the Middle Ages Yoder suggests that

> The hierarchy had a power base and a self-definition which enabled independent judgment. An emperor or a prince could really be forced to listen to the bishop by ban or interdict. The criteria of just war theory and other limits on the prerogatives of princes...had real effect....[But] the Reformation does away with the church's institutional autonomy, Renaissance skepticism destroys the power of the interdict, and in the Reformation confessions the just war theory becomes an affirmation where previously it had been a question. Evidently, each further shift,

---

[17]Yoder, "The Constantinian Sources of Western Social Ethics," The Priestly Kingdom, 143. See also his, "The Disavowal of Constantine: An Alternative Perspective in the Interfaith Dialogue," 53; and "Christ, the Hope of the World," The Original Revolution, 148-150.

[18]Yoder, "The Constantinian Sources of Western Social Ethics," The Priestly Kingdom, 143-144. In contrast, Yoder suggests that "Christian unity is the true internationalism" in his "Let the Church Be the Church," The Original Revolution, 123.

[19]It may seem strange that Yoder, who is so closely identified with Anabaptism, would view "catholicity" as a virtue. He appears to use the term in a way intended to call Christians, regardless of denominational affiliation, back to the crux of the faith: the faithful discipleship of Jesus Christ as he is portrayed in the New Testament. He does not want to be ignored by "mainline" Christians as simply a theologian for Anabaptists. Of course, Yoder's view of the center of Christianity reflects clearly his particular theological tradition. See Yoder's references to what is binding upon all Christians in "Radical Reformation Ethics in Ecumenical Perspective," The Priestly Kingdom, 113-122; and "Introduction," The Priestly Kingdom, 1-12.

as the church seeks to hang on to a status slipping from her hold, decreases even further the capacity to be concretely critical. Least of all can one be concretely critical of a projected future.[20]

Yoder sums up his view of the abiding significance of Constantinianism in the following two claims:

1) that the fourth-century shift continues to explain much if not most of the distance between biblical Christianity and ourselves, which is a distance not simply of time and organic development, but of disavowal and apostasy;
2) that many efforts to renew Christian thought regarding power and society remain the captives of the fallen system they mean to reject.[21]

An important theological line of critique of the various incarnations of Constantinianism is, in Yoder's thought, Christological. For

if kenosis is the shape of God's own self-sending, then any strategy of Lordship, like that of the kings of this world, is not only a strategic mistake likely to backfire but a denial of gospel substance...What the churches accepted in the Constantinian shift is what Jesus had rejected, seizing godlikeness, moving in hoc signo from Golgatha to the battlefield. If this diagnosis is correct, then the cure is not to update the fourth-century mistake by adding another "neo-" but to repent of the whole "where it's at" style and to begin again with kenosis.[22]

When this Christological point is linked with Yoder's discipleship ethic,

---

[20]Yoder, "The Constantinian Sources of Western Social Ethics, The Priestly Kingdom, 144. See Yoder's conclusions on the Reformation's destruction of just war theory as a restraint on the Christian approval of war in his "The Reception of the Just War Tradition by the Magisterial Reformers," History of European Ideas 9 (1988): 20-21; and in When War Is Unjust, 32ff.

[21]Yoder, "The Constantinian Sources of Western Social Ethics," The Priestly Kingdom, 144. See Yoder's "The Authority of Tradition," The Priestly Kingdom, 63ff., for his discussion of the difference between "the wholesome growth" of tradition and apostasy. That Yoder is so critical of the presiding forms of Christianity since the fourth century A. D. is a reflection of his view of the abiding corruption of history "between the times." The risen Christ's victory over the powers has not yet culminated in the clear manifestation of God's rule throughout the world, or throughout much of what passes for "church."

[22]Yoder, "The Constantinian Sources of Western Social Ethics," The Priestly Kingdom, 145. Yoder elaborates on Christ's paradigmatic humility and obedience in The Politics of Jesus, 124-126, 190-192, 240ff.

it becomes clear that for him an unstated assumption of Constantinian reasoning is the claim that "'of course we cannot ask of Caesar that he live like a Christian (i. e., like what the earlier Christians had thought Jesus wanted their pattern of life to be).'" Against what is for Yoder an historically dominant assumption of Christian ethics, that "what it takes to be a Caesar is firmly defined by 'nature'" or a deterministic account of how things must be, he suggests that logically Caesar "would be just as free as anyone else to take risks in faith," to live like a Christian in the imitation of Christ's non-resistant love. On the possible results of such an endeavor Yoder comments that

> It might happen that the result would be that his enemies would triumph over him, but that often happens to rulers anyway. It might happen that he would have to suffer, or not stay in office all his life, but that too often happens to rulers anyway, and it is something that Christians are supposed to be ready for. It might happen that he would be killed: but most Caesars are killed anyway...[I]t might also have been possible that...there could have been in some times and in some places the possibility that good could be done, that creative social alternatives could be discovered, that problems could be solved, enemies loved and justice fostered.[23]

So in sum, Constantinianism is, in Yoder's thought, a metaphor for a shift in the relationship between church and world that has had, and continues to have, a profoundly bad influence on Christian moral reason. It has similarly corrupting ramifications for Christology, ecclesiology, and eschatology. It symbolizes, more dramatically than any other aspect of Yoder's thought, the historically dominant shape that infidelity to the Gospel has taken.

In order to gain a critical perspective on Yoder's argument, it is important to analyze the historical plausibility of his account of Constantine and the shift in moral reason which his reign allegedly embodied. For if Yoder's critique of Constantinianism is to be affirmed, significant aspects of his

---

[23]Yoder, "The Constantinian Sources of Western Social Ethics," The Priestly Kingdom, 146. See also "Armaments and Eschatology," 54ff.

description of what Constantine's rule entailed must be corroborated by historical research.

Yoder comments that his "concern is not with Constantine the man--how sincere his conversion was, what he believed, how he intended to use the church," but with "the new era" of Christian moral reason which his Christian empire began.[24] The significance of this new era of Christian history, which was begun with the conversion of the emperor, has received much historical and theological attention across the centuries.

Eusebius wrote of him in, for example, De Vita Constantini and Historia Ecclesiastica.[25] Alistair Kee comments on these volumes that while

> Eusebius is regarded as the first historian of the church, his Historia Ecclesiastica is actually written to illustrate and confirm a philosophy (or theology) of history. Similarly, De Vita Constantini is not simply a biography of the Emperor. It deals with the transformation in the life of the church which was brought about by Constantine. It is in fact a doxology, a work of faith offered to the glory of God.[26]

Eusebius praised God for Constantine as a divinely appointed ruler who fulfilled God's intention for the governance of the world. Says Eusebius,

> As the Universal Saviour renders the entire heaven and earth and highest kingdom fit for His Father, so His friend [Constantine], leading his subjects on earth to the Only-Begotten and Saviour

---

[24]Yoder, "The Constantinian Sources of Western Social Ethics," The Priestly Kingdom, 135. See also his Christian Attitudes to War, Peace, and Revolution, 39ff.

[25]A Select Library of Nicene and Post-Nicene Fathers (Second Series) Vol. 1, trans. E. C. Richardson (Oxford and New York, 1890), 481-540, contains an English translation of De Vita Constantini. Ecclesiastical History, trans. H. J. Lawlor and J. E. L. Oulton (London: Society for the Promotion of Christian Knowledge, 1927) provides an English text of Historia Ecclesiastica.

[26]Alistair Kee, Constantine Versus Christ (London: SCM Press, Ltd., 1982), 51. See also Timothy Barnes, Constantine and Eusebius (Cambridge, Massachusetts: Harvard University Press, 1981), 245-275; W. H. C. Frend, The Rise of Christianity (Philadelphia: Fortress Press, 1984), 473-505; Lloyd B. Holsapple, Constantine the Great (New York: Sheed & Ward, 1942), especially chapters 19 and 20; and Hermann Doerries, Konstantin der Grosse (Stuttgart: W. Kohlhammer, 1958), 146-171, for historical analysis relevant to Eusebius' view of Constantine.

Logos, makes them suitable for His Kingdom (II, 85)....He has modelled the kingdom on earth into a likeness of the one in heaven, toward which He urges all mankind to strive, holding forth to them this fair hope. (IV, 88).[27]

Paul Keresztes, a modern interpreter of Constantine, approvingly cites as evidence of the Christian nature of Constantine's rule the fact that he enacted laws designed to make divorce difficult, to aid indigents, to facilitate manumission in certain circumstances, and to stop gladiatorial games. He also notes, however, that Constantine imposed some laws which, when viewed from a modern Christian perspective, seem to embody a "shocking brutality."[28]

Keresztes comments on Constantine's rule.

The Emperor simply wanted to preserve the essential social structure of the Empire. If the laws were in many instances harsh, they were nevertheless to be obeyed by all concerned...Does not Holy Scripture unequivocally tells [sic] slaves that they are to obey their masters and keep their places? The classical passages of the New Testament from Saint Paul and the first Pope, Saint Peter, instruct slaves that they should obey their masters in fear and trembling, doing the will of God, since when they suffer patiently it is acceptable to God, and that in doing this they follow, as they always should, the example of Christ. It is important that Christ, the founder of the Christian religion, gave this very example to be followed, and His own mission,--in contrast to the avowed mission of many churchmen of our own days--to be followed by Christians, was not to change the social order but to lead people to the performance of the will of God, namely that they be holy. If he was supposed to change the social order, then Constantine could not learn it from the Holy Scriptures, and still less from the leaders of the Christian Church, the bishops and priests.[29]

---

[27]Eusebius, Oratio de Laudibus Constantini, as cited by Kee, Constantine Versus Christ, 30. The most recent English translation of the oration is found in H. A. Drake, In Praise of Constantine: A Historical Study and New Translation of Eusebius' Tricennial Orations (Los Angeles: University of California Press, 1975).

[28]Paul Keresztes, Constantine: A Great Christian Monarch and Apostle (Amsterdam: J. C. Gieben, 1981), 173-175.

[29]Keresztes, Constantine: A Great Christian Monarch and Apostle, 176-177.

104

Keresztes suggests that what Constantine did learn from Scripture was to display "brotherly love" toward fellow Christians: "[H]is faith in Christianity shone brilliantly in the generosity of his material and moral support for the Holy Church of God." By legalizing Christianity, granting to "the Church privilege after privilege with the single purpose of making it possible for the Church and its representatives...to dedicate themselves completely to its mission of spreading the true teachings of Christ," Constantine was a true servant of God.[30]

Kee challenges such positive readings of Constantine's rule in Constantine Versus Christ: The Triumph of Ideology. It is his argument that a careful reading of Eusebius' writings, and of other ancient texts, reveals that Constantine was not a Christian; indeed, that he used Christianity as an ideology to support a regime that was in many respects anti-Christian. Kee suggests that Constantine shrewdly used the monotheistic language of Christianity as a rhetorical strategy to enhance his stature as the one ruler of the empire. His religious discourse, according to Kee, had no place for Jesus Christ, and portrayed himself as God's chosen Messiah whose rule was an earthly manifestation of God's heavenly reign.[31]

---

[30]Keresztes, Constantine: A Great Christian Monarch and Apostle, 177.

[31]Kee, Constantine Versus Christ, especially chapters 2 and 3. Juergen Moltmann, The Trinity and the Kingdom (San Francisco: Harper & Row Publishers, 1981), 195, notes that Christian monotheism lent itself to such ideological use. For Moltmann, it is "easy to understand why Constantine the Great tried to make out of Christianity a permitted and then a state religion, instead of a persecuted one. The doctrine of sovereignty suggested by Christian monotheism is...more absolutist than the theories based on Aristotle or the Stoics: the one almighty emperor is to a pre-eminent degree, the visible image of the invisible God. His 'glory' reflects God's glory. His rule represents God's rule. Hence the one God is venerated in him. He is not merely the regent; he is the actual lord and possessor of the imperium. The law which applies to all does not bind him; his will is law, makes laws and changes them. He is ultimately in duty bound to extend the imperium to all peoples, in order to allow everyone to enjoy the peace uniting them: 'The one God, the one heavenly king and the one sovereign nomos and logos corresponds to the one king on earth.' The idea of unity in God therefore provides the idea of the universal, unified church, and the idea of the universal, unified state: one god--one emperor--one church--one empire."

See Erik Petersen, "Monotheismus als politsches Problem," Theologische Traktate
(continued...)

Kee describes Constantine's reign as marking the advent of "The Great Reversal" through which the emperor, and his rule, became the basis for a politically projected view of God. Of Eusebius' praise of Constantine, he observes that

> Eusebius has not had these things supernaturally revealed to him, nor has he as in a theophany beheld the Sovereign who is invisible. No, he has looked upon the known and the visible and projected them into objectivity. It is not that by a cosmic alchemy the sovereign takes the form of the Sovereign. Rather, by simple projection, the Sovereign takes on the form of the sovereign, though of course much enlarged.[32]

Kee notes that this reversal characterizes the entirety of Constantine's political career.

> Long before Constantine's "conversion," he had determined by any means possible to become sole ruler of the Empire. Did that change when he associated himself with the God of the Christians? No, the same project was now given divine blessing. Long before his "conversion," he had decided that persecution was counter-productive. Did his conversion mean that he was at the disposal of the church? Far from it; the church was incorporated into his grand plan and became an instrument in his unification of the Empire. But above all, what of his values? Was he so changed at his "conversion" that he now conducted himself according to the will of God as revealed in Jesus of Nazareth? Under no circumstances...If Constantine had been a Christian, even if he had called himself a Christian, then we might have expected his life and actions to have been conformed to the values of Jesus Christ...But in fact it is clear that Constantine's values did not change. Through the Great Reversal these values, which stand in contradiction to those of Christ in matters of wealth, power, ambition, personal relations, social organization and religion, are now assumed to be Christian values. It is in this way that

---

[31](...continued)
(Munich: Hochland Buecherei, 1951), especially 88-105, for a similar account of the political usefulness of monotheism for the sustenance of the empire. See his Eis Theos: Epigraphische, formgeschichtliche und religiongeschichtliche Untersuchungen (Goettingen: Dandenhoed & Ruprecht, 1926) for an in depth discussion of monotheism in the ancient world.

[32]Kee, Constantine Versus Christ, 133.

European history is determined by the values of Constantine, as if they were the values of Christ. But this is the essence of ideology, that the underlying reality is the inversion of what appears to be the case.[33]

While it is beyond the scope of this study to reach definitive historical conclusions on whether Constantine was a Christian and how his alleged conversion may have informed his rule of the empire, this brief historical analysis of Constantine should help to place Yoder's account of Constantinianism in a critical context. The discussion appears to warrant two tentative conclusions.

First, Yoder's account of Constantine's use of Christianity as an ideology to foster his political agenda is not without support from historical studies, such as Kee's volume. Through exacting historical analysis on Constantine of the sort which Yoder does not seem to have undertaken, Kee portrays the emperor and his reign in a fashion that is clearly congenial to Yoder's account.[34] Second, even those who portray Constantine as a faithful Christian, such as Eusebius and Keresztes, suggest that he pursued policies which, on Yoder's terms, are antithetical to the discipleship of Jesus. Whether the use of deadly force or the alliance of the church with the empire, they portray Constantine acting in a fashion of which Yoder would not approve morally.[35]

The thrust of this second conclusion is that even the more positive interpreters of Constantine agree that something radically new, the alliance of church and empire, began with him.[36] In light of their "Catholic" theological

---

[33]Kee, Constantine Versus Christ, 139-140.

[34]Kee, Constantine Versus Christ, 153ff.

[35]See, for example, Keresztes, Constantine: A Great Christian Monarch and Apostle, 175ff.

[36]As noted above, Helgeland, Daly, and Burns suggest in Christians and the Military: The Early Experience, 88, that the clearly new relationship between church and empire which came about with the conversion of Constantine was "a fairly natural and logical development from the kind of experience Christians were having...throughout the previous century." Despite their argument that Christians were involved in the government and the military before the emperor's
(continued...)

orientations, Eusebius and Keresztes interpret this development positively, indeed as the will of God for church and society. Yoder, given his Anabaptist insistence on a discipleship ethic and a clear distinction between church and world, reaches a radically different conclusion.[37] The main point of controversy, then, between Yoder and Kee, on the one hand, and Eusebius and Keresztes, on the other, is theological, and not simply historical, interpretation. Comments Kee,

> The evidence is not in dispute in the case of Constantine. He had a policy towards the church, and this not only included matters of status and property, but extended to the calling of ecumenical councils and the resolution of theological disputes. But how these things are to be interpreted depends on the perspective adopted.[38]

As what is at stake in Yoder's account of Constantinianism is largely the adequacy of his theological interpretation of an historical event and its continuing ramifications, it is important to display more fully, and in greater detail, the major assumptions which inform his critique. Toward that end, the rest of this chapter elucidates and engages critically some of the more important theological and moral commitments that inform Yoder's interpretation of Constantinianism.

Constantinianism's Eschatological Assumptions

As noted briefly above, Yoder thinks that Constantinianism assumes an eschatology that is at odds with a properly biblical eschatology. Yoder, in light of his "biblical realism" orientation, identifies the disagreement clearly.

> The apostolic church confessed Jesus Christ as Lord; risen, ascended, sitting at the right hand of the Father, i. e., ruling (1 Cor. 15:25ff.) over the not yet subdued kosmos. The principalities

---

[36](...continued)
conversion, their claim does not compromise the conclusion that a radically new alliance of church and empire began with Constantine.

[37]See, for example, Yoder's explicitly Anabaptist critique of Constantinianism in "The Recovery of the Anabaptist Vision," 20-21.

[38]Kee, Constantine Versus Christ, 24.

and powers, though not manifestly confessing His Lordship, could not escape from His hidden control or from the promise of His ultimate victory. In ways that took account of their rebelliousness He denied them free rein, using even their self-glorifying designs with His purpose. A latter term for this same idea is "Providence." But with the age of Constantine, Providence no longer needed to be an object of faith, for God's governance of history had become empirically evident in the person of the Christian ruler of the world. The concept of millennium was soon pulled back from the future (whether distant or imminent) into the present. All that God can possibly have in store for a future victory is more of what has already been won.[39]

Rather than seeing the church as living during "the overlapping of two aeons" when Christ's lordship over the world is unconsummated and hidden, the Constantinian sees the new aeon as clearly victorious in the dominant social order.[40] On the moral seriousness of this orientation, Yoder notes that the "new view of the meaning of history" wrought by the Constantinian shift "is deeper than the change in the ethics" which is dependent upon it. "[T]he level on which the shift matters the most" is the question "how does God work in history?"

Yoder suggests that in the New Testament God works "on two distinguishable levels." One is "the visible, confessing community, the church...This voluntary minority body is an organ of the work of God in history." The other level is God's invisible work "through the fact that the risen Christ is at the right hand of the Father."

> The risen Christ at the right hand of the Father governs the universe. We can't see how. We can't immediately say that certain events in secular history or in cultural history have been providentially governed so that they must come out this way in the end, but we do (or the early church does) confess that, as a hidden meaning, and as a meaning which the church can know sometimes through the prophets, sometimes through experience and

---

[39]Yoder, "The Constantinian Sources of Western Social Ethics," The Priestly Kingdom, 136-137.

[40]Yoder, "If Christ Is Truly Lord," The Original Revolution, 55.

discernment. Thus the risen Lord uses the powers despite themselves, including the economic and political powers, including Caesar, somehow for his hidden purposes...So you know for a fact that there is a church and that God is using the church for certain ministries of proclamation and service, fellowship, etc. You have to take it on faith that God is governing the world.[41]

But "after Constantine, that has fundamentally changed." Says Yoder,

Eusebius and Augustine...work out an alternative. God is governing history through Constantine. Constantine is not only the person who happened to take the lid off so the Christians could have religious liberty. That is far too little. He is a kind of savior, a kind of bishop, a kind of theologian. The Empire is the church.[42]

Yoder notes that "When the Church of the fourth century wished to honor Constantine, she interpreted him in the light of her eschatology." Eusebius saw "the Christian Imperator" as being just beneath "Christos Pantokrator." This arrangement assumed that "the State was unequivocally in the realm of

---

[41]Yoder, Christian Attitudes to War, Peace, and Revolution, 42-43. See also "The Otherness of the Church," 289; and "Discerning the Kingdom of God in the Struggles of the World," 371ff.
   This passage reflects the fact that an aspect of Yoder's criticism of Constantinianism is that it has wrongly discerned the union of church and empire, which began with Constantine, to be an act of Providence. Yoder thinks that, instead of boldly proclaiming any such event in the history of the world to be the work of God, Christians must take it on faith--in some unspecified way--that God is working in history "for his hidden purposes."
   This formulation raises two critical issues. First, how can Yoder know that God did not raise up Constantine providentially? We can speculate that Yoder would say that God would not work through a ruler who, on Yoder's terms, brought about an historically pervasive distortion of Christian faith. But, again on Yoder's terms, it is apparently impossible to know for sure how God is governing history. It does not appear, then, that Yoder may consistently rule out the possibility that God may have used Constantine for the Almighty's "hidden purposes."
   Second, Yoder's view of the inscrutable nature of God's governance of the world raises an interesting epistemological issue to keep in mind for the following chapter's analysis of Yoder's view of Christian social action. Namely, how will Christians be able to discern what role they should take in governing the world, given that God's designs for the governance of the world are unknowable? Does Yoder's "non-Constantinian" political project assume a greater knowledge of God's action in history than he is able to justify on his own terms? The fourth chapter will examine these questions in detail.

[42]Yoder, Christian Attitudes to War, Peace, and Revolution, 43. See, for example, Kee's account of Constantine's involvement in ecclesiastical affairs in Constantine Versus Christ, 102-114.

redemption" and a manifestation of God's reign.

This view of the state is also evident for Yoder in the magisterial Reformation's call for "the territorial State" to be the agent of its reforms, as the state was again affirmed as the main agent of God's rule in history.

> The conviction that the center of the meaning of history is in the work of the Church, which had been central in the pre-Constantinian Church and remained half alive in the Middle Ages, is now expressly rejected. The prince is not only a Christian, not only a prominent Christian; he is now the bishop. True faith and the true Church being invisible, the only valid aims of innerworldly effort are those which take the total secular society of a given area as the object of responsibility...The Church confesses in deed and sometimes in word that not she, but the State, has the last word and incarnates the ultimate values in God's work in the world.[43]

The Constantinian assumes that "God's goal, the conquest of the world by the church, had been reached (via the conquest of the church by the world)," and in particular by the state. Yoder suggests that this approach compromises the eschatological nature of God's judgment.

> If the kingdom is in the process of realization through the present order, then the state is not simply a means or reconciling competing egoisms in the interest of order; it can be an agent of God's defeat of evil and may initiate disorder...[T]he function of judgment which the New Testament eschatology leaves to God, becomes also the prerogative of the state....[T]he purpose of exterminating, rather than subduing, evil is shifted from the endtime to the present.[44]

Yoder comments that this was also the error of Thomas Muenster, who "attempted, just as did Constantine, to take into human hands the work which will be done by the Word of God at the end of the age--the final victory of the church

---

[43]Yoder, "The Otherness of the Church," 291.

[44]Yoder, "If Christ Is Truly Lord," The Original Revolution, 66.

and defeat of evil."[45] Implicit in this orientation is the claim that

> God has no way to make history come out right except that we run
> it, so it's God's responsibility, not ours, when we change our
> ethics so as to help him win. We are unselfish in the matter. We
> are just helping God run his world. That's the first deep new
> assumption about the logic of ethics. We have to enable Caesar,
> who's our [and God's] man, to win.[46]

Yoder's account of eschatology is clearly at odds with that of
Constantinianism. While Yoder espouses, within the context of a "biblical
realism" hermeneutic, an "already but not yet" view of the presence of God's
kingdom which locates the Christian life between Christ's decisive and final
victory, Constantinianism identifies the fullness of God's reign with the present
order. While, for Yoder, Christ's lordship is hidden before the Parousia and
most evident in the church, for the Constantinian it is clearly manifest in the
state, which is the chief agent of God's action in history.

While Yoder's eschatological vision of the victory of the Lamb requires
the present imitation of Jesus in obedience to God without primary regard for
punctual results in moral reason, the Constantinian pursues what will work in
sustaining the status quo: Christian ethics is at the service of the empire. From
Yoder's perspective, Constantinianism corrupts the Christian life by interpreting
history in a fashion that calls for the unfaithful modification of the "one particular
social political-ethical option" called for by Jesus.[47]

As noted earlier, one problematic aspect of Yoder's critique of the
eschatology of Constantinianism is his claim that it is virtually impossible to
discern God's providential governance of history. The difficulty with Yoder's
assertion is that it effectively rules out any knowledge of God's action in history,
as "you have to take it on faith [in some unspecified way] that God is governing

---

[45]Yoder, "If Christ Is Truly Lord," The Original Revolution, 69.

[46]Yoder, Christian Attitudes to War, Peace, and Revolution, 51.

[47]Yoder, The Politics of Jesus.

112

the world."[48]

Yoder's formulation casts serious epistemological doubt on his, or anyone else's, ability to argue that God did not providentially bring Constantine to power, or to speak substantively on any question concerning God's action in history. Given Yoder's denial of any such knowledge of the workings of Providence, it appears that one simply cannot know whether God was governing history through Constantine's reign. As an important thrust of Yoder's critique is the denial that God was acting providentially through Constantine, it is hard to see how his claim may be substantiated on his own epistemological grounds.

Moreover, Yoder's denial of knowledge of God's providential purposes in history should be kept in mind for the next chapter's evaluation of Yoder's proposal for Christian political involvement. An important task of the chapter will be to determine whether Yoder assumes a more substantive knowledge of God's purposes for his own project than he allows to the Constantinians.

The Significance of Constantinianism for the Church/World Relationship

A very important implication, for Yoder, of the Constantinian synthesis of church and empire is its shaping influence for the relationship between the church and the world. Yoder places the issue in a larger theological context.

> "World" (aion houtos in Paul, kosmos in John) signifies in this connection not creation or nature or the universe, but rather the fallen form of the same, no longer conformed to the creative intent. The State, which for present purposes may be considered as typical for the world, belongs with the other exousiai in this realm. Over against this "world" the Church is visible; identified by baptism, discipline, morality, and martyrdom. It is self-evident for the early centuries as a part of this visibility of the fellowship of disciples, that the Church's members do not normally belong in

---

[48]Yoder, Christian Attitudes to War, Peace, and Revolution, 42-43.

the service of the world and <u>a fortiori</u> in that of the pagan state.[49]

This "visible dichotomy" assumed, however, "a believed unity." Namely, "the Church believed that her Lord was also Lord over the world." In this light, Yoder suggests that Christians "could take on a prophetic responsibility for civil ethics without baptizing the State" by calling it to "human <u>justitia</u>...not because of any belief in a universal innate moral sense, but because of her faith in her Lord." Says Yoder,

> This attitude was meaningful for the Church because she believed that the State was not the ultimately determinative force in history. She ascribed to the State at best a preservative function in the midst of an essentially rebellious world, whereas the true sense of history was to be sought elsewhere, namely in the work of the Church.[50]

---

[49]Yoder, "The Otherness of the Church," 287. See also his "The Theological Basis of the Christian Witness to the State," On Earth Peace, 139ff.; and Sawatsky, "John Howard Yoder," Non-violence: Central to Christian Spirituality, 251-255; Van Gerwen, "The Church in the Theological Ethics of Stanley Hauerwas," 129-142; and Zimbleman, "Theological Ethics and Politics in the Thought of Juan Luis Segundo and John Howard Yoder," 218ff.

[50]Yoder, "The Otherness of the Church," 287-288. See also The Christian Witness to the State, 12ff. Yoder fails to provide any historical examples of pre-Constantinian Christians who addressed civil authorities in this way. Hence, it is hard to know whom he is describing in these passages, and even harder to know whether he is describing them with historical accuracy.

One example of a pre-Constantinian Christian who commented on the theological significance of the state is Tertullian. He suggests in "Apology," The Ante-Nicene Fathers, vol. III, eds. A. Roberts and J. Donaldson (Grand Rapids, Michigan: William B. Eerdmans Publishing Company, 1980), (21) 35, that, in praying for the empire, "we are lending our aide to Rome's duration." He goes on to say, (32) 42-43, that "We respect in the emperors the ordinance of God, who has set them over the nations. We know that there is that in them which God has willed; and to what God has willed we count an oath by it a great oath." In "To Scapula," (2) 105-106, he makes the similar comment that "A Christian is enemy to none, least of all to the Emperor of Rome, whom he knows to be appointed by his God and so cannot but love and honor; and whose well-being moreover, he must needs desire, with that of the empire over which he reigns so long as the world shall stand--for so long as that shall Rome continue." In "On the Resurrection of the Flesh," (24) 562-563, he suggests that the fall of Rome will be a sign of the coming of the Antichrist. Tertullian's remark in "On Idolatry," (18) 73, that all the "powers and dignities of this world are not only alien to, but enemies of, God," seems to be in tension with his claim that God has appointed the emperors of Rome to rule until the end of the

(continued...)

Yoder argues that it is precisely this claim that "Church and world were visibly distinct, yet affirmed in faith to have one and the same Lord" that the rise of Constantinianism altered. Indeed,

> The most pertinent fact about the new state of things after Constantine and Augustine is not that Christians were no longer persecuted and began to be privileged, nor that emperors built churches and presided over ecumenical deliberations about the Trinity; what matters is that the two visible realities, Church and world, were fused. There is no longer anything to call "world"; State, economy, art, rhetoric, superstition and war have all been baptized.[51]

As it was obvious to astute theological minds like that of Augustine that "compulsory baptism" had not made the empire fully faithful to the Gospel, Yoder notes that "the doctrine of the invisibility of the true Church" arose "in order to permit the affirmation that on some level somewhere the difference between belief and unbelief, i. e., between Church and world, still existed." Under the new governmental/ecclesial arrangement, however, "this distinction had become invisible, like faith itself."[52]

---

[50](...continued)
world. See Geoffrey Wainwright, "Praying for Kings: The Place of Human Rulers in the Divine Plan of Salvation," Ex Auditu 2 (1986): 121, 125.

In order for Yoder to substantiate the validity of his claim about the political involvement of pre-Constantinian Christians, he would do well to engage explicitly a figure such as Tertullian.

[51]Yoder, "The Otherness of the Church," 288. See also his "Christ, the Hope of the World," The Original Revolution, 146ff.; and Gerhard Lohfink's brief critique of Augustine as a Constantinian in Jesus and Community, 181-185.

[52]Yoder, "The Otherness of the Church," 289; and Christian Attitudes to War, Peace, and Revolution, 43. It is fair to ask Yoder, then, for a lucid account of what it means for the church to be visibly distinct from the world. Surely, aspects of the particulars of visibility will vary from situation to situation, from a Constantinian arrangement to a "neo-Constantinian" arrangement, etc... This observation leads to two critical comments. First, Yoder nowhere displays in concrete detail what the visibility of the church requires in given historical situations, or how Christians will go about determining that in such situations. Hence, it is hard to know precisely what he means by reference to a visible church. Second, Yoder's own approach to Christian social involvement will need to be of a piece with his call for right separation from the world. A task
(continued...)

Moreover, by the new arrangement's identification of God's rule with the dominant cultural order, "the eschatology of the New Testament stood on its head."[53] Says Yoder,

> Previously Christians had known as a fact of experience that the Church existed, but had to believe against appearances that Christ ruled over the world. After Constantine one knew as a fact of experience that Christ was ruling over the world, but had to believe against the evidence that there existed a believing Church. Thus the order of redemption was subordinated to that of preservation, and the Christian hope turned inside out.[54]

Yoder's eschatology plays an important role in shaping his critique of Constantinianism on this point, for the church is, in his thought, a "foretaste of His ultimate loving triumph in His kingdom, [and] has a [unique] task within history."[55] The rebellious world is the "social manifestation" of the old aeon, while the church proleptically embodies the new age begun in Christ's victory over the powers.[56] In this perspective,

> [T]he meaning of history lies not in the acquisition and defense of the culture and the freedoms of the West, not in the aggrandizement of material comforts and political sovereignty, but in the calling together [in the church] of "men for God from every tribe and tongue and people and nation," a "people of His own

---

[52](...continued)
of the next chapter will be to determine to what extent Yoder's project succeeds in meeting his own criteria.

[53]Yoder, Christian Attitudes to War, Peace, and Revolution, 44.

[54]Yoder, "The Otherness of the Church," 289.

[55]Yoder, The Christian Witness to the State, 10.

[56]Yoder, "If Christ is Truly Lord," The Original Revolution, 55. As noted earlier, Yoder never displays with historical or sociological clarity precisely what group or ecclesiastical structure he is describing in his discourse on the church. To that extent, it is hard to grasp with precision the boundaries between church and world, as well as the discrete moral relevance of the distinction between the two realms.

who are zealous for good deeds."[57]

Against the assumptions of Constantinianism, Yoder thinks that "the class of true Christians continues to be a minority," for the fact that "the name of Jesus is now intoned over a...culture without changing its inner content" does not transform the old aeon, and those who live according to its standards, into a socially embodied foretaste of the new age.[58] Such uncritical "baptizing" of the larger society does not give it the "shared discerning process" under the guidance of the Spirit, embodied only in a visible church, that Yoder thinks is necessary to sustain Christian discipleship.[59]

Indeed, the conflation of church and world wrought by Constantine destroys the minoritarian, communitarian stance which Yoder thinks is an essential social standpoint for the proper interpretation of Scripture and pursuit of the moral life. Comments Yoder on this point,

> [I]t is not obvious to all modern readers why it should be significant to take account of the minority status of a faith community in understanding its ethical imperatives. To understand the perspective of the book of the Apocalypse, or the prophecies of Jeremiah and Ezekiel, or for that matter of the records of the message of Jesus, many of our contemporaries do not stop to take account of what it contributes to the shape of the writer's ethical guidance that he is not assuming that his listeners dominate the society where they live. The reader of such literature knows that to be a fact, but often does not take account of that fact as helping to explain why the ethical orientation projected in such literature takes the shape that it does.[60]

Whereas Yoder sees church and world as conflictive social

---

[57]Yoder, "The Otherness of the Church," 293. See also "The Spirit of God and the Politics of Men," 66ff.

[58]Yoder, "The Constantinian Sources of Western Social Ethics," The Priestly Kingdom, 136-137.

[59]Yoder, "The Hermeneutics of Peoplehood," The Priestly Kingdom, 35. See also "A People in the World: Theological Interpretation," The Concept of the Believers' Church, 259, 276-277.

[60]Yoder, "The Kingdom as Social Ethic," The Priestly Kingdom, 82.

manifestations respectively of the new and old aeons, which will exist in tension until God's consummated victory over the rebellion of the world in the eschaton, Constantinianism collapses the distinction into an organic cultural union of church and the dominant social order. Thereby, the church loses its unique, minoritarian status as foretaste of the new aeon and the chief instrument of God's work in the world. God's reign is now identified with the empire, and this orientation, in Yoder's view, decimates crucial resources of Christian moral discernment.

As noted above, Yoder's critique of the problematic relationship between church and world entailed by the Constantinian synthesis is not displayed with historical accuracy. He fails to demonstrate both what the precise historically displayed relationship was between church and world before the union of church and empire, and how the conversion of Constantine altered that relationship in a negative way. Likewise, he does not describe with precision the nature of the continuing Constantinian flaw which he detects throughout the history of Christianity since the fourth century A. D.

While it is clear that Yoder thinks that with the rise of Constantine the "proper" relationship between church and world was compromised, he never provides an exacting account what the "proper" relationship would require in a given historically, culturally located situation. To that extent, his critique of the relationship between church and world entailed by Constantinianism appears to operate more as abstract rhetoric than as a lucidly displayed, historically located account of how church and world should interact.

The Significance of Constantinianism for Christian Moral Reason

Yoder suggests that Christian moral rationality was, and continues to be, distorted by the new reading of eschatology and of the relationship between church and world which were entailed by the Constantinian synthesis. Perhaps the most basic aspect of this distortion is the assumption that, in light of the clear demonstration of God's rule in the dominant social order, the chief "source of moral knowledge will have to be other than Jesus in the New Testament" because the sustenance of this order requires a mode of moral rationality distinct from, and contradictory to, what Jesus embodied and proclaimed.[61]

With a Christian empire and emperor, the "realistic" requirements of statecraft take precedence over the calling of obedience to Jesus' non-resistant love. Says Yoder on the logic of this position,

> [W]e cannot tell him to be like Jesus or do what Jesus said. We can't give the emperor the guidance of a pre-Constantinian ethic; that won't work. Why won't that work? Because he couldn't stay in power, and staying in power is necessary...And a ruler does after all what needs to be done. God wants him to stay in power, in order to rule the world, even if that means accepting a non-Jesus ethic.[62]

Implicit in this line of argument is for Yoder the assumption that

> [W]e derive our ethics from the imperative to make history come out right through our actions. God has no way to make history come out right except that we run it, so it's God's responsibility, not ours, when we change our ethics so as to help him win. We are unselfish in the matter. We are just helping God run his world.[63]

This description of the role of Christians in society entails an ethic of responsibility for managing the larger social order that assumes

> an inherent duty to take charge of the social order in the interest of its survival or its amelioration by the use of means dictated, not by love, but by the social order itself. "Responsibility" thus becomes an autonomous moral absolute.[64]

---

[61]Yoder, Christian Attitudes to War, Peace, and Revolution, 46. Kee, in Constantine Versus Christ, 161, likewise comments that, with the Constantinian shift, "the historical Jesus is no longer the norm of conduct or values for the church."

[62]Yoder, Christian Attitudes to War, Peace, and Revolution, 49.

[63]Yoder, Christian Attitudes to War, Peace, and Revolution, 50-51. See also Zimbleman, "Theological Ethics and Politics in the Thought of Juan Luis Segundo and John Howard Yoder," 219ff.

[64]Yoder, "Reinhold Niebuhr and Christian Pacifism," 113. See also Yoder, The Christian Witness to the State, 66ff.

It is for Yoder an autonomous moral absolute that entails a crass pragmatism: "the prosperity of our regime is the measure of good, all morality boils down to efficacy. Right action is what works."[65] This orientation is radically at odds with Yoder's ethic of obedience, which, as noted above, he formulates in an explicit critique of consequentialist reasoning that does not take account of Jesus' lordship over history.[66]

The consequentialist reasoning of the Constantinian appears inappropriate from the perspective of Yoder's account of eschatology, which locates Christians within a narrative, "between the times" of Pentecost and Parousia, the culmination of which will be the consummated vindication of the way of the crucified Lamb, who embodied obedience to God's non-resistant love to the point of death without concern for effectiveness or making history come out right.[67] When that narrative is replaced by, or at least interpreted in light of, one of God's unique blessing of, and even identification with, a particular empire, it is not hard to see how notions of obedience may become subservient to those of responsibility or effectiveness in the sustenance of the empire.

In the Constantinian approach, the standard for judging effectiveness is the strengthening or service of the status quo, which is understood to be the present manifestation of God's rule. As obedience to Jesus' non-resistant love would often not appear to serve that goal, it is rejected as an inappropriate moral orientation.

Yoder interprets such social orders, moreover, in an eschatological perspective which claims that they are not embodiments of God's kingdom, that their success is not the highest value. To the contrary, the crucified Lord, who

---

[65]Yoder, "The Constantinian Sources of Western Social Ethics," The Priestly Kingdom, 140.

[66]Yoder, The Politics of Jesus, 237ff. See also "To Serve Our God and to Rule the World," 11-13; and "Armaments and Eschatology," 55ff.

[67]Yoder, The Politics of Jesus, 240-241. See also "Armaments and Eschatology," 56-58.

rejected the violence on which empires rely, is the key to the meaning and redemption of history. His way of non-resistant love in obedience to God is the ultimately victorious way. Hence, the pursuit of a consequentialist ethic of responsibility that contradicts the requirements of obedience does not succeed ultimately. It is the moral reason of the old aeon which is passing away under the lordship of the Lamb who was slain.[68]

The Constantinian option for a norm of responsibility over a standard of obedience is for Yoder a prime instance of "wrong traditioning" or "error, into which believers are seduced by evil powers seeking to corrupt the church and to disqualify her witness."[69] By adopting the goal of responsibility, and its attendant consequentialist mode of moral reason, Christians have made a so-called "'natural'" source of moral knowledge a more determining norm of their discernment than the teaching and example of Jesus as portrayed in the New Testament.[70]

Yoder suggests that the issue here is not simply a matter of Scripture versus tradition, but whether an aspect of tradition "is counter to the Scriptures; not that it is an ancient idea insufficiently validated by ancient texts, but that it is a latter introduction [possibly] invalidated by its contradicting the ancient message." Indeed, "The issue is (as Jesus said it) the traditions of men versus the commandment of God."[71]

---

[68]Yoder, "The Hermeneutics of Peoplehood," The Priestly Kingdom, 37; and "If Christ Is Truly Lord," The Original Revolution, 55ff.

[69]Yoder, "The Authority of Tradition," The Priestly Kingdom, 69.

[70]Yoder, "The Authority of Tradition," The Priestly Kingdom, 72.

[71]Yoder, "The Authority of Tradition," The Priestly Kingdom, 76. This formulation indicates the difficulty of Yoder's hermeneutical strategy of biblical realism. Namely, Yoder does not attend to the methodological complexity of interpreting Scripture in a way which is influenced by one's theological tradition and one's choice of certain findings of biblical scholarship. He refers to "the ancient message" or the "biblical point of view" without providing an explicit account of how the substance or meaning of those notions is produced. As such, his method of testing
(continued...)

A further aspect of Yoder's critique of the consequentialist moral reasoning of Constantinianism concerns his account of the often unwarranted assumption that moral agents may predict the results of their actions. Such reasoning presupposes a certain "determinism" about the likely response to a given action, as well as a measure of "control of the situation" to enable the agent to do as he or she pleases.[72] Likewise, the agent who is aiming for results must possess, "if not omniscience, at least very full and very reliable information" about the myriad of particulars concerning any historical situation.[73]

Yoder suggests that this way of thinking inadequately describes the options available to a moral agent.

> If there is such a thing as Resurrection, or if the Resurrection is in some sense a model for the believers' life,...then we have to look at the available options in the conviction that there are more options. The present meaning of Resurrection for ethics is that we are never boxed in...Many saving events in history were unforeseeable, unplanned, but they happened. There Resurrection was an impossible unforeseeable new option, and it happened.[74]

Whether martyrdom, a "'providential' escape" through God's intervention, or the hope of resurrection, Christians have resources for describing their options that exceed those of a calculating pragmatism.[75] As "Christian ethics calls for behavior [and discernment] which is impossible except by the miracles of the Holy Spirit," which our concern for effectiveness cannot control,

---

[71](...continued)
tradition by "the commandment of God" appears not to be informed by a sound understanding of the role of tradition in influencing how a particular view of "the commandment of God" is formulated.

[72]Yoder, "What Would You Do If...?,"Journal of Religious Ethics 2 (1974): 82-83.

[73]Yoder, "What Would You Do If...?," 84.

[74]Yoder, Christian Attitudes to War, Peace, and Revolution, 437.

[75]Yoder, What Would You Do?, 26-42.

Yoder calls for simple obedience.[76] It is through obedience to the way of Jesus that Christians may order their lives in a manner appropriate to the service of God's new age.

Yoder also thinks that Christian ethics loses its minoritarian context with the Constantinian "conversion" of the larger society. As there is no longer a world visibly distinct from the church, Christian moral reason becomes the moral reason of society at large, not of a distinct minority group. With a social arrangement in which the ruler claims Christian faith, all citizens are considered Christians and Christianity becomes the official religion of the society; thereby, an identity of dominance replaces that of minority.[77] This new social status has a profound impact, for Yoder, on Christian moral reason.

---

[76]Yoder, "Let the Church Be the Church," The Original Revolution, 115. It will be important to keep in mind Yoder's strong insistence on an ethic of obedience when we consider his proposal for Christian social involvement in the next chapter.

[77]Yoder, "The Kingdom as Social Ethic," The Priestly Kingdom, 82-83. As noted above, Yoder suggests in "The Otherness of the Church," 289, that Augustine recognized that not all those claiming membership in the church were faithful Christians. Hence, Augustine espoused the doctrine of the invisibility of the church to reflect the fact that true Christians compose only a part, and perhaps even a minority, of those identifying with the church. Moreover, Augustine saw human history as characterized by the co-existence of the city of God and the city of the world. "So, too, as long as she is a stranger in the world, the city of God has in her communion, and bound to her by the sacraments, some who shall not eternally dwell in the lot of the saints. Of these, some are not now recognised; other declare themselves, and do not hesitate to make common cause with our enemies in murmuring against God, whose sacramental badge they wear. These men you may to-day see thronging the churches with us, to-morrow crowding the theatres with the godless....these two cities are entangled together in this world, and intermixed until the last judgment effect their separation." Augustine, The City of God (New York: Random House, Inc., 1950), 38 (1.35). See also Justo L. Gonzalez' discussion of Augustine on this point in A History of Christian Thought Vol. 2 (Nashville: Abingdon Press, 1971), 48-53.

Augustine's awareness that, within a social order characterized by the union of church and empire, faithful disciples may very well be in the minority, and will never transform human society into God's unambiguous reign, challenges Yoder's claim that the rise of Constantine clearly changed the identity of Christians from that of a minority to a place of dominance. There was an awareness, at least on the part of some theologians and segments of the church, that not all of society was rightly Christian.

Yoder's formulation of the distinction between church and world obviously seeks to be visible in a way that Augustine's was not. Yoder's failure to display in concrete historical and sociological detail the boundaries of church and world in particular settings, however, compromises the usefulness of his emphasis on the visible church. As we noted above, it is not clear where or how Yoder would draw the lines between church and world.

It will now be appropriate to speak about nature and grace in such a way as to affirm the knowability through "nature" of kinds of moral insight which correspond to the new [consequentialist] ethic. It will be assumed that the moral insights of Gentile antiquity and the teachings of the Old Testament are for some reason closer to "nature" than are the teachings and example of Jesus. The general tone of the argument will be formal: i. e., a discussion of why one should believe in general that those other sources of moral guidance may have some validity. Yet the stake in the argument is material, i. e., the fact that those other moralities are more affirmative than is the New Testament about the uses of coercion, violence, wealth, status, tradition, and the justification of means by ends.[78]

Yoder's critique of the loss of minority status is based on the assumption that "the only way in which the faith can become the official ideology of a power elite in a given society is if Jesus Christ ceases to be concretely Lord."[79] Other values which the dominant order requires for its success, such as "power, mammon, fame, efficacy.... responsibility, nature, efficiency, wisdom," are employed "at the expense of fidelity to the jealousy of Christ as Lord."[80]

Christian ethics, in its new role of guiding the responsible administration of the larger society, must find ways of supporting the exigencies of statecraft, even if they compromise faithfulness to the way of Jesus. Indeed, Christian ethics is now held accountable to "Everyman--baptized but not necessarily thereby possessed of the resources of faith." It has to face the logic of universalizability: "What would happen if everyone did it?" Can the dominant order be sustained

---

[78]Yoder, "The Kingdom as Social Ethic," The Priestly Kingdom, 84. It is important to observe that not all approaches to Christian ethics which look to nature for moral guidance make Jesus Christ morally irrelevant. For example, O'Donovan, in Resurrection and Moral Order, 15, views the resurrection of Jesus as "the reaffirmation of creation" in a way which enables Christians to appreciate God's ordering of nature as a guide to the moral life. It is important not to take Yoder's claim to the extreme point of denying that an appreciation of the moral significance of nature, which is of course God's creation, is necessarily opposed to the discipleship of Jesus.

[79]Yoder, "The Kingdom as Social Ethic," The Priestly Kingdom, 85.

[80]Yoder, "The Kingdom as Social Ethic," The Priestly Kingdom, 86.

by faithfulness to Jesus? If not, the ethic must be altered.[81]

Also lost through the demise of the church's minoritarian identity are its peculiar communal resources for the guidance of moral reason. The "vision of the place of the believing community in history, which vision locates moral reasoning" as the discernment of a distinct community of discipleship with particular traditions, structures, and norms, is compromised through the fusing of church and world.[82] No longer does the church embody "an alternative consciousness" that "represents the promise of another world, which is not somewhere else but which is to come here" through Christ's eschatological victory. No longer is the church in a position "to trust in the power of weakness" and "to see through the weakness of power" because of God's victory through the weakness of the cross.[83]

Yoder thinks that the church, as a minority community which resists the rebellion against God of the dominant order, has resources which enable it to interpret the events of history "more truly" than does the establishment, for the church does "not assume that the only way to read national and political history is from the perspective of the winners": it has no stake in siding with or comforting the victors. Because the minority community is skeptical about the grand claims for itself of the dominant culture, it may critique its "absences of creativity or shortness of will, impatience or evil will, so that the story as it is

---

[81]Yoder, "The Constantinian Sources of Western Social Ethics," The Priestly Kingdom, 138-139. Of course, one could argue against Yoder that "faithfulness to Jesus" may require an interpretation, in certain historical situations, which would guide Christians in performing actions which are not identical with those performed by Jesus. Ramsey, for example, suggests that Christians should follow Jesus' commandment to love the neighbor selflessly by using deadly force, if necessary, to protect the neighbor from unwarranted assualt. For Ramsey, faithfulness to Jesus may require a strategy which Jesus rejected for his own ministry. Ramsey, Basic Christian Ethics, 171ff.

[82]Yoder, "The Hermeneutics of Peoplehood," The Priestly Kingdom, 29. See also "To Serve our God and to Rule the World," 12.

[83]Yoder, "The Kingdom as Social Ethic," The Priestly Kingdom, 94.

told is a subject for repentance and not merely remembering" or eulogizing.[84]

The church is able to discern God's action in history, in a critical manner, through the gift of the Spirit. Says Yoder,

> The promise of the presence of the Holy Spirit is clearly correlated in the New Testament with the need for the church prophetically to discern right and wrong in the events of the age. Not all visible events are God at work, not all "action" is divine, not every Spirit is of Christ....The church is qualified to be such an agent of discernment...because she has in her allegiance to Jesus Christ criteria of good and evil which are significantly different from those which prevail in even the most respectable segments of the larger society.[85]

Likewise, the church, because it is not responsible for managing the entire society, may take the time to pursue "pilot programs to meet previously unmet needs or to restore ministries which have collapsed." It may manifest "a subculture in which some truths are more evidently meaningful and some lines of logic can be more clearly spelled out than in society as a whole."[86] It may function as "the conscience of a society" by voicing "the claims of unrepresented

---

[84]Yoder, "The Kingdom as Social Ethic," The Priestly Kingdom, 95. Yoder does not provide, however, a sufficiently detailed analysis of how the church, in given historical situations, actually has or will go about such moral discernment. Yoder is here making a call to the church to employ its peculiar resources of moral reason and historical interpretation for the sake of prophetic action and proclamation. But, apart from an in-depth display of how such action works and of what it requires in concrete circumstances, Yoder's argument provides little real guidance for the Christian life. It is hard to know precisely what he is calling the church to do and to be.

[85]Yoder, "A People in the World: Theological Interpretation," The Concept of the Believer's Church, 259, 276-277. It is interesting to ask what Yoder means by "church" in this passage. If he is actually describing the church as a body whose working criteria of moral judgment are significantly different from those of society at large, it would appear that he would have to be carefully limiting his reference to certain congregations who measure up to rigorous ethical standards. It seems unlikely that Yoder, with his minoritarian approach, would suggest that all those who profess faith in Jesus Christ, or who claim to be part of the church, employ criteria of moral judgment which are conspicuously Christian. Another possibility is that Yoder is speaking prescriptively of the church. He may be identifying the sort of community which the church ought to be without attempting to describe any existing community as church. This brief discussion reflects the difficulty of determining precisely what Yoder means when he speaks of the church.

[86]Yoder, "The Kingdom as Social Ethic," The Priestly Kingdom, 93.

people and causes, when they do not yet have the ear or the heart of the majority."[87]

But when the minority status of the church is compromised, the resources, goals, and standards of moral analysis change drastically. Says Yoder,

> When Christians count among their number a monarch, or the majority in a democratic system, or a sizable and significant minority in a pluralistic democratic system, it can be practically taken for granted that one way, perhaps the only right way to do moral deliberation is to work out a consequentialist calculation of the direction one wants the whole social system to take. For a small minority such calculation would be an irrelevant or at best utopian way of looking at things.[88]

Yoder suggests that the dominant Constantinian and Weberian mode of social ethics assumes that "concern for effectiveness" in managing the larger society is the most determining aspect of what social "responsibility" requires, and that minoritarian approaches consequently lack moral seriousness. Says he,

> Seldom would the advocate of this Weberian patter[n] of division recognize that it is itself based upon the establishment perspective. Only the person who believes that the "responsible use of power" from a position of domination is necessary in order to be useful will then presuppose that the alternative is moral purity at the price of ineffectiveness.... [T]here may well be dimensions of effectiveness to a minority position even though its logic works on other levels.[89]

As noted above, Yoder describes the norm of effectiveness in light of his

---

[87]Yoder, "The Kingdom as Social Ethic," The Priestly Kingdom, 99.

[88]Yoder, "The Kingdom as Social Ethic," The Priestly Kingdom, 96.

[89]Yoder, "The Kingdom as Social Ethic," The Priestly Kingdom, 96. Yoder comments that Weber asserted that "an ethic of rules will be unconcerned for the results to be expected from a given line of action. In that perspective it might even be taken as a sign of unfaithfulness that one should give as much attention as this study does to how the minority ethic 'really works.' Concern for effectiveness, we are told, is only fitting for those who can live up to that concern by actually managing the world. True obedience to suffering love must therefore presuppose that one disavows concern for results." Such a view is, for Yoder, Constantinian because it describes the task of social ethics primarily in terms of managing society, and finds minoritarian positions morally unimportant.

eschatological description of history: that Jesus has inaugurated a new aeon of God's reign which will find consummation in the eschaton. What is effective, or good or true, may not be described rightly apart from that eschatological consciousness. As the church is a minority community that pursues obedience to the non-resistant way of Jesus, Yoder rejects the way questions of "responsibility" and "effectiveness" are usually framed. In contrast to the conventional Constantinian wisdom, he suggests that

> The entire landscape looks different from a position of weakness. If you could not have stopped something, then you are not to blame when it happens...No longer have we simply the two categories of "right" which we must foster and even enforce, and "wrong" which we must prohibit and punish....There are things which we cannot control, which nonetheless are going to happen, which are going to impinge upon the situation where we ourselves are trying to do something else. This means that it will be an expression of wisdom, and not of self-righteousness or unconcern or isolation, if we accept the fact that those deeds are going to be done and that we cannot stop them, and concentrate for ourselves on doing other things which no one will do. This looks to our friends of a majoritarian cast of mind like acquiescence in evil. It is; one of the differences between being powerful and powerless is that one has thought more about the fact that there are evils one cannot prevent.[90]

Rather than aiming for effectiveness in imposing the best possible solution from a position of strength, Yoder suggests that "since the situation is decisively controlled by other powers, one does the best one can to serve as can be served and save what can be saved in a bad situation."[91] The responsibility of Christians is, in Yoder's view, to pursue faithfulness from a position of weakness within situations that call for the redemptive ministry of the new aeon. Such an approach, he suggests, appears irresponsible only from the Constantinian perspective of those who define responsibility from a majoritarian point of view

---

[90]Yoder, "The Kingdom as Social Ethic," The Priestly Kingdom, 100-101.

[91]Yoder, "The Kingdom as Social Ethic," The Priestly Kingdom, 101.

that seeks to control history.

Throughout the formulation of his critique of Constantinianism, it is clear that Yoder is not simply attempting to make an historical point about the realignment of church and empire begun in the fourth century A. D. Rather, in light of his theological commitments concerning the appropriateness of an ethic of discipleship, a certain view of the relationship between church and world, and a given eschatology, he advances a number of critiques against Constantinianism as a metaphor for a mode of moral reason that he thinks is a longstanding and widespread perversion of the Gospel.

While, as noted in the first section of this chapter, Yoder's description of Constantine's reign has historical plausibility, his grandiose use of Constantinianism as a metaphor to describe a dominant mode of Christian ethics since the fourth century, covering a period of almost seventeen hundred years, raises at least one very important question: Is Constantinianism a metaphor appropriately broad and sufficiently rich to describe the various approaches to Christian ethics, in diverse social and political situations, which have gained dominance at various points and in various places throughout the last seventeen centuries?

Yoder attempts to demonstrate the applicability of the designation "Constantinian" to modes of moral reason that operate in social spheres which are clearly different from that of ancient Christendom through his references to various "neo" Constantinianisms. Whether in the magisterial Reformation, the officially secular state of the Enlightenment, or the anti-religious Marxist regime, Yoder suggests that dominant ways of construing Christian ethics reflect "the identification of a civil authority as bearer of God's cause" in a fashion that conflates the distinction between church and world. Christian ethics comes to serve the dominant cultural order; indeed, "Christian," in his view, ceases to designate an ethic formulated with decisive and proper reference to Jesus Christ.[92]

It is interesting to ask, in this light, why Yoder uses the term "Constantinian" in its several "neo" forms to articulate his critique of these different orientations. Why, for example, does he augment one term in various ways instead of employing different terms for different eras and political contexts?

It appears that one factor in Yoder's preference for the language of Constantinianism is the radical historical critique of Anabaptism. By looking back to the paradigmatic "established church" of Christendom, Yoder identifies the first historical instance of the alignment of church and state which Anabaptism has, from its origins, opposed. Says Yoder of his tradition,

> The Anabaptists did not reject the present for its failure to be Eden, or the New Jerusalem...Their indictment was rather that one particular set of decisions, accepted by the churches at large in the fourth century, symbolized by Constantine, had been wrong when measured by the New Testament. It was not wrong because it was later than the New Testament, but because wrong fourth-century options were chosen rather than right fourth-century options. Anabaptist historiography sees the pre-Constantinian fathers in a strikingly favorable light. If apostasy...is inexcusable, it must also have been evitable. Faithfulness must also be possible. We should then expect to find faithfulness in history as well. Locating the Fall in the age of Constantine means granting the benefit of the doubt to over two centuries of fallible, divided, confused church life, during which nonetheless the vision of the major teachers was structurally sound...This respect for the early centuries continues to this day to be edifying in Anabaptist circles.[93]

Yet interest in Constantine is obviously not limited to Anabaptists. By focusing critical attention on a reign which most branches of the Christian church

---

[92]Yoder, "The Constantinian Sources of Western Social Ethics," The Priestly Kingdom, 141-143. See also "Christ, the Hope of the World," The Original Revolution, 140ff.

[93]Yoder, "Anabaptism and History," The Priestly Kingdom, 129. See also his "The Recovery of the Anabaptist Vision," 20-21; and Christian Attitudes to War, Peace, and Revolution, 23ff.

have praised across the centuries, Yoder virtually ensures that his arguments will not simply be ignored as sectarian or overly provincial, for they strike at the heart of the language of "Christian civilization" and have obvious reference to an extremely important event in the history of Christianity. In this sense, Yoder's choice of terms is strategic, designed to convey that his position "is pertinent today as a call for all Christian believers."[94] By framing his critique with reference to Constantine, Yoder directs attention to an event which is recognized as significant in the history of virtually all Christian traditions.

Moreover, Yoder's account of the significance of Constantinianism appeals to an even earlier and more central source of authority for Christians: the teaching and example of Jesus as portrayed in the New Testament.[95] By playing Constantine against Jesus in a fashion designed to show the former's lack of faithfulness to the latter, Yoder shrewdly advances his attack against "the established church" and all that he thinks it entails for the Christian life. By making explicit reference to Jesus and the New Testament, Yoder attempts to frame his attack in a way that simply cannot be ignored by any Christian tradition.[96]

Another shaping factor of Yoder's strategy is his aim of responding critically to the contemporary conventional wisdom about Jesus' irrelevance for social ethics.[97] By placing the work of Troeltsch and the Niebuhrs within the "Constantine versus Jesus" debate, he finds theological and historical resources for arguing against their "prior acceptance of the irrelevance of Jesus to the

---

[94]Yoder, The Priestly Kingdom, 8.

[95]See, for example, Yoder, The Politics of Jesus, 23; and "But We Do See Jesus," The Priestly Kingdom, 60-62.

[96]Yoder, The Priestly Kingdom, 8.

[97]Yoder, The Politics of Jesus, 15-19.

political existence of his disciples."[98] His discourse on Constantinianism, when combined with his account of the "one particular social-political-ethical option" of Jesus, enables him to portray ethicists with whom he disagrees on these matters as being more the followers of Constantine than of Jesus. Thereby, he seeks to demonstrate their theological and moral inadequacy.

It may prove helpful, in evaluating the appropriateness of Yoder's designation of various modern approaches to Christian ethics as in some respects Constantinian, to examine briefly whether that appellation is applicable to a particular modern ethicist whom Yoder discusses, namely, Reinhold Niebuhr. Yoder writes of Niebuhr's emphasis on "responsibility" as a norm for ethics that

> As used by Niebuhr this means not our obligation to concern ourselves with all needs around us in terms of the love ethic; it means rather an inherent duty to take charge of the social order in the interest of its survival or its amelioration by the use of means dictated, not by love, but by the social order itself. This social order being sinful, the methods "necessary" to administer it will also be sinful. "Responsibility" thus becomes an autonomous moral absolute, sinful society is accepted as normative for ethics, and when society calls for violence the law of love is no longer decisive.[99]

Yoder suggests that Niebuhr "derives his ethics from the fact of man's predicament" in a manner contradictory to the New Testament's portrayal of the moral life "from the fact of God's redemption" in Jesus. He also thinks that Niebuhr views the United States of America as God's chief agent in history, and that the church has no significant role in his thought.[100] Indeed, the main stumbling block of his work for Yoder is Niebuhr's "un-Biblical assumption of

---

[98]Yoder, "The Authority of Tradition," The Priestly Kingdom, 79.

[99]Yoder, "Reinhold Niebuhr and Christian Pacifism," 113. See also his references to Niebuhr in The Politics of Jesus, 13, 16, 110ff.; and in Christian Attitudes to War, Peace, and Revolution, 343ff.

[100]Yoder, "Reinhold Niebuhr and Christian Pacifism," 115.

responsibility for policing society and for preserving Western civilization" which leads him to a militarism that is antithetical to the example of Jesus.[101] Niebuhr is a Constantinian, in Yoder's view, due to his description of social ethics primarily as the task of managing society effectively in a fashion for which Jesus' example of obedience to God is not directly relevant.

In evaluating Yoder's reading of Niebuhr as a Constantinian ethicist, it is necessary to attend briefly to certain aspects of Niebuhr's project in order to determine whether Yoder has read him fairly. It is important to note, first, that the dichotomy of love and justice is central to Niebuhr's approach to ethics. Niebuhr found the commandment for sacrificial, forgiving love to be at the heart of Jesus' teaching. Says he, "The height of love is certainly more unprudential and uncalculating than mutual love and it contains universalistic demands which challenge any particular community."[102] However, this norm finds its source in "purely religious and not in socio-moral terms." It is essentially concerned with the individual's relationship with God, not with other people. "It has only a vertical dimension between the loving will of God and the will of man."[103]

Niebuhr thought that this standard of love could never be embodied or manifest in actual life, for it presupposes a sinless, non-estranged moral agent. Jesus' law of love is not, then, an obligation for the Christian: it is a paradox, a goal with which compliance is impossible under the estranged conditions of historical existence.[104] Within this context, Niebuhr construes justice as an approximation of love which allows Christians to seek a balance of power in society. Says he, "The very essence of politics is the achievement of justice

---

[101]Yoder, "Reinhold Niebuhr and Christian Pacifism," 117.

[102]Reinhold Niebuhr, Reinhold Niebuhr on Politics, eds., Harry R. Davis and Robert C. Good (New York: Charles Scribner's Sons, 1960), 131-133.

[103]Niebuhr, An Interpretation of Christian Ethics, 23-28.

[104]Niebuhr, Reinhold Niebuhr on Politics, 135-136.

through equilibria of power."[105]

Duane Friesen makes the point that Niebuhr's project is

a serious distortion of the Christian faith because it does not
sufficiently emphasize the basic thrust of the whole biblical story:
God's redemptive activity in history to make his people into a new
people who, because of their trust in God, are given new
possibilities of obedience to God's will.[106]

Niebuhr, says Friesen, makes the mistake of construing theology as a discourse
primarily about human "possibility" in a fashion that makes sin inevitable and
true faithfulness to Jesus impossible.[107]

Friesen's claim on the centrality of anthropology for Niebuhr is borne
out by Niebuhr's eschatology, which is formulated primarily in terms of a
"dialectical conception of time and eternity" in which the human as a finite
creature with an infinite horizon is inevitably caught.[108] In formulating his
eschatology, Niebuhr moves from an analysis of human self-consciousness to
claims about history which provide a context for the inevitably estranged
human.[109] God's kingdom functions for him as an ideal, atemporal realm above
human history which symbolizes our estrangement, for we always fall short by
its standard of love. The approximation of justice is the best that humans can do.

It appears that Niebuhr's eschatology plays an important role in his
description of justice as an approximation of love the content of which is not

---

[105]Niebuhr, An Interpretation of Christian Ethics, 116.

[106]Duane Friesen, Christian Peacemaking and International Conflict (Scottdale, Pennsylvania:
Herald Press, 1986), 98.

[107]Friesen, Christian Peacemaking and International Conflict, 98-99.

[108]Niebuhr, The Nature and Destiny of Man, vol. 2 (New York: Charles Scribner's Sons,
1943), 289. See also Hughes' discussion of Niebuhr's eschatology in "The Ethical Use of Power:
A Discussion with the Christian Perspectives of Reinhold Niebuhr, John Howard Yoder, and
Richard J. Barnet," 70-71.

[109]Niebuhr, The Nature and Destiny of Man, vol. 1 (New York: Charles Scribner's Sons,
1941), 17.

determinatively informed by the discipleship of Jesus. Even as humans are, for Niebuhr, estranged from the eternal kingdom by the paradoxical conditions of historical existence, we are likewise alienated from the love ethic of Jesus by the pragmatic requirements of life in a sinful world. Indeed, Niebuhr largely collapses Christian expectation for the coming of the kingdom into a symbol of the inevitable alienation of human existence. For Niebuhr, in contrast to Yoder, humans are not located "between the times" within a narrative scheme the end of which will be the fulfillment of God's reign; instead, we are caught in a static dialectic between time and eternity. As Niebuhr put it,

> Placing the final fulfillment at the end of time and not in a realm above temporality is to remain true to the genius of prophetic religion and to state mythically what cannot be stated rationally. If stated rationally the world is divided between the temporal and the eternal and only the eternal forms above the flux of temporality have significance....The apocalypse is a mythical expression of the impossible possibility under which all human life stands...the Kingdom of God is therefore not here. It is in fact always coming but never here.[110]

As Dennis McCann suggests, Niebuhr's was primarily "an ethic for politicians" that called for the achievement of balances of power as the best strategy for precluding injustice in society.[111] Niebuhr approached Christian social ethics primarily in terms of the pursuit of justice as a quality manifest in social situations characterized by a balance of power.[112] Jesus functioned systematically in his project as the preacher and example of an impossible ideal of sacrificial love that stands above the approximation of justice, holding its historical manifestation in creative tension with the eternal ideal. Moral reason is for Niebuhr the discernment of how to "coerce the anarchy of conflicting

---

[110]Niebuhr, An Interpretation of Christian Ethics, 35-36.

[111]Dennis McCann, Christian Realism and Liberation Theology (Maryknoll, New York: Orbis Books, 1981), 87-103.

[112]Niebuhr, An Interpretation of Christian Ethics, 69.

human interests into some kind of order," to pursue justice in an inevitably sinful world. It is the practical task of achieving balances of power in society.[113]

This brief, and obviously less than exhaustive, reading of one aspect of Niebuhr's project appears, at first glance, to support Yoder's designation of him as a Constantinian.[114] First, it is clear that Niebuhr's ethic was focused primarily on the goal of managing society effectively in a way not directly informed by Jesus' example. While Niebuhr thought that Jesus demanded an ethic of sacrificial love, he found that ethic inappropriate for life in a sinful world. Hence, he construed justice, as the pursuit of balances of power, as an imperfect approximation of Jesus' ethic which enables Christians to participate in the responsible management of the larger society. Thereby, justice, the working goal of social ethics, took precedence over Jesus' ethic of love, even justifying the rejection of Jesus' pacifism, which was for Niebuhr the paradigmatic commitment of love.[115] In this sense, the goal of effectiveness in running society took precedence over obedience to Jesus' example.

Second, Niebuhr qualifies as a Constantinian, by Yoder's standards, due to his conflation of church and world. Indeed, the church had no distinctive, let alone unique, moral significance in his approach. The social order with which the Christian life was most strongly identified was the dominant cultural order: the government and economic structures. Far from a visible sign and foretaste of God's reign with unique moral resources, the church, at most, was just another social institution, like any other group of people, which would seek the common good of the nation. The ethic of the church was not materially different from that of the larger society. It served the ends of society in pursuing a norm of justice

---

[113]Niebuhr, An Interpretation of Christian Ethics, 64, 85.

[114]Yoder should properly identify Niebuhr as a "neo-neo-Constantinian," due to Niebuhr's commitment to constitutional democracy. Yoder, "The Constantinian Sources of Western Social Ethics," The Priestly Kingdom, 142.

[115]Niebuhr, An Interpretation of Christian Ethics, 22ff., 114, 137ff.

for which Jesus was not directly relevant.[116]

Third, Niebuhr's eschatology seems to bear a resemblance, at least in its practical ramifications, to that of Constantinianism. While Niebuhr clearly did not identify God's kingdom with the social order of his day, neither did his view of God's reign allow the present to be contextualized and criticized by its location "between the times." For Niebuhr, there was no future aspect to the kingdom of God. Humanity was caught statically in between the temporal and the eternal: the kingdom was a symbol of an estrangement which no future could overcome.[117] Hence, Niebuhr's view seems to have an affinity with Yoder's description of the eschatology of Constantinianism: the kingdom is as present now as it will ever be. "All that God can possibly have in store for a future victory is more of what has already been won."[118]

An ethics appropriate to a new aeon, or an approach to the moral life which seeks to foreshadow the future of God's salvation, clearly has no place in light of Niebuhr's static eschatology. The institutions which reign now, the state and economic structures, are of most interest to Niebuhr, for they are the most important loci of power in society. They are where responsibility may be exercised. As the church does not, in his view, foreshadow and embody proleptically the future of God's reign, "the civil authority" must be the "bearer of God's cause." It is the chief agent of God's governance of history.[119]

It is important to observe, as a further critical note, that Yoder's designation of Niebuhr as a Constantinian reflects a lack of historical and sociological precision in the formulation of the critique. To put it bluntly, the

---

[116]See, for example, Niebuhr's treatment of "The Law of Love In Politics and Economics," An Interpretation of Christian Ethics, 84ff., 103ff.; and Moral Man and Immoral Society (New York: Charles Scribner's Sons, 1932), 257ff.

[117]Niebuhr, An Interpretation of Christian Ethics, 35-36.

[118]Yoder, "The Constantinian Sources of Western Social Ethics," The Priestly Kingdom, 137.

[119]Yoder, "The Constantinian Sources of Western Social Ethics," The Priestly Kingdom, 143.

social order in which Niebuhr lived was obviously quite different from that of Constantine. Hence, the concrete particulars of what Christian faithfulness required in Constantine's setting would clearly differ from those appropriate to Niebuhr's location. As Yoder is not greatly interested in the historical particulars of Constantine's conversion or reign, and neither in the exacting display of what the various "neo" Constantinian social arrangements mean for the relationship between church and society, it is difficult to affirm any more than a quite abstract, vague resemblance between Constantine and Niebuhr. Granted, on Yoder's terms Niebuhr was more interested in effectively managing the social order of a nation than he was in following Jesus' example of obedience to God. But Yoder never demonstrates that the theological, moral, and political particulars of Niebuhr's project have anything substantive in common with those of Constantine. Neither does Yoder show explicit parallels in the sort of policies or moral rationality advanced respectively by Constantine and Niebuhr.

Given Niebuhr's interpretation of the human condition, of the political situation of his day, and of salient aspects of Christian theological tradition, he sought to contribute to public moral discourse in a way that would avoid certain major errors of Protestant liberalism and of traditional orthodox belief.[120] While Niebuhr was obviously concerned with the relevance of Christian faith for questions of public policy, his intellectual agenda was very much a product of twentieth century North America, and addressed a social order far different from the one introduced by Constantine.[121]

---

[120]Niebuhr begins his formulation of "An Independent Christian Ethic" with the claim: "The orthodox churches have long since compounded the truth of the Christian religion with dogmatisms of another day, and have thereby petrified what would otherwise have long since fallen prey to the beneficent dissolutions of the processes of nature and history. The liberal churches, on the other hand, have hid their light under the bushel of the culture of modernity with all its short-lived prejudices and certainties." Niebuhr, An Interpretation of Christian Ethics, 1-2.

[121]The America of Niebuhr's day was characterized, for example, by the legal separation of church and state, American denominationalism, and a lively debate among Christians of various

(continued...)

138

An interesting way of examining further the appropriateness of Yoder's treatment of Niebuhr as a Constantinian is by attending a bit more closely to Niebuhr's eschatology. This is a theme of particular interest because eschatology is an issue of disagreement between Yoder and Niebuhr which appears to play an important shaping role in the moral projects of both figures. Yoder suggests that a failure to incorporate theologically the "between the times" eschatology of the New Testament is a central factor in the problematic moral reasoning of Constantinianism. Niebuhr rejects such a temporal eschatology,[122] and instead sees God's reign in more transcendent terms as an ideal realm from which humans are tragically estranged. As much of Yoder's project, especially his ecclesiology, Christology, and view of the moral life, are, as noted above, informed strongly by his eschatological commitments, it is interesting to note that Niebuhr's more static eschatology is of a piece with a quite different theological orientation. Ecclesiology, Christology, and the moral life are not, for him, construed in light of a new age of God's kingdom. They are approached, rather, from the perspective of the human being who is inevitably held in tension between the historical and transcendent, and whose moral life is therefore focused on approximating the impossible ideal of love into the broken realities of history.[123]

That these different eschatologies seem to be correlated with Yoder and

---

[121](...continued)
persuasions about pacifism, socialism, etc... While Yoder does acknowledge that "neo-neo-Constantinianism" presupposes the separation of church and state, he describes this version of Constantinianism very briefly, and does not display in detail its material similarity to the reign of Constantine. Yoder, "The Constantinian Sources of Western Social Ethics," The Priestly Kingdom, 142.

[122]By "temporal eschatology," I mean to stress the fact that for Yoder the Christian life takes place between two discrete events or times which are understood to occur in a sequence. Hence, the fulfillment of God's reign is an event to occur at some point in the future.

[123]Yoder, "The Constantinian Sources of Western Social Ethics," The Priestly Kingdom, 136-138; Niebuhr, The Nature and Destiny of Man, 1:17; 2:289.

Niebuhr's profoundly different views of the moral life appears, as we noted earlier, to be an important reason for Yoder's critique of Niebuhr as a Constantinian. On Yoder's account, an important theological source of Constantinianism's moral perversion is its failure to incorporate a properly biblical eschatology.[124]

It is important to note, however, that Niebuhr's eschatology, in clear contrast with that which Yoder attributes to Constantinianism, was an important theological source for Niebuhr's critique of overly optimistic indentifications of God's reign with present social orders. According to Yoder, Constantinians assume that God's reign has been virtually fulfilled in the present social order.[125] Such a position appears to be quite close to that of certain forms of Protestant liberalism, which Niebuhr attacked forcefully.

> Liberal Christianity, in adjusting itself to the ethos of this age, therefore sacrificed its most characteristic religious and Christian heritage by destroying the sense of depth and the experience of tension, typical of profound religion. Its Kingdom of God was translated to mean exactly that ideal society which modern culture hoped to realize through the evolutionary process. Democracy and the League of Nations were to be the political forms of this ideal. The Christian ideal of love became the counsel of prudential mutuality so dear and necessary to a complex commercial civilization. The Christ of Christian orthodoxy, true mythical symbol of both the possibilities and the limits of the human, became the good man of Galilee, symbol of human goodness and human possibilities without suggestion of the limits of the human and the temporal--in short, without the suggestion of transcendence.[126]

In this light, Niebuhr's eschatology, though not that which Yoder believes that biblical realism requires, seems to have been an important resource for criticizing a synthesis of Christianity and culture which, if the above citation

---

[124]Yoder, "If Christ Is Truly Lord," The Original Revolution, 55ff.

[125]Yoder, "The Constantinian Sources of Western Social Ethics," The Priestly Kingdom, 136.

[126]Niebuhr, An Interpretation of Christian Ethics, 9.

from Niebuhr is to be believed, bears more than a few points of resemblance to the social arrangement ushered in with Constantine! Indeed, it is precisely Niebuhr's eschatology which enabled his fierce criticism of Protestant liberalism for forgetting that God's kingdom will not be built through the strivings of Western culture.[127] Hence, it is safe to conclude that, at least in this respect, Niebuhr's eschatology may not serve as a warrant for identifying him as a Constantinian.

Yoder could respond to this argument by saying that, while Niebuhr's eschatology is free from the explicit immanentist assumptions of Constantinianism, the practical effect of Niebuhr's theological project is to underwrite an ethic which pursues the effective management of society in a way that compromises fidelity to the example of Jesus, especially in its rejection of pacifism. Given Yoder's theological assumptions, that is an appropriate description for him to make. The more pertinent question, however, is whether it is fitting to describe such a project as Constantinian.

Our conclusion is that Yoder's formulation of the designation "Constantinian," especially when it is applied to figures from quite different historical situations, is problematic, largely due to his failure to display with precision how the projects of those figures are similar in substantive ways to that of the fourth century ruler. Apart from demonstrating in concrete detail important similarities in social strategies and theological and philosophical presuppositions, it is hard to see how Yoder is justified in describing someone as a Constantinian.

As noted above, Yoder shrewdly uses the term as a way of identifying the presence of what he takes to be decisive theological and moral errors which have presided over Christian ethics for almost seventeen hundred years. As such, his references to Constantinianism amount to a rhetorical strategy to call

---

[127]Niebuhr, An Interpretation of Christian Ethics, 62ff.

Christians to abandon ways of compromising with the world which he, in line with Anabaptism, believes are antithetical to the task of Christian discipleship. Playing Jesus against Constantine, as Yoder does, is a provocative way of making his critique. The problem is that it is also an historical way of making his point. In order to show that the appellation is deserved, Yoder needs to attend much more explicitly to the task of demonstrating significant similarities and parallels between Constantine and the figures whom he describes as Constantinians in a way that takes account of the huge societal differences between, for example, fourth century Asia Minor and twentieth century North America.

Apart from a more rigorous engagement of the myriad particulars relevant to the description of the Christian life in any historical period, Yoder's account of Constantianism is too thinly constructed to sustain its adequacy as an historical metaphor for dubious theological and moral judgment. It may serve well as a provocative way of raising the issues of pacifism or of the limits of the church's compromise with the world, but it is not a well warranted, substantive characterization of an historically dominant strand of Christian faith and practice.

In order to portray in greater detail the sort of Christian involvement in secular society of which Yoder approves, and to determine whether that sort of involvement is consistent with his critique of Constantinianism, the following chapter will examine Yoder's rationale for Christian participation in social spheres other than the church. Through this focus, it analyzes, in particular, how Yoder's eschatological commitments shape his agenda for social action in a way that purports to be non-Constantinian.

CHAPTER 4

PRACTICAL APPLICATION: YODER'S ALTERNATIVE VIEW OF
CHRISTIAN INVOLVEMENT IN SECULAR SOCIETY

This chapter analyzes the practical relevance of Yoder's critique of
Constantinianism by examining the sort of political involvement, by Christians in
secular society, of which he approves. The chapter divides into three sections:
(1) a discussion of Yoder's theological basis for political involvement; (2) an
analysis of his position on the use of the larger society's political language by
Christians; and (3) an examination of his view of the proper moral logic for
setting the agenda and identifying appropriate strategies for Christian social
action.

Theological Basis

An important aspect of Yoder's theological basis for Christian political
involvement is his view of the institutions of society as fallen powers which God

uses against their will for God's purposes.[1] Yoder notes, first, that the powers

> were part of the good creation of God. Society and history, even
> nature, would be impossible without regularity, system, order--and
> this need God provided for...The creative power worked in a
> mediated form, by means of the Powers that regularized all visible
> reality.[2]

While the powers are now fallen--"no longer active only as mediators
of the saving creative purpose of God"--God orders them for good. Says Yoder,

> The powers, despite their fallenness, continue to exercise an
> ordering function...Even the pagan and primitive forms of social
> and religious expression, although obviously unworthy of being
> imitated, remain a sign of the preserving patience of God toward
> a world that has not yet heard of its redemption....[T]he Powers
> cannot fully escape the providential sovereignty of God. He is
> still able to use them for good.[3]

God's using them for good, however, does not alter the fact of their
rebellion or their present sovereignty over humans. Indeed, "Man's subordination
to these Powers is what makes him human, for if they did not exist there would
be no history nor society nor humanity." It is the work of Christ, for Yoder, to
conquer the powers.

> If then God is going to save man in his humanity, the Powers
> cannot simply be destroyed or set aside or ignored. Their
> sovereignty must be broken. This is what Jesus did, concretely
> and historically, by living among men a genuinely free and human
> existence. This life brought him...to the cross. In his death the
> Powers...acted in collusion...His very obedience unto death is in
> itself not only the sign but also the firstfruits of an authentic

---

[1]As noted earlier, Yoder's treatment of "the powers" is dependent upon Berkhof's exegetical
work in Christ and the Powers. See also Parham, "An Ethical Analysis of the Christian Social
Strategies in the Writings of John C. Bennett, Jacques Ellul, and John Howard Yoder," 189-190;
Hughes, "The Ethical Use of Power: A Discussion with the Christian Perspectives of Reinhold
Niebuhr, John Howard Yoder, and Richard J. Barnet," 128ff.; and C. Norman Kaus, Review of
The Christian Witness to the State, The Mennonite Quarterly Review 40 (January 1966): 67-70.

[2]Yoder, The Politics of Jesus, 143. See also "Christ, the Hope of the World," The Original
Revolution, 140-141; and Preface to Theology, 176.

[3]Yoder, The Politics of Jesus, 144.

restored humanity...Not even to save his own life will he let himself be made a slave to these Powers. This authentic humanity included his free acceptance of death at their hands. Thus it is his death that provides his victory: "Wherefore God has exalted him highly, and given him the name which is above every name...that every tongue might confess that Jesus Christ is Lord."[4]

In light of Jesus' victory over the powers through resurrection, Yoder affirms that Christ is now lord over them despite their continued rebellion.[5] Says he,

The question may be meaningfully raised, What can lordship mean as long as the powers of this world are still in rebellion? Since lord is fundamentally a term from the realm of political authority, we can best respond to this question by pointing out that many a political sovereign, whose authority no one challenges legally, is still not effectively in total control of all the actions of all the persons and organizations in the territory over which he claims dominion and cannot force total and unconditional obedience even in realms where his sovereignty is confessed.[6]

So it is with Jesus' lordship over the rebellious powers. They remain rebellious, but God has conquered them in principle and seeks to order them according to the divine purposes.[7]

---

[4]Yoder, The Politics of Jesus, 147-148.

[5]Yoder, Preface to Theology, 177-180.

[6]Yoder, The Christian Witness to the State, 11.

[7]Yoder's use of "the powers" appears quite vague, as the term seems to apply to virtually every aspect of creation which has been corrupted by sin. While Yoder does refer to "the most worthy, weighty representatives of Jewish religion and Roman politics" as the powers which acted "in collusion" in crucifying Jesus, he never provides an exacting, precise display of, say, how a particular power functions in a given social and historical context and how the church should go about witnessing to Christ's victory over the powers in relation to it. Yoder, The Politics of Jesus, 147ff.

His The Christian and Capital Punishment and The Christian Witness to the State are efforts in that direction, but both documents lack focused, explicit analysis of the workings of a given power, such as the state, with reference to the particulars of a discrete, historically located problem. The themes "capital punishment in America" and "the witness to the state" are obviously very large questions involving myriad particulars. In order to make clear that the language of "the powers" is useful for guiding focused discrimination in moral judgment, Yoder

(continued...)

146

Yoder comments, in this regard, that Christ's lordship over the powers is "not redemptive but conservative" in purpose.

> The purpose of Christ's dominion over the exousiai and over the states is not to bring in the Kingdom, but simply to keep things from falling apart so that the Church can do the work of the Kingdom. The reason we are to pray for the State, for kings, according to Timothy (1 Tim. 2:1-4), is that God desires that all men should be brought to the knowledge of the truth--but not that the State is going to bring men to the knowledge of the truth. It is because the State is keeping things peaceable that the Church has the chance to bring men to the knowledge of the truth. There is always this distinction between these two areas, or orders, and the duality is defined in that one is redemptive and the other conservative.[8]

Yoder suggests that the "state--speaking now not of any one particular political pattern but of the fundamental phenomenon that society is organized by the appeal to force as ultimate authority--is a deeply representative segment of the 'world.'" This is the case because the state is, for Yoder, an inevitably coercive, violent social structure that does not recognize Jesus' lordship. Says Yoder,

> Whatever the state is or should be in theory, in fact every state wields the sword, and it is that fact that sets the theme for this study. Whether some other kind of institution, which would not wield the sword and would therefore not pose all the same problems for us, should properly be called a state, is here irrelevant.[9]

Yoder cites Romans 13 and 1 Peter 2 as New Testament affirmations of

---

[7](...continued)
would do well to isolate a carefully delimited problem or issue, and analyze it in light of the powers. Apart from such an analysis, his references to the powers are too abstract and broad to be useful for casuistry.

[8]Yoder, "The Theological Basis of the Christian Witness to the State," On Earth Peace, 141.

[9]Yoder, The Christian Witness to the State, 12. Hughes criticizes Yoder's claim that "violence is the essence of the state" in "The Ethical Use of Power: A Discussion with the Christian Perspectives of Reinhold Niebuhr, John Howard Yoder, and Richard J. Barnet," 159ff. See also Zimbleman, "Theological Ethics and Politics in the Thought of Juan Luis Segundo and John Howard Yoder," 260ff., for a critical analysis of Yoder's view of the state.

the state "as God's instrument for the maintenance of order in society." Of Christ's lordship over the state in eschatological perspective, Yoder comments that

> The time between the ascension of Christ and the defeat of the last enemy, when the kingdom of the Son will give place to the consummated kingdom of the Father, is thus characterized by the way in which the reign of Christ channels violence, turning it against itself, so as to preserve as much as possible of the order (taxis) which is the pre-condition of human society and thereby also a vehicle for the work of the church. The state being, in its judicial and police functions, the major incarnation of this channeled evil, it is perfectly logical to find the New Testament teaching on the state most clearly expressed in a context that begins by describing the transformed life of the believer (Romans 12) and ends with an evocation of the coming day (13:11ff.) in the light of which the believer is already called to walk.[10]

Indeed, in this period "between the times," the state and the other institutions and powers of society function

> for the sake of the church's own work...The reason for Christian prayer in favor of the political authorities is that "God our Saviour desires all men to be saved and to come to the knowledge of the truth" (1 Tim. 2). The function of the state in maintaining an ordered society is thereby a part of the divine plan for the evangelization of the world.[11]

Yoder suggests that Christians are not limited, however, in their dealings with the state to calling for the free operation of the church. He thinks that Christians also have a profound concern for the welfare of their neighbors, which is a warrant for addressing the state critically.

---

[10]Yoder, The Christian Witness to the State, 12-13.

[11]Yoder, The Christian Witness to the State, 13. Yoder also comments on the nature of Christ's lordship over the state in "On Divine and Human Justice," On Earth Peace, 210. These, as well as other recently cited, passages appear to reflect a greater knowledge of how God governs history through the agency of the state than do passages passages, such as Christian Attitudes To War, Peace, and Revolution, 42ff., which indicate that God's action in the world is invisible and only rarely comprehended by the church. It is fair to ask, then, where Yoder comes down on the question of how much humans can know about God's governance of history.

"[H]uman welfare" is in itself a value, a criterion, which, although not always abstractly definable, is usually self-evident in a given context of need. When Jesus instructed us to love our neighbors as ourselves, He did not mean to enjoin a certain measure of selfishness, either undergirding or counterbalancing our altruism; the point is much more simply that I know very well, in looking at myself, what I consider to be "good." This criterion of "human welfare" is a concept distinct from what we have been saying about the lordship of Christ; the two can, however, not be basically in opposition to one another.[12]

As part of their witness to the state, Christians are to call upon it to do good and not evil. For Yoder, this claim means, for example, continuing in the tradition of the Hebrew prophets in condemning the idolatry of the state which gives rise to various forms of excessive nationalism.[13] This witness is not, however, that of calling the state to become God's kingdom. Says Yoder,

We need to distinguish between the ethics of discipleship which are laid upon every Christian believer by virtue of his very confession of faith, and an ethic of justice within the limits of prudence and self-preservation, which is all one can ask of the larger society. The distinction is needed to avoid a misunderstanding, perhaps forever banished in its crudest forms with the demise of theological liberalism, but still a latent temptation, namely the tendency to identify the gospel of the kingdom of God with a plan for social betterment independent of changing men's minds and hearts.[14]

Nevertheless, Yoder insists that the act of calling the state, through its

---

[12]Yoder, The Christian Witness to the State, 14. It is hardly of a piece with Yoder's insistence on the importance of moral formation within the community of faith for him to suggest that human welfare is "usually self-evident in a given context of need." Given his emphasis on the importance of communal procedure and structure for discernment in "The Hermeneutics of Peoplehood," The Priestly Kingdom, 22ff., it is far from clear how he can consistently suggest that what is at stake in any moral question is self-evident.

[13]Yoder, The Christian Witness to the State, 15.

[14]Yoder, The Christian Witness to the State, 23. Note that Yoder's formulation underwrites, at the very least, a practical duality of the high demands of discipleship and the lower demands of social justice. Later sections of the chapter will determine to what extent this duality is consistent with Yoder's call for an ethic of uncompromised obedience to God.

leaders, to do good and not evil may be properly described as evangelism.

> It is not the case that a witness to an individual, calling him to
> conversion with reference to his own personal guilt and the
> direction of his life, is biblically speaking evangelism whereas the
> witness either to groups or to persons in social responsibility,
> calling on them to change their dispositions and do in their offices
> what God would have them do, is something else...[T]he good
> news announced to the world has to do with the reign of God
> among men in all their interpersonal relations, and not solely with
> the forgiveness of sins or the regeneration of individuals.[15]

Yet even in this sort of evangelism, there is a personal dimension to the message. Says Yoder,

> Precisely because the message we express is a derivative of, an
> element of, a form of the gospel, we must communicate first of
> all, whatever be the specific political issue with which we are
> concerned, an awareness of our prior concern for the welfare of
> this statesman as a man. We are concerned about his own moral
> integrity, measured first of all by his own moral standards, even
> though from our perspective his highest ideals might still fall short
> of the vision of Christian discipleship. Any such communication
> to the statesman is thus in a sense pastoral; its presupposition is
> that one person has the right to be dealt with as a person, as an
> object of God's and therefore of our esteem, who is honored but
> also brought into judgment as we speak to him of the implications
> of divine righteousness.[16]

Yoder's approach is informed by his assumption that "On whatever level we find a man in the effort to speak to him, what we ask of him is that he accept the Gospel." Not simply a second-rate form of evangelism, calling a person in authority to do good and not evil is a proper instance of calling the powers to serve God's purposes. "It is...the gospel itself in relation to his present situation, that situation in turn being determined largely by his earlier disobedience." Comments Yoder,

If, for example, a subordinate officer in the Korean War had been

---

[15]Yoder, The Christian Witness to the State, 23.

[16]Yoder, The Christian Witness to the State, 24.

challenged to treat his prisoners of war according to the Geneva
Convention, or if a French intelligence officer in Algeria had been
challenged not to torture innocent suspects, the only way he could
have responded to this challenge--even though it was placed before
him fully in terms of his present military involvement and of
military justice--would be to take a step of obedience which would
be costly, would bring upon him suffering and reproach, would be
possible only in the strength of the Holy Spirit and in the name of
Jesus Christ. This call to him therefore differs from that which
the conscientious objector is following only in the level of
involvement in which the message finds the man to whom it
speaks, and in the length of time which each in his place has had
to think through in detail the implications of Christian
obedience.[17]

Yoder's description of such "worldly" discourse in the service of Christ,

indeed of Christ's work through the discourse, reflects his view of the risen

Lord's present hidden dominion over, and active presence in, the world.[18]

Yoder argues that

the passage in Romans [13:1-7] is simply one application of a
New Testament truth which is stated more frequently and more
clearly in other ways. Its broader and more basic claim is the
confession that "Christ is Lord" (Phil. 2:11, 1 Cor. 12:3). This
lordship does not apply only over the church; Christ has been
exalted "far above every principality and power, and might, and
dominion, and every name that is named..." (Eph. 1:21, Phil.
2:10, 1 Cor. 15:27, Matt. 28:18). This lordship is not
acknowledged by the world, but it is nonetheless real...The state,
like any rebellious power, can attempt to be independent, can

---

[17]Yoder, The Christian Witness to the State, 25. In this passage, Yoder seems to assume that
God's involvement with humanity is easily discernable, as people apparently pursue justice only
through the power of the Holy Spirit. Here he appears to presume a knowledge of God's
involvement in history which he expressly denies those who identified the reign of Constantine as
the work of Providence. Yoder might suggest that his tradition embodies resources sufficient to
sustain proper discernment in a way that others do not, and that consequently he may make such
judgments while not allowing others to do so. If he were to make that argument, it would still
not reduce the tension, as noted above, raised by his claim that God governs the world invisibly--
that we can know very little about God's providential work. If that is the case, it appears that
Yoder may be a bit over-confident of his knowledge of how God works through military
personnel.

[18]Yoder, The Christian Witness to the State, 8-9.

claim to be its own master, but Christians know the claim is false and the attempt doomed to failure. Actually, the state does rebel; but ultimately it cannot do so; and the certainty of the accomplishment of God's purposes is what Christians proclaim even to the principalities and powers already in the present age (Eph. 3:10)...If it is Jesus Christ and not some other god or some other lord who rules at the right hand of God, then the purpose, goals, and standards of that rule can be no other than this same Jesus revealed to us while in the flesh, seeking not to destroy, but to save. It cannot, therefore, be argued that under His dominion the state has the right or the duty to destroy life.[19]

The theological basis of Yoder's support for Christian involvement in secular society is, then, the lordship of Christ over the powers, the most prominent of which is the state. Yoder's eschatology plays an important shaping role here, for his understanding of Christ's lordship is precisely eschatological. Jesus is lord because his obedience to God, which was vindicated by resurrection, has ushered in a new aeon of God's reign, an important characteristic of which is the decisive defeat of the powers. Indeed, "the concrete meaning of the term Lord" is for Yoder this eschatological triumph over the powers.[20]

In the time between the inauguration and fulfillment of the new age, God orders or marshals the rebellious powers, against their will, to serve God's purposes.[21] By calling upon society and its leaders to pursue a justice that is consistent with the demands of God's kingdom in, for example, the prohibition of killing and concern for the welfare of the neighbor, Christians participate in

---

[19]Yoder, The Christian and Capital Punishment, 15-16.

[20]Yoder, The Christian Witness to the State, 9.

[21]Yoder, The Politics of Jesus, 24. Yoder fails to provide, however, any well displayed examples of what God's ordering of the powers has meant in the past. He does not show us, for example, how a particular group of Christians in a particular setting came to the conclusion that a given event was the work of God ordering the powers. To that extent, it is hard to know precisely what significance his references to the powers have for the interpretation of God's action in history.

God's ordering of the powers.[22] In light of the confession that "Jesus is Lord," Christians are to call for a social order that serves God's purposes, especially in "preserving the fabric of the human community as the context within which the church's work can be carried on."[23]

As noted in the first chapter, Yoder's approach to the state in light of Christ's lordship reflects Barth's influence upon him. Yoder comments on Barth's Christocentric view of the state:

> Creation order cannot be affirmed or described apart from Christ; if "preservation" has any place, it is not as the shadow which Creation left behind but as the light which Reconciliation casts before itself.. ..Barth sees the state as one of the rebellious powers brought into subjection to the lordship of the risen Christ, but not yet totally defeated....The attitude to take to the state is then not derived from a reading of its performance, but from the confession of Christ's lordship. That "the powers that be are of God" is not an empirical statement about how well some statesmen are doing; it is a dogmatic statement about the triumph of Christ.[24]

Yoder also notes that Barth's Christengemeinde und Buergergemeinde takes the novel approach of framing a Christian view of the state in a fashion that distinguishes, at a fundamental level, between the church and the larger society. "[I]t was never customary [before] to distinguish basically between the morality of the community of faith and that of unbelieving society." Moreover,

> Barth's originality at this point is double: He recognizes that the Church is herself a social body, so that the duality of individual versus corporate morality is not applicable; and he recognizes realistically that in speaking to the civil community he cannot

---

[22]Yoder, The Christian and Capital Punishment, 13-16. See also The Christian Witness to the State, 14.

[23]Yoder, The Christian Witness to the State, 11.

[24]Yoder, Karl Barth and the Problem of War, 124-125. See also The Pacifism of Karl Barth (Scottdale, Pennsylvania: Herald Press, 1968), 5.

presuppose faith in Christ on the part of those to whom his witness is addressed.[25]

Yoder notes, then, in Barth the presence of a novel Christocentric and ecclesially centered approach to "the Christian witness to the state" which has become characteristic of his own project. Following Barth, he comments that, while there will "be a Christian message addressed to the State; there will not be a Christian ethic for the State." Within the context of a clear theological distinction between church and secular society, Yoder, like Barth, seeks to provide an account of how Christians, in light of Jesus' lordship, may call upon those in power to serve God by doing good and not evil.[26]

A few tentative conclusions on the theological basis of Yoder's approach to social involvement are in order at this juncture. As we have indicated at various points in the discussion, a major problem in Yoder's formulation is his epistemological optimism about knowing how God is governing and acting in history. The problem is that Yoder's claims to know how God is ordering the powers for the preservation of human society seem to contradict his claims, made in arguing against Constantinianism, that God's action in the world is invisible, and rarely discernable even by the church. Moreover, his use of "the powers" seems vague and abstract, given his failure to display with precision, and in detail, how this concept is materially useful for moral discrimination in particular, historically located situations. While Yoder's use of "the powers" reflects his attempt to approach social ethics in light of the hermeneutical strategy of biblical realism, it also indicates certain points of tension, as noted earlier, between his reliance on modern biblical scholarship to determine "what the text says" and his commitment to a communal, Christological hermeneutic of Scripture. As Yoder

---

[25]Yoder, The Pacifism of Karl Barth, 9. See also his "Helpful and Deceptive Dualisms," 74ff.; "Karl Barth: How His Mind Kept Changing," How Karl Barth Changed My Mind, 166ff.; and his unpublished essay, "The Basis of Barth's Social Ethics," 6ff.;

[26]Yoder, The Pacifism of Karl Barth, 10-11, 30.

154

has not displayed with clarity how these two interpretative strategies may operate with methodological coherence, there appears to be a point of tension at the epistemological basis of his formulation.

In these respects, there seem to be methodological difficulties in Yoder's account of how Christians are to interpret God's action in history, as well as in how Christians are to discern the particulars of their discipleship in the world. The final section of the chapter will develop these criticisms more fully, and indicate their significance for the evaluation of Yoder's project.

The Use of Society's Language

Yoder suggests that, in most instances, Christians should use "middle axioms" for the expression of their critique of the state and secular society.[27] These axioms are "norms," which are taken from the discourse of society, and used critically by the Christian "to clothe his social critique without ascribing to those secular concepts any metaphysical value outside of Christ." They are "pagan terms" to be used in the service of ordering the powers in a manner appropriate to Christ's lordship. Indeed, Yoder insists that "the ultimate ground for their validity is the love of Christ; in fact, that they do not exist except as a reflection or projection of the relevance of that love."[28]

---

[27]Yoder, The Christian Witness to the State, 35. The term "middle axiom" is most often associated with the work of John C. Bennett, a proponent, along with Reinhold Niebuhr, of Christian Realism. See Parham's discussion of Bennett's use of the middle axiom in "An Ethical Analysis of the Christian Social Strategies in the Writings of John C. Bennett, Jacques Ellul, and John Howard Yoder," 63ff. Given Yoder's strong critique of Christian Realism, it is ironic that he uses the term. As the following analysis will show, Yoder's use of the middle axiom reflects a profound tension in his thought between the affirmation of an ethic of obedience and a social strategy that approximates the demands of the Gospel through language which is chosen by a standard of effectiveness.

[28]Yoder, The Christian Witness to the State, 73. Yoder apparently intends to designate middle axioms as terms, with no moral status in and of themselves, which Christians may use to express the demands of the Gospel to non-Christians in such a way that the non-Christian will be able to comprehend and respond, at least in part, to the Gospel.

This strategy raises a critical question: Why, on Yoder's terms, should Christians be
(continued...)

Yoder refers elsewhere to such norms as "'market place semantics'" which, at least in North America, "have been established by the [Constantinian] likes of Troeltsch, Weber, and the brothers Niebuhr." As an example of how Christians may use such language, Yoder compares three ways of talking about leadership.

[1] The Nations in their own terms: market place semantics: The tyrants let themselves be called "benefactors."
[2] The faith community speaking to the nations: Appeal to the tyrant's language to make him less a tyrant.
[3] The faith community speaking internally: Servant leadership is the way of the cross.[29]

All three sorts of discourse focus on leadership. The third form serves as a basis for the Christian's view of what leadership ideally entails, but that high standard is not directly applicable to secular society, for it does not accept an explicitly Christian social ethic. In this light, Yoder notes that the church may use the language of the ruler against him or her in order to call for the just use of power. To the ruler who claims to be the benefactor of his or her subjects, the Christian would respond: "Then act like a benefactor!" This strategy is "in

---

[28](...continued)

concerned to direct their social criticisms to non-Christian leaders? The answer would appear to be that Christians should do so as part of their effort to participate in God's ordering of the rebellious powers which have been conquered through the resurrection of Jesus Christ. That way of putting it, however, appears to reflect a concern with the state as the servant of God which is in tension with Yoder's claim that there is an "absolute priority of church over state in the plan of God." The Christian Witness to the State, 17, 13. Indeed, given Yoder's claim that God's providential involvement in the world is virtually unknowable, it is hard to know how Christians will be able to discern with any degree of certainty what God intends for the world, let alone what middle axioms are appropriate tools for communication with the world.

These criticisms continue to press the issue that Yoder may very well rely on more optimistic epistemological claims for his own constructive project than he allows to those whom he labels Constantinians. They also raise the possibility that Yoder's program for social action may entail a compromise of the social demands of the Gospel for the sake of effectiveness in communicating with political leaders. Should that be the case, Yoder would be guilty of the charge which he makes against the Constantinians of putting concern for consequences before the goal of obedience to God.

[29]Yoder, "The Christian Case for Democracy," The Priestly Kingdom, 160-161.

between" the often unwarranted pretensions of the ruler to be a servant and the way of servanthood which Yoder thinks that the church should pursue.[30]

The call of the Christian to the ruler is not, then, a direct appeal to agape, but

> to the State's concept of justitia. In France, for example, what we have to say to the French government for the moment is: "Take seriously your talk about 'liberty, equality, and fraternity.' If you have done that, then we will ask a little more." Because the State is already committed to order, our message to the State is an appeal asking it to live up to its own principles.[31]

Yoder recognizes that this approach must face the possibility that "a crudely tyrannical ruler would admit that he is doing us no good; therefore we would have no language with which to criticize him." He thinks, however, that

---

[30]Yoder, "The Christian Case for Democracy," The Priestly Kingdom, 161.

[31]Yoder, "The Theological Basis of the Christian Witness to the State," On Earth Peace, 143. Yoder's reference to justice as a realistic approximation of love is remarkably similar to Niebuhr's formulation in An Interpretation of Christian Ethics, 80: "In the struggle between property-owners and workers, broadly considered, between the rich and poor, which agitates every modern industrial nation, certain moral judgments are possible which are less under the peril of demonic pretension and sinful dishonesty than either individual or national judgments, being less subjective than the former and less dependent upon the relativities of national cultures than the latter. They stand under the criterion of the simplest of all moral principles, that of equal justice. [emphasis mine] That principle has been operative in all the advances made by human society and its application to the modern social situation is obviously valid. In a struggle between those who enjoy inordinate privileges and those who lack the basic essentials of the good life it is fairly clear that a religion which holds love to be the final law of life stultifies itself if it does not support equal justice as a political and economic approximation of the ideal of love." [emphasis mine] Like Niebuhr, Yoder appears to address secular society in a way that tempers the high requirements of agape for the sake of "realistic" concerns about effectiveness in bringing the critical relevance of love to bear upon the world. Yoder seems to recognize this similarity in The Christian Witness to the State, 66-73. While there are obvious points of difference between Niebuhr and Yoder, as discussed in the previous chapter, it is striking that there is such a strong parallel in the shape of their social strategies. Both see agape as the only abiding norm of the Christian life, and call upon the powers of society to approximate that norm by pursuing justice or other norms which are imperfect realizations of love. Yoder seems to accept, then, the Constantinian assumption that "of course we cannot ask of Caesar that he live like a Christian," "The Constantinian Sources of Western Social Ethics," The Priestly Kingdom, 145. See Hughes' perceptive analysis of the similarity of Niebuhr and Yoder on this point in "The Ethical Use of Power: A Discussion with the Christian Perspectives of Reinhold Niebuhr, John Howard Yoder, and Richard J. Barnet," 150-156.

this possibility is "not a very threatening real possibility, because most rulers do claim beneficence" or some other justification for their rule that would enable critique.[32]

In addressing a society's power structure, Yoder suggests that, rather than working from an ideal view of the state or a list of principles that secular society ought to embody, Christians should attend to how, in given circumstances, a particular "state can fulfill its responsibilities in a fallen society." Says he,

> The Christian witness will therefore always express itself in terms of specific criticisms, addressed to given injustices in a particular time and place, and specific suggestions for improvements to remedy the identified abuse. This does not mean that if the criticisms were heard and the suggestions put into practice, the Christian would be satisfied; rather, a new and more demanding set of criticisms and suggestions would then follow. There is no level of attainment to which a state could rise, beyond which the Christian critique would have nothing more to ask; such an ideal level would be none other than the kingdom of God.[33]

The logic of the middle axiom works similarly with reference to particular problems, as

> These concepts will translate into meaningful and concrete terms the general relevance of the lordship of Christ for a given social ethical issue. They mediate between the general principles of Christological ethics and the concrete problems of political application. They claim no metaphysical status, but serve usefully as rules of thumb to make meaningful the impact of Christian social thought.[34]

---

[32]Yoder, "The Christian Case for Democracy," The Priestly Kingdom, 169.

[33]Yoder, The Christian Witness to the State, 32.

[34]Yoder, The Christian Witness to the State, 32-33. As noted earlier, Yoder's method calls for the application of rather vaguely defined middle axioms to particular historical situations. A major difficulty with Yoder's display of this method is that he does not describe in sufficient detail how that application works in real situations in the world. Apart from such a display, which would have to take account of the myriad particulars of a social location, Yoder's discourse on middle axioms seems more a rhetorical strategy to raise the issue of Christian social involvement than a carefully delineated project of moral judgment and social action.

By using middle axioms, which represent the moral language of secular society, Yoder seeks to make neither "the order of nature" nor the conventional political wisdom of a culture a source of revelation or a determining source of knowledge about the nature of the state. As regards the state, God's revelation is that

> there exists also in the unredeemed world an order, a relation to Him who ordains, and who is none other than our Redeemer. This is the concept of order (taxis) and duty (opheilein) which runs through Romans 13:1-7 and which we have referred to as the reign of Christ. On the basis of revelation we can thus speak of a structure of society whose main lines we may ascertain--from revelation, not from nature--and which will be the framework of our judgments about ethics for states. This structure is, however, not a stable ideal order, but an ordering, a historical mediation between continued rebellion and the orderliness of the kingdom to come.[35]

Given the particular historical judgment required for such historically mediated analysis, "the application of these middle axioms should correspond with the most accurate and impartial descriptions of historical reality." In this light, Yoder suggests that "only a Christian orientation permits a truly fair understanding of the facts of history."

He makes this claim, first, because of the "honest objectivity" made possible "only with the fundamental abandon of self-defense involved in Christian faith." He suggests, second, that Christian forgiveness sees that "even the apparent villain in historical conflicts is subject to causes not wholly his fault, and capable of some good." Third, Christian repentance enables a self-criticism which is capable of attributing blame where it is due to "oneself or one's class or nation." Fourth, "Christian hope makes it possible to approach the study of

---

[35]Yoder, The Christian Witness to the State, 33-34. Yoder's reference to "a historical mediation" raises again the question of precisely how Christians are to discern how to make historical mediations of the Gospel in particular situations in the world. Yoder nowhere provides an exacting account of how this process will work in a socially, historically, and culturally located situation.

history in the deep faith that it will somehow make sense" and embody justice. Fifth, Christian concern for the neighbor "enables the Christian historian to seek the meaning of history in personal and moral values, freed from the temptation to interpret primarily the story of regimes and sovereignties."[36]

As the Christian who employs middle axioms does so in light of particular historical judgments, i. e., that term X is particularly useful for the critique of situation Y, the honest and precise interpretation of history is crucial for Yoder's method. Apart from such an interpretative strategy, Christian social ethics may not function properly. It is for this reason that Yoder refers to the importance of the resources for the interpretation of history which Christians possess. Says he,

> This enumeration of ways in which Christian insight qualifies the historian--or rather may and should qualify him--could be extended; but this much should suffice not only to indicate that the Christian's moral commitment should make him a better historian and social analyst, but also to permit the corollary thesis that the properly objective analysis of events will test the rightness of the Christian's moral evaluation.[37]

---

[36]A difficulty with Yoder's references to the objectivity of a Christian interpretation of history is that his analysis does not go beyond a rhetorical level. Namely, he does not provide any well developed, exactingly displayed examples of how such interpretation works or when it has occurred in the history of Christianity. Neither does he attend to the more practical question of how the church may, in resistance to the influences of a sinful world, produce historians who interpret events without improper bias. Gustavo Gutierrez, for example, addresses some of the complexities of historical interpretation in light of economic and political conditions in Latin America in "Theology from the Underside of History," The Power of the Poor in History (Maryknoll, New York: Orbis Press, 1983), 169ff. Yoder's project seems to lack that sort of well developed critical awareness of the influence of culture, class, race, and other factors in the interpretation of history. Yoder manifests a concern for the critical reading of the history of Christian faith in "Anabaptism and History," The Priestly Kingdom, 123ff., but he does not revise his earlier references to objectivity.

Moreover, Yoder's formulation reflects a great epistemological confidence that Christians may discern rightly the ultimate significance of events in human history. That claim, as noted above, appears to be in unresolved tension with his assertion that God's governance of history is virtually unknowable in the midst of history.

[37]Yoder, The Christian Witness to the State, 34-35. Yoder fails, however, to describe in detail how these resources serve in particular historical situations to form the Christian as an apt interpreter of history.

Yoder attends to the term "responsibility" in relation to the state as a middle axiom, the interpretation of which has often "been extremely confusing" in signifying

> a commitment to consider the survival, the interests, or the power of one's own nation, state, or class as taking priority over the survival, interests, or power of other persons or groups, of all humanity, of the "enemy," or of the church.[38]

In contrast to this approach, which assumes "the ultimate priority of the work of the state over that of the church," Yoder suggests, in light of his eschatological commitments, that Christians have a quite different responsibility to society.

> The validity of our witness to society, including the critical address to the state and the statesman, hangs on the firmness with which the church keeps her central message at the center: her call to every man to turn to God and her call to those who have turned to God to live in love. If she fails to keep this call to personal commitment at the center of her life and work, her prophetic witness to society is either utopianism or demagoguery.[39]

Yoder insists that responsibility not be interpreted in a fashion that compromises fidelity to his understanding of the true task of the church and the Christian life.

Through the use of middle axioms, Yoder appears to compromise the high demands of love by holding society accountable to a norm less rigorous than agape. In this light, Yoder's position does not seem to be characterized by an unambiguous plea for society to conform to the standards of God's rule. Yoder, like Niebuhr, addresses society through language intended to convey an approximated version of the demands of love. He does not call directly for conversion or compliance with the way of discipleship. While Yoder may be critical of certain formulations of responsibility as being inappropriate approximations of love, it is important to note that his project is clearly one of

---

[38]Yoder, The Christian Witness to the State, 36. See also Yoder's critique of the language of responsibility in "Discerning the Kingdom of God in the Struggles of the World," 370ff; and "Reinhold Niebuhr and Christian Pacifism," 113.

[39]Yoder, The Christian Witness to the State, 36.

compromise and approximation for the sake of playing a role in the governance of the social order. Yoder, then, is much closer to Niebuhr and other proponents of an ethic of responsibility than Yoder would like to admit.

In addition to the term responsibility, Yoder examines "order" with reference to the state, which he suggests is a "fundamental criterion for historical analysis." In light of Romans 13, 1 Timothy 2, and 1 Peter 2, he concludes that proper order in society "obtains when the innocent are protected and the guilty punished; these are the standards for the legitimacy of the function of magistrate." Such a view of order limits the state's authority to use force.

> [T]he state never has a blanket authorization to use violence. The use of force must be limited to the police function, i. e., guided by fair judicial processes, subject to recognized legislative regulation, and safeguarded in practice against its running away with the situation. Only the absolute minimum of violence is therefore in any way excusable. The state has no general authorization to use the sword independently of its commission to hold violence to a minimum.[40]

Yoder suggests that there is little danger that the state will fail in its task of maintaining order. In fact, "The universal temptation is rather to overdo this function." Too often, "the policeman or the statesman comes to consider himself as being responsible for bringing into existence an ideal order." Such a goal often amounts to idolatry. Says Yoder,

> [S]uch efforts to organize the ideal society from the top will always be less successful than hoped; but what matters more is that the pretention to be, or to be in the process of becoming the ideal society, is pride, the one sin that most surely leads to a fall, even already within history. Thus the state need not ask to be worshiped to be on its way to becoming demonic; it is sufficient that it place the authority of its police arm behind its pretension to represent an ideal order, and it is already making religious

---

[40]Yoder, The Christian Witness to the State, 36-37.

162

claims.[41]

In formulating a critique of such abuses of the state's authority, Yoder suggests that "The Christian social critique will always speak in terms of available, or at least conceivable, alternatives." Not calling for a perfect social order, Christians will demand "the elimination of specific visible abuses." As in the "great days of Puritanism, Quakerism, Wesleyanism, and revivalism," Christian social critique

> always has worked most effectively by combating one visible sin at a time, and has led to the greatest confusion and ineffectiveness when conceived as proposing the establishment of an ideal order. When...he [the Christian] exposes one injustice as a time, pointing each time to a less evil way which the statesman can understand and follow, there can be a real improvement in the tolerability of the social compromise and thus in a certain sense progress...We should not confuse this progress with the attainment of the good life, nor assume that the personal or social salvation of man is thereby achieved. The ideal order would require sinless men; by definition it cannot be attained in this age. At the same time that some dimensions show progress (e. g., Anglo-Saxon civil liberties) others become steadily worse (militarism).[42]

Yoder's hesitation about speaking of unambiguous moral progress in secular society reflects his "between the times" eschatological orientation which recognizes that God's reign over the world is not yet consummated. He comments that

---

[41]Yoder, The Christian Witness to the State, 37. Yoder apparently does not attend to various ambiguities of statecraft, governance, and social policy in his references to the quest for an "ideal society." He does not demonstrate, for example, how Christians, amidst the complexities of American constitutional democracy with its scheme of checks and balances, will be able to discriminate among legitimate calls for order and social improvement and illegitimate projects of national idolatry. Yoder makes reference to the fact that most Christians in Germany did not recognize at the time that Adolf Hitler was leading the nation in an idolatrous fashion. Given, in light of that example, that it likely will not be self-evident to most Christians when abuse of state authority occurs, Yoder needs to provide an account of how Christians may learn to make such discriminations. To the extent that he does not, this aspect of his project appears inadequately formulated.

[42]Yoder, The Christian Witness to the State, 39.

If truly the earnest of the promised triumph has been given to our age, then the discerning both of real "progress" and of real cumulation of evil is not only permissible but mandatory. The dynamic of Bible faith has (with time and sometimes indirectly) created for the first time a sense of world community; it has freed whole peoples from primitive-pagan superstitions in favor of a more rational world view and let the "post-religious" world come of age; it has built schools and factories, fed, and healed. But progress is also regression. The house swept clean is soon inhabited again. Technology becomes prideful and self-confident; the Marxists (or the bankers) become tyrants. The "Peace of God" becomes the Crusade.[43]

Given the ambiguity of moral progress in this age, Yoder notes that "the Christian social critique is therefore always relative." He means by that term that, while the ultimate standard of judgment is God's kingdom, "for there are no other standards," God's fulfilled reign "is not an available possibility, lying beyond both the capacities and intentions of a fallen society." In this context,

The fact that the world to which we speak is in rebellion guarantees that the Christian social critique can never lead too far. The world can be challenged, at the most, on one point at a time, to take one step in the right direction, to approximate in a slightly greater degree the righteousness of love.[44]

Yoder also notes that there is "a level of human values, not specifically Christian but somehow subject to Christian formative influences," which the Christian social critique may affirm and employ in addressing society. He refers

---

[43]Yoder, The Christian Witness to the State, 39.

[44]Yoder, The Christian Witness to the State, 39. It is again apparent that Yoder's project has much in common with Niebuhr's discourse on "The Relevance of an Impossible Ethical Ideal" in An Interpretation of Christian Ethics, 62ff. Both figures call for approximations of love in the social order out of an awareness that secular society is not capable of manifesting unambiguous fidelity to the demands of Gods' reign. Both Yoder and Niebuhr interpret human history in light of eschatological commitments which make the present an age not suited to the world's full compliance with the Gospel. Of course, the two figures formulate their eschatologies quite differently. Yoder's biblical realism sustains a "between the times" eschatology which sees the present as a time before the fulfillment of the kingdom. Niebuhr's more static approach views humanity as timelessly estranged from the ideal perfection of God's reign. Despite these differences, it is clear that the two figures both pursue projects of calling for approximations of love in society.

164

here

> not only to "cultural" activities, but to the entire fabric of human togetherness--to attitudes of honesty and mutual respect, hard work and clean thinking, unselfishness and tolerance, which the Christian witness creates not only among committed church members, but also by what we have called "moral osmosis" among its sympathizers and among the children of Christians even if these children do not themselves choose the path of discipleship.[45]

As Yoder thinks that such "values cannot be and should not be made subject to the control of the state" and that they have value apart from their contribution to the state, he suggests that

> The Christian social critique will therefore distrust every proposal to sacrifice personal values in the present for future institutional benefits, especially if the making of the sacrifice and the later achievement of the good purpose are entrusted to the political authorities and envisaged as the establishment of a better order.[46]

In standing for such values and against the abuse of authority in its address to the state, Yoder recognizes that Christians "should expect most often to be taking the unpopular side." In fact,

> The witness to the state of which we are speaking is, by virtue of the nonresistant Christian commitment which it presupposes, by necessity the expression of a small minority. Such a group cannot speak to every conceivable issue and adds nothing significant when what it has to say is no different from what others say. We have further observed that the Christian witness does not provide any foundation for government, either practically or philosophically,

---

[45]Yoder, The Christian Witness to the State, 40. As in certain other aspects of his project which we have described, Yoder does not describe in exacting detail how Christians should engage this realm of values.

[46]Yoder, The Christian Witness to the State, 40. Yoder's formulation is too vague and abstract for readers to grasp precisely what he means by suggesting that Christians will always distrust calls for the sacrifice of personal values for future social benefits. Surely, there are occasions when the commitments, desires, and preferences of individuals are rightly tempered by concern for the common good. Yoder seems to underwrite such a tempering in his suggestion that Christian social critiques call for the approximation of love out of concern for the reform of society.

but that the Christian rather accepts the powers that be and speaks to them in a corrective way. It is when we speak to those in power and to the dominant majority groups in the population that we plead the case of the minorities and the absent; this does not mean that if we were speaking to the minority groups themselves we should be uncritical or flattering.[47]

Yoder works from the "universal biblical concern for 'the widow and the orphan'" to suggest that the Christian social critique, in its use of the larger society's language, will be informed by the assumption that "in any society certain categories of persons will be excluded from the economic and social privileges of the strong." Even "the much-heralded welfare state" does not ameliorate the facts of poverty and political weakness. By making known the shortcomings of government policies designed to help the impoverished, Christians pursue "a witness reminding those in power of the continuing injustices of their regime."

In addition to concern for the poor, Yoder insists that Christians should undertake advocacy on behalf of the stranger or outsider, such as "the North American Indian, the Negro, migrant workers, and overseas peoples whose immigration is not permitted." Christian concern "extends as well to the enemy" whom the dominant order may very well condemn.[48]

In advancing these various concerns to the state in a language which is intelligible to it, Yoder notes that a common theme is the plea for government to "take the most just and the least violent action possible." For the state to comply with this request will often entail for it the sacrifice of "immediate selfish ends for the sake of principle," whether compliance with the Geneva Convention in the midst of war or calling for free elections that will likely bring in new leaders. Such sacrifice demonstrates that "nothing just is ever cheap." By identifying appropriate middle axioms for raising these issues, Christians will call the state

---

[47]Yoder, The Christian Witness to the State, 41.

[48]Yoder, The Christian Witness to the State, 41.

to "the highest attainable aim" for secular society.[49]

Through such use of the dominant order's language, Christians will seek to order the state toward the service of God's purposes. They will call the powers that be to serve, admittedly in a broken and imperfect way, the lordship of Christ.

Our discussion has indicated that Yoder's approach to Christian social action is, through its strategy of compromise and approximation of the demands of agape, closer to Niebuhr's than Yoder would like to admit. Moreover, Yoder's references to middle axioms are generally vague and abstract, lacking an exacting display of how such norms may be identified and applied in given situations. Yoder's formulation also seems to rely on a more precise knowledge of God's purposes in, and governance of, history than Yoder was willing to grant to Constantinians. As such, there appear to be significant points of tension in Yoder's proposal for Christian social involvement. The final section of the chapter will develop these criticisms more fully, and display their significance for the evaluation of Yoder's project.

The Moral Logic of Setting the Agenda and Identifying
Appropriate Strategies for Social Action

Yoder's approach to the state is based on the theological assumption that

> It is not the world, culture, civilization, which is the definitional category, which the church comes along to join up with, approve, and embellish with some correctives and complements. The Rule of God is the basic category. The rebellious but already (in principle) defeated cosmos is being brought to its knees by the Lamb.[50]

---

[49]Yoder, The Christian Witness to the State, 42.

[50]Yoder, "But We Do See Jesus," The Priestly Kingdom, 54. See also Koontz, "Confessional Theology in a Pluralistic Context: A Study of the Theological Ethics of H. Richard Niebuhr and John H. Yoder," 34ff.; Scriven, The Transformation of Culture: Christian Social Ethics after H.

(continued...)

As noted above, it is precisely because of Christ's lordship over the powers that Yoder believes that Christians are to search for middle axioms to call the state to do good and not evil.

In attending explicitly to Yoder's view of the moral logic of Christian participation in secular society, it is clear that he intends non-resistant love to be the determining norm for discernment. Yoder's conceptual formulation of a Christian social critique recognizes "the norm of love as the only standard in the church...[and expects] the standards and the achievement of the world to be less than love." He also denies "the existence or the knowability of a fixed standard of justice in the realm of unbelief" or the world. Says Yoder,

> We therefore avoid affirming that there is any norm willed by God other than love itself. What holds down the performance and the standards that apply in the world is the weight of sin, not a divinely revealed lower order for secular society. God's only ultimate will is what He has revealed in Christ.[51]

In addressing society, Christians, as noted above, are to use "pagan terms (liberty, equality, fraternity, education, democracy, human rights)" as middle axioms to express the demands of agape in a given situation.[52] In this way, Yoder wants to provide "a challenge to the established system upon its own turf," using its own language, or at least language which it understands, to call it to do good.[53]

Against Constantinian notions of responsibility, which entail that the strategies of identifying with and managing society are the most appropriate

---

[50](...continued)
Richard Niebuhr, 146-158; Parham, "An Ethical Analysis of the Christian Social Strategies in the Writings of John C. Bennett, Jacques Ellul, and John Howard Yoder," 162-165, 183-189; and Zimbleman, "Theological Ethics and Politics in the Thought of Juan Luis Segundo and John Howard Yoder," 260ff.

[51]Yoder, The Christian Witness to the State, 71-72.

[52]Yoder, The Christian Witness to the State, 73.

[53]Yoder, "Civil Religion in America," The Priestly Kingdom, 179.

modes of social involvement, Yoder proposes that Christians, as a distinct minority group,[54] should speak critically to society in light of God's intention for human relations that manifest love, or at least an approximation of love. In opposition to interpretations of the Christian life which uncritically support the dominant culture, Yoder suggests that

> The alternative to the fusion of Christ and culture is not a Christ rejecting culture, but a more radically Christ-oriented transformation of the genuine values hidden amidst the mishmash called "culture."[55]

Yoder thinks that such a critical involvement in the culture of secular society is not unheard of among Christians in North America.

> There were William Lloyd Garrison and Alexander Campbell holding together abolitionism and nonviolence. There were William Jennings Bryan and Norman Thomas and Harold Stassen, perennial near winners, seeing their victors soon defeated and some of their causes winning. There was Judge James E. Horton, who in 1935 sacrificed a judicial career in the attempt to give a fair trial to a black man. There was Martin Luther King, Jr., utterly Baptist when almost despite himself he became the most important churchly instrument of cultural change in our century. Most of them Baptist, most of them pacifist, most of them who would rather be right than president; they were the heralds of the agents of creative cultural change on a national scale precisely because they did not conceive of national power as their goal, but kept their eyes on the higher loyalty of Kingdom citizenship.[56]

Yoder insists that the God who is described in the Bible, as well as the history of faithfulness to that God, demands of Christians such a critical participation in society.

---

[54]Yoder does not define with precision in what ways Christians are "a distinct minority group." There would appear to be numerous points of continuity and discontinuity between Christians and other people in society. Those points would likely vary according to the particular social situation in which Christians find themselves.

[55]Yoder, "Civil Religion in America," The Priestly Kingdom, 180. See also his unpublished essay, "How Richard Niebuhr Reasons: A Critique of Christ and Culture," especially 27ff.

[56]Yoder, "Civil Religion in America," The Priestly Kingdom, 181.

The God-language of the Bible does not point inward to the renewed heart alone, nor upward to the "higher power," nor forward to the "hereafter," but backward to the salvation story, outward to the claims of the rest of the world, the enemies to love and the slaves to free, and forward to a city not of our own making...The irreducible historicity of Abraham and Moses, Jeremiah and Jesus, the demonstrable wrongness of Constantine and Charlemagne and the Crusades, the providential rightness of the renewals...[and] of the call to obedience to a God whose sovereignty is not at the service of human dominion but who rather calls human power into servanthood; these are the memories that can best give substance to our hopes. The transcendence that counts is not a power from beyond that is now leashed to favor us, but the affirmation of values beyond our control to which we are committed, calling us to be ministers of peace and of justice above, beyond, and maybe even against our own interest.[57]

Yoder pursues this sort of critical involvement, for example, by trying "to keep the question open about whether and why (or when and where) democracy is really the best form of government."[58] Two basic points of orientation for his analysis of this question are:

1) A New Testament realism about the nature of governmental power, as exemplified in the political choices of Jesus and the apostles;
2) a free-church realism about the [moral] ambivalence of "Christendom."[59]

Against the Constantinian assumption that the paradigmatic moral agent of Christian ethics is the ruler whose chief aim is the administration of the entire society in the name of God, Yoder suggests "a non-Christendom alternative stance" which operates with "the conscious anachronism and oversimplification of reaching back to the New Testament" for "a provocative paradigm" to guide

---

[57]Yoder, "Civil Religion in America," The Priestly Kingdom, 188. See also "The Original Revolution," The Original Revolution, 31-33.

[58]Yoder, "The Christian Case for Democracy," The Priestly Kingdom, 152.

[59]Yoder, "The Christian Case for Democracy," The Priestly Kingdom, 153.

Christian involvement.[60]

He cites Jesus' statement that "'The rulers of the nations lord it over them'" as an indication that it is a fact of life that there are political rulers who have dominion over subjects. Moreover, "'Those who exercise authority let themselves be called benefactors.'" They claim to be working for the good of their subjects. Jesus also says to his disciples "'But it shall not be so among you; you shall be servants because I am a servant.'" Comments Yoder,

> After having described realistically both the fact of rule and the fact of value claims being made for that rule, Jesus locates himself and his disciples in a different ethical game. They are not to take over that game of "rulers-making-a-case-for-their-benevolence" nor are they to attempt to interfere with it. They are called simply to do something else. The meaning of that "something else" is the alternative answer to the question of government which is represented by the servant Messiah.[61]

Yoder observes that Jesus' statements reflect three levels of moral analysis. First, there is the simple descriptive statement that there is political dominion. Second, there is "a level of moral rhetoric used by the bearers of power to legitimize themselves." Third, there is the alternative language and ethic of discipleship. Yoder's complaint is that

Since Constantine we have fused those three levels: the facticity

---

[60]Yoder, "The Christian Case for Democracy," The Priestly Kingdom, 155.

[61]Yoder, "The Christian Case for Democracy," The Priestly Kingdom, 156. Yoder's formulation does not appear to take account of the fact that the New Testament does not portray Jesus as someone who used middle axioms or any other strategy of approximation for the proclamation of God's kingdom. Indeed, it was Jesus' bluntness in denouncing the rulers of his society which seems to have led to his crucifixion (e. g., Matt. 23, 27:11). Yoder urges Christians to follow Jesus in calling the powers to serve God's purposes, but he does not acknowledge that his strategy is, in the above respect, significantly different from that of Jesus in the New Testament. This criticism raises a question about Yoder's allegiance to biblical realism. Namely, is Yoder's social project an unambiguous embodiment of "the biblical point of view," as he suggests? At least in its use of middle axioms to compromise the demands of love, Yoder's project appears to affirm something other than "the world view of the Bible." With its approximation of the demands of the kingdom for the sake of effective communication, Yoder's project seems to manifest something like a Constantinian concern for managing the social order.

of dominion, the language of legitimation, and the differentness of the disciples...Since Constantine, when talking about government, we have assumed (as Jesus could not have) that we are talking about government of Christians and by Christians. We have thus lost the distance which Jesus maintained between his realism about power and his messianic liberty in servanthood. We have not distinguished between an ethic which can claim the authority of incarnation for the content of messianic servanthood and that other discourse which talks with the rulers about their claim to be benefactors.[62]

Against this fusion of discourse, Yoder suggests that Christians, as they seek to address the state, should "accept as normal the diaspora situation in which Christians find themselves in most of the world today," and give up the illusion that they do or should run the world. From the perspective of a resistant minority group, Christians will then be "freer than before to make fruitful use of the self-justification language of the rulers...as the instrument of our critical and construction communication with them." Comments Yoder,

If the ruler claims to be my benefactor, and he always does, then that claim provides me as his subject with the language I can use to call him to be more humane in his ways of governing me and my neighbors. The language of his moral claims is not the language of my discipleship, nor are the standards of his decency usually to be identified with those of my servanthood. Yet I am quite free to use his language to reach him.[63]

Even in democratic societies, which claim that the people govern, there is still a division between the ruler and the ruled. Says Yoder,

We are still governed by an elite, most of whose decisions are not submitted to the people for approval. Of all the forms of oligarchy, democracy is the least oppressive, since it provides the strongest language of justification and therefore of critique which the subjects may use to mitigate its oppressiveness. But it does not make of democracy, and especially it does not make of most regimes which today claim to be democracies, a fundamentally

---

[62]Yoder, "The Christian Case for Democracy," The Priestly Kingdom, 157.

[63]Yoder, "The Christian Case for Democracy," The Priestly Kingdom, 158.

new kind of sociological structure.[64]

The various restraints on government entailed by democratic structures "do not constitute the fact of government; they only mitigate it." For Yoder, it is simply "the nature of the civil order itself that its coercive control is prior to any justifications or qualifications thereof."[65] Democracy is not, for Yoder, a qualitatively new form of social organization.

Rather than virtually identifying, like the Constantinian, God's reign with the state and expounding an ethic to sustain the dominant order, Yoder suggests that Christian participation in secular society is an exercise in "the stewardship of scare resources, allocating the available Christian leadership discriminatingly in the places where it is most strategically significant."[66] In this moral stewardship, no norm, whether that of responsibility or effectiveness, "has moral autonomy over against the structure of the servanthood of Jesus." In pursuing discipleship, Christians will "decide how to be active in the wider society" in light of a preference "for servant roles."

This orientation entails that

the paradigmatic person by whose situation my ethic must be tested would not the oppressor but the oppressed, not the most powerful or even the most righteous powerful person, not my representative or my ruler, but the one with whom Christ in his servanthood is first of all identified.[67]

In pursuing this sort of Christ-like servanthood, the Christian moral

---

[64]Yoder, "The Christian Case for Democracy," The Priestly Kingdom, 158-159.

[65]Yoder, "The Christian Case for Democracy," The Priestly Kingdom, 159.

[66]Yoder, "The Christian Case for Democracy," The Priestly Kingdom, 161.

[67]Yoder, "The Christian Case for Democracy," The Priestly Kingdom, 162. Apparently even the plea on behalf of the oppressed will be framed in a way designed for maximum effectiveness with the oppressor, even if that framing will require a compromise of the social requirements of God's reign. Despite Yoder's description of his project as non-Constantinian, it is clear that he has a strong concern for Christians to be effective in the governance of the social order, even if compromise for the sake of results is required. This is a significant point of tension in Yoder's thought.

agent is to be "an agent of reconciliation." Yoder thinks that all Christians have this "general call" to embody non-resistant love in imitation of Jesus' obedience even to the point of death.[68]

Yoder describes Christian involvement in secular society, then, in light of the following claims: (1) There exist rulers and states which exercise political dominion, often in ways not consistent with the demands of love; (2) Christians should recognize Jesus' lordship and pursue a minoritarian ethic that will look for opportunities of loving service in society; and (3) Christians may use whatever language is available in their situation to call for society to do good and not evil.

Perhaps the clearest example of Yoder's method is contained in his The Christian and Capital Punishment, a pamphlet which calls for Christians to "support efforts to abolish the death penalty as a legal way of dealing with offenders." Yoder begins his argument with an account of "The Basic Christian Testimony About Human Life," which draws from the teachings of Jesus, other passages from both the Old and New Testaments, and the writings of Menno Simons, to suggest that killing is illicit because human life is sacred and a necessary condition for "being reconciled with God and man."[69]

Yoder then interprets the Old Testament's allowance for the death penalty as a limitation of vengeance. It assumed that "Vengeance is happening; the necessity is that it be controlled" by limiting it to "an eye for an eye."[70] Moreover, he suggests that for the Hebrews "it is not so much a legal or an ethical as a ceremonial requirement that blood must be paid for with blood." But with Jesus' fulfillment of the Old Testament's ceremonial requirements,

> no more blood is needed to testify to the sacredness of life, and no

---

[68]Yoder, The Christian Witness to the State, 56-57.

[69]Yoder, The Christian and Capital Punishment, 4-5. See also The Christian Witness to the State, 49-50; and Parham, "An Ethical Analysis of the Christian Social Strategies in the Writings of John C. Bennett, Jacques Ellul, and John Howard Yoder," 173-174.

[70]Yoder, The Christian and Capital Punishment, 7.

more sacrifices are called for to expiate for man's usurping of the power to kill. With the cross of Christ the moral and the ceremonial basis of capital punishment is wiped away.[71]

He next attends to "Killing and the Function of the State," arguing that Jesus' disruption of an execution, as portrayed in John 8, is "our first orientation point" for thinking critically about the state's authority, or lack thereof, to take life. Yoder notes that Paul's reference to "the sword" in Romans 13 is an affirmation of judicial authority, not an approval of executions. Hence, he finds no New Testament justification for a view of the state on which capital punishment is its prerogative. In this light, it becomes the task of Christians to critique the state in light of what they know to be true. Says Yoder,

If Christ is not only prophet and priest but also king, the border between the church and the world cannot be impermeable to moral truth. Something of the crossbearing, forgiving ethics of the Kingdom must be made relevant to the civil order.[72]

Yoder then shifts his attention to an analysis of the argument that the death penalty is justified because it is a deterrent to murder. He rejects this claim on psychological grounds, as most murderers "are driven by forces of emotion or outright insanity such that no reasoning, no weighing of consequences, takes place at all as they decide to kill." He also argues statistically that states without the death penalty often have a substantially lower murder rate than states with the penalty.[73] He points, moreover, to the possibility of "judicial error which can never be made right" in "an erroneous sentence of death." The very fallibility of the criminal justice system is a warrant for rejecting such a final punishment:

---

[71]Yoder, The Christian and Capital Punishment, 9.

[72]Yoder, The Christian and Capital Punishment, 10-11.

[73]Yoder, The Christian and Capital Punishment, 16-17. Although there are some studies which provide relevant statistical analysis of this issue, Yoder provides no evidence for his assertion that murderers do not consider the consequences of their actions, and are not "normal people."

"never make decisions about men's fates which cannot be reviewed."[74]

Yoder concludes by briefly answering the question

What should Christians do? First of all, we should become informed. Our convictions on this matter should be as well thought through as those concerning military service. We should contribute to the awakening of public opinion by speaking to our neighbors and writing to newspapers. We should witness to legislators, especially if and when abolition legislation is being considered. We should assure our church leadership, locally, and on a state-wide and denomination-wide level of our support in any approaches they might make to legislative committees, through conference resolutions, or through other channels of testimony. Underlying all this effort, justifying it, and enabling it, we should remind ourselves that when we are instructed to "pray for kings and all who are in high places" it is concrete things like this which we are to have in mind. "That we may lead a quiet and peaceable life" does not mean that Christians are to be interested primarily in their own tranquility; it means that the purpose of government is to keep all violence within society at a minimum. In our land and in our day one of the best ways to testify to this divine imperative is to proclaim to the state the inviolability of human life.[75]

Perhaps more clearly than any other example which he provides, Yoder's way of framing a response to the death penalty displays his understanding of how Christians may participate in secular society. The theological basis for Yoder's concern is the lordship of Christ. Jesus undertook a non-violent ministry, stopped an execution, satisfied the Old Testament ceremonial laws which required the shedding of blood, and now reigns over the rebellious powers of the world. These Christological claims provide the theological basis for Yoder's position. Likewise, Yoder acknowledges the existence of the state as a realm not fully obedient to Christ, but which nevertheless is limited in its authority by God's reign. Yoder's advocacy is designed to order the state, as a

---

[74]Yoder, The Christian and Capital Punishment, 18-19.

[75]Yoder, The Christian and Capital Punishment, 23.

fallen power, to serve God's purposes, to do good and not evil.

Yoder attends to the issues of deterrence and judicial error in ways that may prove persuasive to the authorities on their own terms. He seems to use these points as middle axioms to call for reforms; but these are reforms, proposed here in a language which the leaders of society may accept, which are ultimately justified in light of Jesus' lordship.

Yoder's treatment of this issue warrants two tentative criticisms. First, it is clear that his references to judicial error and deterrence amount to an approximation or compromise of the demands of agape. Yoder notes that Jesus stopped an execution, as recorded in John 8, on the grounds that those guilty of sin are not worthy to take the lives of others. It would appear, then, that faithfulness to "the politics of Jesus" would require a strategy that conveys a similarly stringent message on the nature of the relationship of humans to God. In a way distinct from such blunt prophetic speech, Yoder suggests that Christians make prudential arguments about deterrence and judicial error in order to be effective in persuading government officials to eschew capital punishment. Thereby, Yoder appears, by his own standards, to compromise the integrity of the Christian social witness by placing concern for effectiveness over the pursuit of communicating unambiguously the call for obedience to God.[76]

Second, Yoder's call for Christian opposition to capital punishment reflects a rather substantive knowledge of what sort of political order God desires for the world. On the basis of Yoder's argument against the Constantinians, that God's governance of the world is virtually unknowable in this age, it is not at all clear how Christians may know with such clarity that they are to address governmental officials in this way. Indeed, given Yoder's claim that God acts in history primarily through the agency of the church, and that Christians must

---

[76]Yoder's method appears to be in tension with his claim that Christian social action should operate according to a norm of obedience, out of faithfulness to Jesus' example, which rejects calculating concerns about the effectiveness of moral action. The Politics of Jesus, 233ff.

simply "take it on faith that God is governing the world," it is puzzling that he so strongly advances Christian participation in the administration of the state. God's designs for the world would seem, on Yoder's terms, to be virtually unknowable. Why, then, should Christians be so invested in matters of public policy? As noted above, there appears to be an unresolved tension in Yoder's account of what humans may discern of God's purposes in, and governance of, history.[77]

Another example of Yoder's method of Christian social action is his treatment of just war theory. While Yoder thinks that just war reasoning "rejects the norm of the cross and the life of Jesus Christ as the way of dealing with conflict" in its legitimation of killing, he does not refrain from arguing according to its standards to call just warriors, regardless of whether they are Christians, to live up to the theory's restraint on the use of force.[78]

Yoder suggests that just war thinking operates in light of certain "very broad assumptions," each of which, "if they are to be respected as morally honest," will call resort to arms into serious question. The standard of intention, for example, requires that advocates of just war thinking make "a conscious commitment to the willingness to pay the price of the refusal which becomes imperative when the doctrine applies negatively" in judging participation in a war

---

[77]See Yoder, Christian Attitudes to War, Peace, and Revolution, 42-43; and The Christian Witness to the State, 16ff. Yoder would likely respond to this criticism with the claim that Christians know, in light of Jesus' example and victory over the fallen powers, what sort of social order they are to seek, one which would embody God's ordering of the powers to serve God's purposes. This claim, however, is in tension with his remarks against the Constantinians that God's governance of, and purposes for, the fallen world are virtually unknowable.

[78]Yoder, "The Authority of Tradition," The Priestly Kingdom, 75. See also Christian Attitudes to War, Peace, and Revolution, especially chapters 4-7, and 20; and The Christian Witness to the State, 45-49. It is clear that Yoder, in his use of just war theory, is employing language designed to convey effectively an approximation of the demands of agape. As just war theory obviously falls short of the pacifism which Yoder believes is normative for Christians, Yoder is not, on his own terms, calling for right obedience to God. He has chosen just war language for the sake of effectiveness, even though it compromises the demands of the Gospel. Once again, we find Yoder pursuing a social strategy which bears a resemblance to that of Constantinianism.

as unjust. Thereby it would entail that the agent should conscientiously object to the war. Similarly, in cases where there is no legitimate authority or just means to defend a just cause, the just warrior must refuse to fight. Yoder suggests that "most people using just-war language" have not made "that serious choice," and that important questions of intention and legitimacy are often brushed aside by the nationalism and militarism of just war advocates.[79]

Likewise, concerning the criterion of last resort, Yoder thinks that advocates of just war reasoning in the United States have not established structures designed to pursue the non-violent resolution of conflicts of the sort that would have to be tried before the use of force properly could be described as the last available option. When equal amounts of time and effort have not been invested in finding non-violent alternatives to, for example, the use of the military or the CIA to achieve the policy goals of the nation, violent means are hardly a last resort. Says Yoder, "Last resort can only be claimed when other resorts short of the last have been faced seriously."[80]

Yoder fears, in this light, that just war theory is often employed as an uncritical ideology for unrestrained militarism and nationalism.

> If on the one hand the possibility of surrendering can be shown to be real in the minds of moralists, citizens, and decision-makers; if scenarios for loss-cutting and face-saving, plans for peacemaking and for civilian based defense were pursued, with seriousness equal to that invested in contingency strategic plans and battle models, the JWT [just war theory] could claim its millennial tradition as an intrinsically moral position.
> If on the other hand there is no right of the enemy's subject people's which cannot yield to our judgment of "supreme emergency," and no calculus to distinguish an authentically "supreme" emergency from all the others, if there is no condition under which if losing we should sue for peace, if there is no offense against the rules of war which we would not commit "if

---

[79]Yoder, When War Is Unjust, 74-75.

[80]Yoder, When War Is Unjust, 76-79.

we (really) had to," then what calls itself JWT is in fact merely a polite camouflage for an ultimate national egotism, respecting the welfare of others only under the limits of a single-scale consequentialism.[81]

Yoder suggests that, by calling the state to abide by its espoused just war standards, Christians may participate in God's ordering of the powers of the old aeon in a more tolerable fashion by seeking certain restraints on the state's use of violence. Even though Yoder thinks that non-violence is normative for Christians, he insists that Christians may contribute to moral discourse about war in this way:

> The continuum of increasing tolerability, leading from total disorder to the kingdom of God, can be spoken to by the church at any point, in terms of the choice between greater and lesser evils available at that point. When the church's testimony against war has not been heard, the church does not therefore become silent or irrelevant; she still has a word about the ways of waging war.[82]

In this light, Yoder is critical of "the slogan 'unconditional surrender'" which aims "not at setting right a particular iniquity but at eliminating the enemy." Such reasoning threatens to destroy "the fabric of society to a degree far graver than the original offense [which signaled the beginning of hostilities] and therefore creates more problems than it resolves." Yoder, pointing to an instance of the unfortunate implications of such an approach, comments that

> The unconditional surrender mentality contributed in a major way to the present East-West problem by creating a power vacuum in central Europe and favoring a too unqualified alliance of the Western Powers with the U.S.S.R. before 1945. In the same way, the systematic anti-communism of the Western states since 1950, accepting any kind of alliance even with dictators and feudal tyrants, is equally unwholesome.[83]

---

[81]Yoder, "Surrender: A Moral Imperative," The Review of Politics 48 (Fall 1986): 592.

[82]Yoder, The Christian Witness to the State, 48.

[83]Yoder, The Christian Witness to the State, 48.

In contrast, a "police conception of limited war, while not intrinsically legitimate," has the advantage of operating according to certain standards and controls which provide resources for a mediated end to hostilities short of the destruction of an entire society which is assumed to be an embodiment of evil worthy only of annihilation. Yoder notes that it was precisely such a goal of "the extermination of the enemy" that lead the United States to use atomic bombs against Japan in 1945, when the leaders of that nation had already sued for peace. He argues that, while the bombs were not necessary to end the war, they were used "only to make the surrender unconditional."[84]

Yoder finds the criteria of just war thinking to be "useful attempts to delimit, in terms of the function of the state, the cases in which the use of violence is the least legitimate." Christians, in their attempt to call the state into line with God's purposes, may use the language of just war against the state as a middle axiom to limit its violence in light of Christ's lordship. Comments Yoder,

> That there can be a just war in the Christian sense of the word just or righteous is, of course, excluded by definition; we can make the point only negatively. When the conditions traditionally posed for a just war are not fulfilled, then a war is unjust to the point that even a state, resolved to use violence, is out of order in its prosecution.[85]

Capital punishment and just war theory, then, are two public issues of the sort which Yoder thinks that Christians may address redemptively. In both instances, Yoder begins with the Christologically based assumption that taking human life is wrong; he then proceeds to argue in a fashion designed to call

---

[84]Yoder, The Christian Witness to the State, 48-49.

[85]Yoder, The Christian Witness to the State, 49.

society to policies more consistent with the demands of the lordship of Christ.[86]

In evaluating the overall coherence of Yoder's position, it is interesting to examine, first, whether his view of discipleship is of a piece with his treatment of Christian involvement in secular society. This question arises in light of Yoder's claim that what is normative for Christians in Jesus' example is

> the concrete social meaning of the cross in its relation to enmity and power. Servanthood replaces dominion, forgiveness absorbs hostility. Thus--and only thus--are we bound by New Testament thought to "be like Jesus."[87]

Yoder describes Jesus' acceptance of the cross as "a substantial, binding, costly social stance."[88] Through his obedience to God, which culminated in his crucifixion, Jesus demonstrated God's love through "non-resistance, bearing the other's sinfulness, bearing, literally, his sins." It was only non-resistance that would respect the freedom of humanity to reject him, and fulfill God's salvific intention non-coercively.[89]

It may be asked, however, in what sense the voting, lobbying, and use of middle axioms for which Yoder calls may be described as non-resistant. Is it not, rather, a form of dominion, and even of resistance, to use political power in advancing a certain agenda, even an agenda influenced by Jesus' teaching and non-violent example? Ramsey argues that the non-violent resistance of political action is quite far from Jesus' ethic of non-resistance.

> It is plain that Jesus did not substitute the milder coercion of law courts and a system of claims and counter-claims for exacting an

---

[86]See Yoder, The Christian and Capital Punishment, 4ff.; and The Christian Witness to the State, 45-49. The operative term here is "more consistent." In calling for the stringent use of just war criteria, Yoder knows that he is not calling society to proper discipleship. Instead, and for the sake of effectively approximating the demands of agape, Yoder calls for a limitation of the state's use of force by traditional just war standards.

[87]Yoder, The Politics of Jesus, 134.

[88]Yoder, The Politics of Jesus, 130-131.

[89]Yoder, Preface to Theology, 229.

eye for an eye...He did not say, Do not resist by violent means which necessarily bring death, but you may resist non-violently by using all means such as passive non-cooperation and civil disobedience which fall short of directly killing another man....Non-violent or passive resistance and violent resistance are equally far removed from non-resistance. Non-resistance is incommensurable with any form of resistance.[90]

In analyzing this issue, it is important to remember that Yoder sees Jesus' non-resistant acceptance of the cross as the culmination of his lifelong way of active obedience to God. By his ministry of God's kingdom, Jesus offended and challenged the rebellious powers of the world, and in particular the political and religious leaders of Palestine. He resisted the sinful ways of the world in his obedient ministry, but did not resist the final test of his obedience: death on a cross as "the political, legally to be expected result of a moral clash with the powers ruling his society."[91] It is precisely in this sense of refusing to defend himself, from the charges brought against him on account of his active ministry, that Yoder thinks that Jesus was nonresistant.[92]

When Yoder describes Jesus as nonresistant, then, he does not intend to describe him as a passive or "do nothing" figure. To the contrary, he

---

[90]Ramsey, Basic Christian Ethics, 68-69; he engages Yoder specifically on these issues in Speak Up for Just War or Pacifism, 115ff.; and generally on the distinction between nonresistance and nonviolence in Basic Christian Ethics, 68ff. See Zimbleman's critique of Yoder's norm of nonresistance in "Theological Ethics and Politics in the Thought of Juan Luis Segundo and John Howard Yoder," 310ff.; and Hughes' analysis of Yoder's view of power in relation to politics in "The Ethical Use of Power: A Discussion with the Christian Perspectives of Reinhold Niebuhr, John Howard Yoder, and Richard J. Barnet," 147-156.

For other examples of Yoder's treatment of Christian political action, see "The National Ritual: Biblical Realism and the Elections," Sojourners 5 (October 1976): 29-30; "Why I Don't Pay All My Income Tax," Sojourners 6 (March 1977): 11-12; and The Christian and Capital Punishment, 23. See also Parham, "An Ethical Analysis of the Christian Social Strategies in the Writings of John C. Bennett, Jacques Ellul, and John Howard Yoder," 172ff.

[91]Yoder, The Politics of Jesus, 132, 147-148. See also "Jesus and Power," On Earth Peace, 365-372.

[92]Yoder, The Politics of Jesus, 100; "The Political Axioms of the Sermon on the Mount," The Original Revolution, 51.

understands Jesus to have been actively deviant from the conventional social, political, and religious norms of his day, and to be the paradigm of obedience before God whom Christians are to follow in their lives.

There is a point of ambiguity, however, in Yoder's claim that, while "there is no general concept of living like Jesus" demanded by New Testament authors, there is throughout Scripture the call for Christians to follow their Lord "at the point of the concrete social meaning of the cross in its relation to enmity and power. Servanthood replaces dominion, forgiveness absorbs hostility."[93] The ambiguity is that it is not clear whether Yoder is suggesting that the non-resistance embodied by Jesus' actual acceptance of the punishment of the cross is normative for the Christian life, or that what may be described as Jesus' non-violent resistance of challenging the religious and political authorities of his day, which led to the crucifixion, is what is normative. To the extent that it would be quite puzzling for Yoder to call for social activism in imitation of a Lord whose most characteristic action was the passive acceptance of a sentence of death, it is safe to conclude that he intends Jesus to be a model for Christians in both his ministry of non-violent resistance and his non-resistant death.

In order to avoid the entirely passive connotations of the term "nonresistance" (which would make it hard to see how a nonresistant Jesus could be a model for Christian activism), it may serve to elucidate Yoder's account if references to Jesus' nonresistance are precisely and explicitly limited to his acceptance of the cross--i. e., to his refusal to defend himself from the repercussions of his active ministry.[94] Indeed, Jesus' ministry, according to

---

[93]Yoder, The Politics of Jesus, 134. Yoder makes his case on this point by numerous references to New Testament texts on pages 115-134.

[94]See, for example, Yoder's discussion of Jesus' active ministry as a model for Christians in "The Original Revolution," The Original Revolution, 28ff.; "Christ, the Light of the World," The Original Revolution, 128ff.; and "The Hermeneutics of Peoplehood," The Priestly Kingdom, 37.

184

Yoder's reading of the gospels, amounts to the demonstration of a "social-political-ethical option" for living a life of "social nonconformity."[95] Throughout his ministry, Jesus resisted the sovereignty of the fallen powers "by living among men a genuinely free and human existence" in a fashion so provocative as to bring about his death.[96]

It appears, then, that Yoder, for the sake of clarity, would do well to distinguish more clearly between the non-resistance, or rejection of self-defense, of Jesus' acceptance of the cross, and his active, though non-violent, resistance to evil throughout the entirety of his ministry. When seen in this light, Yoder's suggestion that Jesus is an example for Christians "only on one subject...his cross" seems consistent with his call for Christians to pursue an active obedience to God relative to the social orders in which they find themselves.[97] It appears consistent because, for Yoder, Christians are to follow Jesus in the ministry of God's kingdom in a fashion that challenges and resists the sovereignty of the corrupted powers over human life. We are, for example, to call for the abolition of capital punishment because killing violates God's will for human relations. It was precisely this sort of active resistance which led to the nonresistance of the cross, to Jesus' death at the hands of the political authorities of his day.

Yoder suggests that Christians are, likewise, to follow Jesus' non-resistant example in accepting punishment, and even death, without defending themselves.[98] We are to follow Jesus in calling humanity to serve God and in accepting the often harsh response of the world to our proclamation and action. The whole of Jesus' ministry, and of the Christian life, is, for Yoder, characterized by resistance against the forces of evil; it is uniquely in the face of

---

[95]Yoder, The Politics of Jesus, 23, 97.

[96]Yoder, The Politics of Jesus, 147.

[97]Yoder, The Politics of Jesus, 97.

[98]Yoder, He Came Preaching Peace, 18-21.

the cross, or similar retribution, that Jesus' followers are to resist by not resisting evil, by letting even death come without abandoning the way of obedience. Indeed, to follow Jesus in laying down one's life, to be non-resistant, is ironically a strong form of resistance, of placing the norm of obedience to Jesus' example over the conventional wisdom of self-defense. It is this call for resistance to norms and structures which challenge fidelity to Jesus that appears most characteristic of Yoder's view of the Christian life.[99]

Another, and more troubling, aspect of Yoder's approach to Christian social involvement, as noted earlier, is his reliance on middle axioms to provide the working language of a Christian social critique.[100] Hauerwas suggests, on this point, that Yoder's use of middle axioms "avoids making clear what criteria and conception of the just society is used for the individual judgments about society." Through his reliance on the language of the larger society, it is not clear, says Hauerwas, how the precise content or definition of moral terms employed by Christians in public discourse, such as "innocent" or "injustice," will be determined. Hauerwas suggests that

> If such criteria were made more explicit it might be possible to suggest in a more positive fashion what stake men of faith have in the maintenance of such criteria of justice; or at least it might make somewhat problematic Yoder's assertion that a sufficient Christian ethic can be based solely on revelation. Yoder may object that such criteria are not necessary as the Christian simply works within the alternatives of the historically contingent state, but then it seems that the Christian is always in danger of accepting the status quo as normative--i. e., just the problem that

[99]See Yoder, The Politics of Jesus, 23, 130-131; He Came Preaching Peace, 18-20, 47-56; "The Original Revolution," The Original Revolution, 23ff.; and "But We Do See Jesus," The Priestly Kingdom, 62.

[100]Yoder, The Christian Witness to the State, 35, 71-73. See also "The Christian Case for Democracy," The Priestly Kingdom, 160ff.

Yoder most wants to avoid.[101]

Parham raises the similar objection that Yoder's use of middle axioms is "somewhat obscure." He argues that Yoder has not made clear, for example, how Christian moral reason is to operate "in complex situations where principles [or middle axioms] are in conflict."[102] Zimbleman, likewise, suggests that Yoder has "neither formulated as well-defined precepts nor raised to...[a] high level of specificity" his account of moral norms other than that of nonresistant love.[103] He thinks that Yoder has failed to make lucid how Christians should discriminate between the various values, norms, and axioms which they will likely employ in addressing social issues.[104]

While Yoder has apparently not responded directly to these charges, it seems likely that he would defend his method by reference to the communal context in which Christians, in his approach, have unique resources of moral discernment that will guide them in judging which language or norms to use in addressing particular matters in light of Jesus' lordship. Right judgment, for him, occurs "only in the actual encounter between a believing community and the next challenge. The only way to see how this will work will be to see how it will work."[105]

Yoder understands the church to embody, through its procedures and offices, a society of discipleship with resources sufficient to train and sustain its

---

[101]Hauerwas, "The Nonresistant Church: The Theological Ethics of John Howard Yoder," Vision and Virtue, 217-218. See also Huetter's criticism of Yoder on this point in "The Church: Midwife of History or Witness of the Eschaton?," 49.

[102]Parham, "An Ethical Analysis of the Christian Social Strategies in the Writings of John C. Bennett, Jacques Ellul, and John Howard Yoder," 198.

[103]Zimbleman, "Theological Ethics and Politics in the Thought of Juan Luis Segundo and John Howard Yoder," 310-311, 266ff.

[104]Zimbleman, "Theological Ethics and the Politics in the Thought of Juan Luis Segundo and John Howard Yoder," 311, 334.

[105]Yoder, "The Hermeneutics of Peoplehood," The Priestly Kingdom, 45.

members in discerning what discipleship entails. The Spirit, present with the church since Pentecost, guides the community in its pursuit of fidelity to Jesus as a socially embodied foretaste of God's new age. It is part of this fidelity or obedience to call the fallen powers of society to serve God's ends through the use of middle axioms, language which the powers can understand.[106]

Yet, even when Yoder's view of middle axioms is interpreted within this communal context, there remains a great deal of ambiguity about his proposal. It is simply not clear what precise standards or procedures of moral judgment are to be employed by the community, and in what precise fashion, to guide the critical appropriation of middle axioms. Yoder's discussion of these norms, such as "liberty, equality, fraternity, education, democracy, [and] human rights," fails to develop any one of them in detail or to discriminate between various definitions of, for example, human rights, equality, or justice.[107] While it is clear that Yoder wants to discriminate among various axioms in light of Jesus' lordship, it is by no means clear how that discrimination is to proceed.[108]

While Yoder praises certain public figures, such as Harold Stassen and Martin Luther King, Jr., for proper political involvement in light of "the higher loyalty of Kingdom citizenship," he fails to display in detail why he praises them, or how the community of faith is to discern that their use of society's language was more congenial to the demands of the Gospel than that of, say, Harry S.

---

[106]Yoder, "The Hermeneutics of Peoplehood," The Priestly Kingdom, 22-37; He Came Preaching Peace, 96-107; The Christian Witness to the State, 10ff.; 22ff.; and "A People in the World: Theological Interpretation," The Concept of the Believers' Church, 259, 264-271, 276-277.

[107]Yoder, The Christian Witness to the State, 73. For discussions of certain complexities in defining "justice" as a moral term, see MacIntyre, After Virtue, 244-245; L. Gregory Jones, "Should Christians Affirm Rawls' Justice as Fairness? A Response to Professor Beckley," The Journal of Religious Ethics 16 (Fall 1988): 251-271; and Friesen, Christian Peacemaking and International Conflict, 112-122.

[108]Yoder, "The Christian Case for Democracy," The Priestly Kingdom, 155-166.

188

Truman or William F. Buckley, Jr. While it is easy to assume in broad scope why Yoder surely would approve of the former pair more than the latter, especially in light of their respective views of militarism, it is still not clear how Christians are to discern, amidst the myriad particulars of a concrete social situation, and the possibility of conflicting moral norms, why and how King's discourse would be approved over that of Buckley. Apart from displaying in concrete detail how such a judgment would be made on the address of Christians to the state, Yoder's account is inadequate.[109]

Although Yoder's treatments of capital punishment and just war theory appear more precise--in that he employs, on the former issue, particular notions of deterrence and, on the latter issue, traditional criteria such as intention and last resort--it is unclear how the ethicist is to determine which norms are most applicable in a given debate on capital punishment or in the evaluation of a particular war effort. Surely, the particulars of such debates will vary depending on a plethora of historically contingent factors. Still, it is not apparent how Yoder's communally located method of discernment would cope with such vicissitudes. Neither is it clear how Christian moral reason is to function in a situation where proposed norms conflict, or how the precise content or definition of a norm is to be determined.[110]

Moreover, Yoder does not seem to have analyzed carefully the possibility that Christians might discern, in a given situation, that a plea to the state for a pragmatic pacifism might be more appropriate than would arguments for just war standards. It is not clear how Yoder's method would determine when, where, and how such a strategy, which would seem to be more in keeping with his commitment to non-violence, would be a more appropriate work of

---

[109]Yoder, "Civil Religion in America," The Priestly Kingdom, 181.

[110]Yoder, The Christian and Capital Punishment, 17ff.; When War Is Unjust, 74-79.

obedience to God than would a call for the logic of just war theory.[111]

Apart from not providing a well displayed, historically located demonstration of how ethicists should make the large number of discriminations and judgments necessary for the successful use of middle axioms, Yoder does not lucidly "bridge the gap" between talk of fidelity to Jesus and particular, historically located moral and political judgments. In this sense, it does not appear that Yoder's project is methodologically adequate for guiding the discernment of what obedience to God entails for specific instances of Christian political involvement.[112]

Yoder's lack of a substantive, detailed display of how middle axioms function suggests that his use of the term is more a provocative rhetorical strategy designed to call Christians to social involvement than a rigorously developed method of moral discourse. Even as the previous chapter concluded that Yoder's references to Constantinianism are not elucidated with historical, sociological, and theological precision, the present discussion finds that Yoder's supposedly non-Constantinian method for social involvement is flawed by a similar lack of exactitude.

Another troubling aspect of Yoder's use of the middle axiom is that, as noted above, it embodies a concern for effectiveness or consequential moral reasoning which appears to be in contradiction with Yoder's call for an ethic of obedience. For the sake of effective communication with societal leaders, Yoder suggests that Christians are to approximate the requirements of agape through the use of terms which will be acceptable to their hearers, even though those terms

---

[111]Yoder, Nevertheless, 128-132; When War Is Unjust, 20-22; and The Christian Witness to the State, 45-49.

[112]Gustafson, in Ethics from a Theocentric Perspective, 1:75-76, rightly comments that Yoder's "Concentration on practical moral reasoning limits the area of consideration; it needs to be pushed to its theological boundaries. Ethos criticism has the merit of asking the big questions that casuistry avoids, but its own stance must be pressed to some practical conclusions on specific areas of human activity."

190

do not manifest the fullness of the call to obedience to God.[113]

Indeed, the very notion of a middle axiom seems to reflect a concern for effectiveness, for finding secular language that is capable of making efficacious the social critique of the Gospel. While being effective in this sense may very well be, for Yoder, a task of obedience to what God demands, he has not offered an explicit rationale for why this particular strategy of approximation is consistent with his anti-Constantinian critique of consequentialist moral reasoning. To that extent, there is a profound tension and lack of coherence in this aspect of Yoder's work. It is hardly consistent for him to denounce seventeen hundred years of Christian moral reasoning as having been characterized by the compromise of the demands of the Gospel for the sake of effectiveness in governing society, and at the same time to advance a project which clearly has those same characteristics.

Likewise, Yoder nowhere demonstrates that such a method of compromise for the sake of effectiveness is an implication of the "one particular social-political-ethical option" embodied by Jesus in the New Testament. He portrays Jesus as a Messiah who unambiguously proclaimed the implications of God's reign for human relations, and who challenged the dominant order of his society out of pure obedience to God uncompromised by considerations of effectiveness. Yoder's method of social action calls for the compromise and approximation of the social demands of Gospel for the sake of effective communication with societal leaders; as such, Yoder's method is in discontinuity with his portrayal of Jesus. To that extent, Yoder's method also seems in tension with his espoused loyalty to biblical realism. This criticism challenges Yoder's central claim for the distinctiveness of his project, that it calls Christians to the discipleship of Jesus as he is portrayed in the New Testament.[114]

---

[113]Yoder, The Christian Witness to the State, 71-73; "Christ, the Hope of the World," The Original Revolution, 153ff.; The Politics of Jesus, 238ff.

[114]Yoder, The Politics of Jesus, 23.

There exists, moreover, a difficulty with Yoder's claim that sound Christian analysis of political situations "will usually coincide with the best informed secular analysis [and be] confirmed by the most objective of those who analyze similar problems on common-sense grounds."[115] The problem is that it is by no means clear by what standards a given social scientist or other political commentator will evaluate or describe a particular situation, and from what perspective any such analysis may be called "objective." Indeed, the content of such an evaluation will likely depend on the analytical method and interpretative commitments of the examiner in question.[116]

Michel Foucault, for example, argues against the ideal of objectivity in interpretation through a method of "geneology...a form of history which can account for the constitution of knowledges, discourses, [and] domains of objects" through a radical historicism which locates human knowledge within matrices of power and regulation which amount to the standards in light of which truth claims are advanced.

He argues that

Truth is a think of this world: it is produced only by virtue of multiple forms of constraint. [It concerns] "the ensemble of rules according to which the true and the false are separated and specific effects of power attached to the true." [Hence, the political problem] is not changing people's consciousness...but the political, economic, institutional regime of the production of

---

[115]Yoder, The Christian Witness to the State, 45.

[116]It is curious that Yoder, who places a great deal of importance on communal moral formation and the unique resources of the church for discernment and moral description, would refer so easily to agreement between Christians and others on the interpretation of complex matters. Comments Yoder in "Introduction," The Priestly Kingdom, 11, "The church precedes the world epistemologically. We know more fully from Jesus Christ and in the context of the confessed faith than we know in other ways. The meaning and validity and limits of concepts like 'nature' or of 'science' are best seen not when looked at alone but in light of the confession of the lordship of Christ."

truth.[117]

Foucault insists that standards of truth are the products of socially embodied forces of power in society. Hence, analysis of intellectual projects, and claims to truth and objectivity, may not remain at the level of pure theory; it must attend to the forces and interests of its production.

Foucault's comments suggest that it is quite problematic to speak simply of "the best secular analysis" or "objectivity" apart from an explicit critical awareness that the standards by which a method is judged sound, or an evaluation determined to be objective, are socially produced, based on certain historically relative presuppositions, and not self-evidently justified. As Yoder does not attend to how Christian ethicists may discriminate among various secular construals which claim to be "objectively true," or at least "sound," his project will face difficulty in responding to societal issues about which "the facts" are in dispute. How, for example, will Christians determine whether "the best secular analysis" confirms or contradicts their judgments?

An example of the sort of secular analysis which would appear to be important for Yoder's project is the work of Bryan Turner in the sociology of religion. Turner has examined the role of religion within late capitalist societies, such as the U. S. A., and suggests that they are

> characterized by a thick network of regulatory institutions which order and contain human activity. The compensation for containment is located in a hedonistic mass, consumerism and privatized leisure.[118]

In these societies, "private systems of meaning have become uncoupled from public modes of social legitimation." Hence, pursuing a particular view of the good life, such as Christian discipleship, or

---

[117]Michel Foucault, "Truth and Power," The Foucault Reader, ed. Paul Rabinow (New York: Pantheon Books, 1984), 59.

[118]Bryan Turner, Religion and Social Theory: A Materialist Perspective (London: Heinemann Educational Books, 1983), 225.

opting for abstinence or orgy is now an idiosyncratic choice without major social significance; both asceticism and hedonism are highly commercialized, operating outside zones of political regulation and administration.[119]

In Turner's view, the only link between the private realm of freedom and "the objective regulation of public activities" is "a commercialized popular culture that employs sexual idioms to extend the market for consumer goods."[120] Turner's position is important because, if it is true, it demonstrates that, due to the power structures and social conditions of late capitalism, Christianity, as well as the political activity of Christians, is simply irrelevant for the functioning of contemporary society.

If that claim is warranted, it would likely influence the sort of strategy which Yoder, or any other Christian ethicist, would advocate for Christian social involvement. The problem is that Yoder's method does not appear to be able to evaluate critically such clearly important, and morally relevant, positions. He simply states that Christians should rely on the best available information. Without an account of how an ethicist will discriminate among or test various claimants to truth in the analysis of society, Yoder's project seems inadequate, because it is not clear how he will go about distinguishing "the best informed secular analysis" from the not so well informed.[121]

Yoder's suggestion that Christians incorporate the best available information, apart from a critical awareness of the complexity of that task, amounts to a vague suggestion that ethicists remain open to the findings of non-theological discourses. Absent a detailed display of how that incorporation should work, Yoder's approach remains imprecise rhetoric. It does not represent a lucidly demonstrated method by which Christians might take account of other

[119]Turner, Religion and Social Theory, 239-240.

[120]Turner, Religion and Social Theory, 240-241.

[121]Yoder, The Christian Witness to the State, 45.

fields of enquiry.

Because Yoder's account of Christian political involvement relies on "the most accurate and impartial descriptions of historical reality" for the proper identification and use of middle axioms, this inadequacy is profoundly important.[122] Without a rigorous method for discrimination among various accounts of "what's happening" in the world in which Christians are to pursue discipleship, how will ethicists be able to discern what obedience to Jesus' example requires in given situations or how to use middle axioms well? The methodological gap between the language of following Jesus and the moral complexities of historical situations remains, for Yoder, largely unbridged.

Yoder's apparent failure to recognize that his non-Constantinian project is, in important ways, dependent historically upon the Constantinian synthesis of church and world is yet another difficulty. This appears to be the case in light of Yoder's confidence that there will usually be points of moral and linguistic continuity between the church and the dominant order sufficient to enable a Christian critique which will not be entirely ignored by the powers that be.[123] According to Yoder, states are now in the habit of seeking the approval of the churches, while the churches generally support what the state and other cultural institutions desire.[124] It appears that this mutual support has made church and state, in many times and places, largely comfortable with one another. Absent, at least from the "'neo-neo-Constantinian'" social arrangement characteristic of the nation in which Yoder lives, is the mutual rejection by church and state of one another which characterized, with varying degrees of severity, the period

---

[122]Yoder, The Christian Witness to the State, 34.

[123]Yoder, "The Christian Case for Democracy," The Priestly Kingdom, 155ff.

[124]Yoder, "Civil Religion in America," The Priestly Kingdom, 177.

preceding Constantine's conversion.[125]

It is likely, only as a result of this history of good relations between church and state, that it would occur to an avowed non-Constantinian such as Yoder to be so concerned with Christian involvement in political affairs, or even to describe his method as "non-Constantinian." Were it not for the historical demonstration that churches may influence society as a whole, the dominant form of which he critiques, it is doubtful that Yoder would undertake a Christian witness to the state, particularly in the form of approximating the demands of agape for the sake of effectiveness. Indeed, a good many of Yoder's publications are explicit responses to Constantinian approaches to ethics. At least in this sense, his "enemy" has largely shaped the agenda which he has pursued throughout his career.[126]

As an Anabaptist, Yoder brings his tradition's critique of "the established church" to bear upon the history of Constantinian social structures. By critically analyzing how Constantinian moral reason has operated, and continues to influence Christian ethics, he has identified errors and temptations which he believes Christians should avoid in their political action.[127]

That Yoder's project is historically located in this sense directs attention, once again, to the problematic nature of his "biblical realism." Yoder claims throughout his writings that he is expounding "the biblical point of view" and bringing it to bear upon questions of the Christian life. As noted in the second chapter, however, it is clear that Yoder brings to biblical interpretation certain hermeneutical presuppositions of the sort which call into question the adequacy

---

[125]Yoder, "The Constantinian Sources of Western Social Ethics," The Priestly Kingdom, 142. See also Frend, The Rise of Christianity, 318ff.; 452ff.

[126]See, for example, Yoder's "Reinhold Niebuhr and Christian Pacifism;" The Christian Witness to the State; "If Christ Is Truly Lord," The Original Revolution; and The Politics of Jesus, especially chapter 1. It is clear in these works that Yoder is responding polemically to Constantinian projects.

[127]Yoder, "The Recovery of the Anabaptist Vision," 14-21.

of a simple appeal to "the world view of the Bible." Especially in light of the post-Constantinian nature of his critique of Constantinianism, it is safe to conclude that Yoder is interpreting Scripture from a particular historical vantage point in a fashion that belies the language of biblical realism.[128]

As indicated earlier, Yoder does not demonstrate how certain forms of participation in the affairs of a constitutional democracy through the use of middle axioms are to be construed as direct implications of "the biblical point of view."[129] Rather, he pursues such social action as an historically mediated implication of his reading of Scripture as an Anabaptist and a critic of Constantinianism. While Yoder is obviously aware of certain ways in which theological tradition shapes biblical hermeneutics, he has not reformulated his references to biblical realism in this light. In this respect, Yoder's account of Christian political involvement is not adequately informed by a critical appraisal of how theological tradition and post-Constantinian historical location have shaped his use of Scripture.[130]

A final critical point to make is that there is an unresolved epistemological tension in Yoder's thought between the apparently contradictory claims that: (1) God's governance of history is virtually unknowable; and (2) Christians may discern with no great difficulty what God's intentions are for governance of the world. Yoder makes the first argument against the Constantinian assertion that God raised up Constantine as a providential act for the furtherance of the Christian faith.[131] The second claim is a presupposition

---

[128]See Yoder's "The Use of the Bible in Theology," The Use of the Bible in Theology/Evangelical Options, 113ff.; The Politics of Jesus, 5-6; Christian Attitudes to War, Peace, and Revolution, 425ff.; and "Biblicism and the Church," Concern Pamphlet #2, 26-69; for discussions of biblical hermeneutics.

[129]Yoder, The Christian Witness to the State, 32-33;72-73.

[130]Yoder, "The Authority of Tradition," The Priestly Kingdom, 66-67.

[131]Yoder, Christian Attitudes to War, Peace, and Revolution, 42-43.

of Yoder's plea for Christians to participate in God's ordering of the powers in, for example, opposing the death penalty and calling for the state's stringent observation of just war standards.[132]

The tension arises, perhaps, because Yoder is concerned to condemn what he takes to be an historically presiding view of God's providential action in the reign of Constantine, while at the same time wanting to speak in a substantive way about God's purposes in history in order to advance his own plan of social action. Yoder would appear to have various options for reducing this tension. He could, for example, provide an explicit account of how and why some groups of Christians may discern God's purposes in history better than others.[133] On the other hand, Yoder could modify the severity of his rejection of the knowledge of God's governance of the world, or even formulate a method of moral discernment which could operate without claiming to know God's purposes for history.

Apart from such a resolution of tension, Yoder's project has a profound epistemological problem. He cannot give a fully coherent account of why the Constantinian appeal to knowledge of God's purposes in history is less adequate than his own. To the extent that Yoder's argumentation about the knowledge of God's governance of history is flawed in this way, his project appears to totter on the brink of epistemological incoherence. As Yoder has not provided a convincing account of how Christians may discern or know God's involvement

---

[132]Yoder, The Christian and Capital Punishment, 10ff.; The Christian Witness to the State, 16ff., 48-49. Yoder's great concern with communicating effectively with societal leaders raises, moreover, the issue of how great a role the state, and other societal institutions, have in God's governance of history. While Yoder suggests that God's direction of history reflects "the absolute priority of church over state in the plan of God," The Christian Witness to the State, 17, he goes to great pains, even compromising the demands of agape, to enable Christians to have a role in guiding the state in a way pleasing to God. Yoder's stress on the importance of such political involvement seems to indicate a point of tension with his "ecclesiocentric" views of God's action in history and of the Christian life.

[133]Yoder appears to be headed in this direction in "The Hermeneutics of Peoplehood," The Priestly Kingdom, 15ff.

in and purposes for the world, ethicists will find it hard to glean much discrete moral guidance from his constructive proposal, or to affirm the cogency of his critique of Constantinianism.

In an effort to display the practical implications of Yoder's eschatologically informed critique of Constantinianism, this chapter has examined and evaluated Yoder's moral rationale for Christian political participation. We have concluded that, while Yoder describes his approach as non-Constantinian, his method displays a number of significant parallels to Constantinianism. Yoder's eschatology does not appear to have sustained a project of social involvement which is markedly different from that which he critiques. Throughout Yoder's formulation, there are significant points of tension and incoherence which severely call into question the adequacy of his proposal. The following, and concluding, chapter will briefly reiterate the significance of these conclusions for the overall evaluation of Yoder's work, and demonstrate the importance of this study in that light.

CHAPTER 5

CONCLUSION

This final chapter concludes the analysis of Yoder by summarizing the basic conclusions of the study. It divides into three brief sections: (1) a summary of the study's significance; (2) an assessment of the import of eschatology for Yoder's moral analysis; and (3) a description of his eschatologically informed view of appropriate Christian political action.

Summary of the Study's Significance

This study has examined the import of eschatology for the formulation of Yoder's critique of Constantinianism. The first chapter began the discussion through an overview of Yoder's project and an analysis of the state of research on Yoder, which indicated that the importance of eschatology for his critique had not received exacting scholarly attention.[1]

---

[1]The rather general comments of McClendon, Ethics: Systematic Theology, 1:73-74, 318-321; and of Zimbleman, "Theological Ethics and Politics in the Thought of Juan Luis Segundo and John Howard Yoder," 218-219, are perhaps the most focused of those in the secondary literature on this particular aspect of Yoder's work.

200

In laying the conceptual groundwork for a direct examination of his view of Constantinianism, the second chapter considered Yoder's eschatology, attending to how his position is informed by a particular use of Scripture, together with the relationship between his eschatology and views of Christology, ecclesiology, and Christian ethics. Through this analysis, the chapter examined Yoder's eschatology in a more detailed fashion than have previous studies.[2]

The third chapter analyzed in detail the rationale of Yoder's critique of Constantinianism, especially noting its eschatological assumptions, significance for the relationship between church and world, and importance for Christian moral reason. By focusing on Yoder's view of Constantinianism, the chapter brought this aspect of Yoder's work under a scrutiny more rigorous than that of earlier examinations.[3]

In an effort to demonstrate the practical relevance of Yoder's eschatologically informed critique, the fourth chapter examined his alternative view of Christian involvement in secular society, attending in particular to the theological basis of such participation, his account of how Christians may use society's language in addressing the state, and his method for identifying appropriate agendas and strategies for Christian social involvement. The chapter displayed how Yoder's eschatological commitments shape his view of proper Christian political involvement, and evaluated his proposal critically in a more

---

[2]Cf., for example, the brief discussions of Yoder's eschatology in Hughes, "The Ethical Use of Power: A Discussion with the Christian Perspectives of Reinhold Niebuhr, John Howard Yoder, and Richard J. Barnet," 124-126; Zimbleman, "Theological Ethics and Politics in the Thought of Juan Luis Segundo and John Howard Yoder," 215ff.; Hauerwas, "The Nonresistant Church: The Theological Ethics of John Howard Yoder, Vision and Virtue, 207ff.; and McClendon, Ethics: Systematic Theology, 1:73-74, 318-321.

[3]See, for example, Parham, "An Ethical Analysis of the Christian Social Strategies in the Writings of John C. Bennett, Jacques Ellul, and John Howard Yoder," 149ff.; Zimbleman, "Theological Ethics and Politics in the Thought of Juan Luis Segundo and John Howard Yoder," 218ff.; and Sawatsky, "John Howard Yoder," Non-violence: Central to Christian Spirituality, 251ff.

exacting fashion than have previous studies.[4]

Throughout these chapters, the discussion has sought to make lucid, through a close reading of relevant primary and secondary sources, how Yoder's eschatology shapes and informs his description and critique of Constantinianism, as well as his alternative account of Christian political involvement. In addition, the discussion has tested Yoder's position at various points for internal coherence, and has noted points of both strength and weakness.

Eschatology and Moral Analysis

Eschatology shapes Yoder's approach to moral analysis in important ways. First, Yoder suggests that his "between the times" eschatology requires the Christian to interpret the world in which he or she lives as existing at the overlapping of two aeons.[5] A new aeon has begun with the ministry and resurrection of Jesus, which event is the beginning of God's reign which will not find fulfillment until the eschaton.[6] Jesus of Nazareth, whose paradigmatic obedience to God even to the point of death on a cross was the sign of the beginning of the new age, is the example of the moral life for Christians "between the times."[7]

Through Jesus' obedience to God in embodying non-resistant love, and especially through his resurrection, the Almighty has conquered in principle the rebellious powers of the world. It is through this conquest that the new age has

---

[4]See, for example, Parham, "An Ethical Analysis of the Christian Social Strategies in the Writings of John C. Bennett, Jacques Ellul, and John Howard Yoder," 191ff.; Zimbleman, "Theological Ethics and Politics in the Thought of Juan Luis Segundo and John Howard Yoder," 266ff.; and Hauerwas, "The Nonresistant Church: The Theological Ethics of John Howard Yoder, Vision and Virtue, 209-210.

[5]Yoder, "If Christ Is Truly Lord," The Original Revolution, 55ff.

[6]Yoder, The Christian Witness to the State, 8-10.

[7]Yoder, The Politics of Jesus, 130-131; "The Hermeneutics of Peoplehood," The Priestly Kingdom, 37.

begun; "Jesus is Lord" is precisely an eschatological claim which anticipates the coming fullness of God's reign.[8]

Yoder suggests that Jesus is a moral example for Christians primarily in his non-resistant acceptance of the cross as the "political, legally to be expected" retribution for his socially disruptive ministry of God's kingdom.[9] Christians are to follow Jesus, according to Yoder, in both his nonresistant acceptance of punishment and in his non-violent resistance to the powers that be. The way of Jesus must be our way of living in the new age.[10]

A further implication of eschatology for ethics, in Yoder's approach, is its establishment of the church as a foretaste of the new age which empowers, through the presence of the Spirit, the pursuit of discipleship. The church, as a distinct minority community which embodies procedures and structures necessary for the sustenance of the Christian life, constitutes a social order which embodies proleptically the obedience to God which the consummated kingdom will entail for all reality. Through its common life, Christians are to be guided in discerning what the Christian life entails.[11]

The sort of moral reason which the church, as a foretaste of the new age, sustains is precisely that of obedience to God in the imitation of Jesus' obedience. Yoder formulates his account of obedience in a way that is critical of consequentialist views of morality, because they describe what it would mean to be effective in a fashion which is not informed by the eschatological claim that the risen Lord will one day conquer all reality, that the crucified Lord is the key

---

[8]Yoder, Preface to Theology, 229ff.; The Politics of Jesus, 147-162; The Christian Witness to the State, 9.

[9]Yoder, The Politics of Jesus, 132.

[10]Yoder, "But We Do See Jesus," The Priestly Kingdom, 62; The Politics of Jesus, 23; "Christ, the Light of the World," The Original Revolution, 129.

[11]Yoder, "The Hermeneutics of Peoplehood," The Priestly Kingdom, 28ff.; The Christian Witness to the State, 10; "The Otherness of the Church," 286-296.

to history's meaning and final fulfillment.[12] Because Jesus' way of obedience has been uniquely vindicated through his resurrection, as the way of all reality upon its completion, obedience to God is "aligned with the ultimate triumph of the Lamb."[13] While obedience is not without positive punctual results, Yoder insists that the controlling norm of Christian moral reason be obedience to God in the fashion exemplified by Jesus' ministry.[14]

In light of his eschatologically shaped view of the Christian life, Yoder criticizes Constantinianism for underwriting a number of serious theological and moral errors. First, this orientation replaces the "between the times" eschatology with the view that God's reign is manifest in the present social order. The present is no longer seen within the context of God's future fulfillment. God's reign is for all practical purposes identified with the status quo.[15]

Moreover, Constantinianism conflates what Yoder sees as the proper distinction between church and world. The church, no longer a minority community of discipleship which is uniquely empowered by the Spirit, is now but one of many cultural institutions whose chief aim is to sustain the dominant order. Indeed, rather than pursuing obedience to the example of Jesus, Constantinianism seeks the furtherance of the aims of the present regime. In the name of "responsibility," the norm of fidelity to Jesus is replaced, or at least interpreted in light of, the exigencies of running the empire. It makes punctual effectiveness a determining standard of moral discourse in a fashion that, from Yoder's perspective, denies that true success resides purely in obedience to the way of the

---

[12]Yoder, The Politics of Jesus, 233-250; "Armaments and Eschatology," 53ff.; "To Serve Our God and to Rule the World," 3ff.; "Christ, the Hope of the World," The Original Revolution, 153ff.

[13]Yoder, The Politics of Jesus, 245.

[14]Yoder, "The Kingdom as Social Ethic," The Priestly Kingdom, 91-101.

[15]Yoder, "If Christ Is Truly Lord," The Original Revolution, 55ff.; "The Constantinian Sources of Western Social Ethics," The Priestly Kingdom, 136-138.

crucified and risen Lord.[16]

Yoder nuances his account of Constantinianism by the addition of "neo"s to designate post-Byzantine social arrangements which have in common, despite certain variations, these main problematic characteristics. He suggests that they agree in designating the state as the chief agent of God's action in history in a fashion which compromises the ecclesially located moral task of Christians, namely the pursuit of obedience to God in a manner appropriate to location "between the times."[17]

The discussion has demonstrated several major points of tension in Yoder's formulation of the moral import of eschatology. We have noted difficulties with Yoder's use of Scripture, as he seems to affirm the "what the text says" approach of biblical realism without displaying how that orientation coheres with his requirement that Scripture be read communally and Christologically. We have also suggested that Yoder has failed to display with clarity in what sense there are substantive theological and moral parallels between the reign of Constantine and the projects of more recent figures whom Yoder describes as Constantinians, such as Reinhold Nieubhr.

The study has further demonstrated that Yoder's ecclesiology is not developed with sufficient clarity or precision for it to be clear what historically located community Yoder is describing as church and how this community does or should relate to the world. Neither has Yoder made lucid how the moral discernment of the church and the social action of Christians is to procede materially. He has presented relatively vague notions of a communally sustained discipleship which employs middle axioms for the sake of constructive

---

[16]Yoder, "The Otherness of the Church," 286-296; "Reinhold Niebuhr and Christian Pacifism," 113-117; "The Constantinian Sources of Western Social Ethics," The Priestly Kingdom, 135-136.

[17]Yoder, "Christ, the Hope of the World," The Original Revolution, 141-152; "The Constantinian Sources of Western Social Ethics," The Priestly Kingdom, 141-144.

engagement in society, without displaying in detail or with the support of well developed examples how such moral analysis is to procede in historically located situations.

Perhaps the most troubling criticism of Yoder is that his proposed alternative to Constantinian moral reasoning embodies important characteristics of Constantinianism. Like the orientation which Yoder seeks to avoid, his approach approximates and compromises the social demands of the Gospel for the sake of effective communication with the leaders of society. In order to be effective in playing a role in the governance of society, Yoder suggests that Christians temper their speech in a manner conformed to the realistic possibilities of the situation. Hence, by Yoder's own standards, he is guilty of compromising the demands of agape for the sake of consequentialist concerns.

While Yoder seeks to articulate a moral project which is markedly distinct from that of Constantinianism, we have found that his approach is remarkably similar to the orientation which he criticizes. Despite Yoder's attempt to approach Christian ethics in a manner appropriate to a "between the times" eschatology, he has not produced a clear alternative to Constantinian moral reasoning for which eschatology has a decisive, lucid import. Both the formulation of his critique of Constantinianism and his proposed alternative lack precise historical display and support, as well as coherent conceptual development. In these respects, he has not successfully brought eschatology to bear upon the moral discernment of the Christian life.

Political Action in the New Age

Yoder seeks to provide an alternative account of Christian involvement in society which is informed by his eschatological commitments. He suggests that Christians should view the institutions of society, especially the state, as fallen powers of the world which have been conquered in principle by God through

Jesus' resurrection.[18] Even as God now orders the powers to serve God's ends against their will as a sign of the new age, Christians are to participate in society in a fashion that calls the powers to serve the God known in Jesus.[19]

In this participation, Christians are to follow Jesus' example of denouncing and resisting evil as part of the ministry of God's kingdom. Yoder suggests that Christians will identify middle axioms, or terms understandable to the larger society, to voice their critiques of policies or situations that contradict God's design for human relations.[20]

Yoder has used the language of just war, for example, in calling for a limitation on the state's use of violence.[21] He suggests that virtually every social order attempts to justify itself through language, such as beneficence or freedom, which Christians may use in critique of it.[22] Yoder's approach to political involvement purports to be non-Constantinian to the extent that it maintains the distinction between church and world, the "between the times" eschatology, and Jesus as moral norm in ways that avoid the theological and moral pitfalls of Constantinianism.

As indicated above, some of the most serious points of difficulty which the study has identified concern Yoder's proposed view of political action. In addition to his compromise of the social implications of the Gospel for the sake of effectiveness in political advocacy, which bears a strong resemblance to the Constantinian method which he rejects, we find that Yoder has not displayed with clarity how middle axioms are to be identified, discriminated among, or employed

---

[18]Yoder, The Politics of Jesus, 135ff.; The Christian Witness to the State, 12ff.

[19]Yoder, The Christian and Capital Punishment, 15-16.

[20]Yoder, The Christian Witness to the State, 32-33, 35ff., 72-73.

[21]Yoder, When War Is Unjust, 74ff.; "Surrender: A Moral Imperative," 576ff.; The Christian Witness to the State, 49.

[22]Yoder, "The Christian Case for Democracy," The Priestly Kingdom, 158ff.

in morally complex situations. Neither has he demonstrated how Christians are to incorporate critically the sources of secular wisdom which he thinks are important for formulating a Christian social critique. In light of these problems, Yoder's method contains significant methodological flaws which severely challenge the ability of his approach to guide well Christian political action.

The basic theological thrust of Yoder's critique of Constantinianism suffers, as well, from points of tension concerning epistemology. Yoder assumes more epistemological certainty for his knowledge of God's purposes in history than he allows to the Constantinians. While he suggests that the judgment that God providentially brought Constantine to power as a Christian emperor is unjustifiable, as God's governance of history is virtually unknowable, Yoder speaks confidently of his knowledge of God's purposes and action in the world. This is a significant point of tension which severely compromises the adequacy of Yoder's method of moral discernment, especially in light of the fact that Yoder's social agenda is strongly shaped by his knowledge of God's action in history through the ordering of the powers.

The conclusions of this study, then, are largely critical of Yoder's eschatologically informed critique of Constantinianism and of his proposed alternative for Christian social action. As indicated above, Yoder's account lacks a precise, adequate display through sufficiently developed examples from the history of Christianity, as well as internal coherence at many points.

There are, however, some more positive conclusions of the study. Yoder has found a way, in his discourse on Constantinianism, provocatively to raise issues which are central to the moral concerns of his Anabaptist heritage. With his critique of Constantinianism, Yoder has developed a metaphor for the perversion of the Gospel which occurs when the church uncritically aligns itself with the dominant order of a society. While his formulation is less than precise and is informed by the moral distinctiveness of Anabaptism, Yoder's argument ought to be accessible and somewhat interesting to all Christians. Because he has framed the issue in terms of faithfulness to the way of Jesus as opposed to the way of crass political pragmatism, the main thrust of his critique may hardly be ignored, even by Christians whose denominational heritage is that of "the established church."

At the very least, Yoder has advanced a provocative attack on modes of Christian moral reason which would attempt to justify an unwarranted compromise of the social implications of the Gospel. His is a call to vigilance against such corruption. Despite the methodological difficulties that are present in both his critique and proposed alternative, Yoder has raised shrewdly a number of issues which are relevant to those who seek to embody "the politics of Jesus" in a world which has not yet come under the consummated rule of God.

As someone who has learned much from Yoder, and who is generally in sympathy with his "discipleship" approach to Christian ethics, I am more than a bit surprised at the severity of my criticisms of this aspect of Yoder's work. Far from a thoroughgoing repudiation of Yoder's project, of the moral relevance of Anabaptism, or of an ethic of discipleship, these critical points represent demands for greater systematic clarity and methodological precision in the construction of a Christian social ethic. Most specifically, they are calls for greater perspicuity in displaying the import of eschatology for the critique of Constantinianism.

The largely negative conclusions of the study suggest that this aspect of Yoder's project would benefit from a number of conceptual revisions. First, Yoder would do well, especially in light of his affirmation of the problematic hermeneutical strategy of biblical realism, to provide a more coherent account of the authority and use of the Bible for constructive work in theology and ethics. In particular, he should find a way of describing the church's interpretation of Scripture which explicitly recognizes that, in every theological use of the Bible, a representative of a particular branch of the Christian church is interpreting Scripture in a way that is influenced by a given historically conditioned reading of theological tradition. Yoder's reliance on certain findings of modern biblical scholarship further complicates his account of the theological use of Scripture, as it raises the issue of the authority of that scholarship for the theological discourse of the community of faith. The obvious complexity of these hermeneutical issues renders dubious, as noted above, Yoder's simple references to the "what the text says" approach of biblical realism. As Yoder seeks to hold Christian ethical discourse accountable to the example of Jesus, as portrayed in the New Testament, these issues seem to strike at the heart of Yoder's method. A more adequate treatment of them appears necessary for the furtherance of his project.

Second, a successful revision of Yoder's critique of Constantinianism would need to embody greater historical and sociological acumen in order to display in convincing detail how Constantine's reign marked the beginning of a deviant, and historically pervasive, form of Christian social ethics. An exacting account of the particulars of the moral life of Christians in various times, places, and social situations would be required, it appears, in order to make clear in what sense Constantinianism has been an historically presiding corruption of the Christian life. The same sort of rigor would be required to display the commonality of Constantinianism with the various "neo" Constantinianisms which Yoder identifies. Apart from such a detailed display, Yoder's references to Constantinianism, as we have argued, seem largely rhetorical and less than historically precise.

Third, Yoder's stance on the nature of God's governance of history, and of human knowledge of that divine involvement, would benefit from revision and clarification at at various points. As noted earlier, it appears somewhat inconsistent for Yoder to argue that Constantinians cannot know, because God's governance of history is inscrutable, that God brought Constantine to power as an act of providence, while at the same time basing his alternative approach to Christian political involvement on a quite substantive knowledge of God's purposes for the governance of the world.

In addition, while Yoder claims that God's involvement in human history is uniquely manifest and known in the church, he calls for Christians to compromise the rigorous demands of agape, and of obedience to the Gospel, through a mode of political action which is to be conformed to a standard of effectiveness in communicating with the leaders of secular society. If, as Yoder claims, God's governance of history "between the times" is focused on the life of the church, and if Christians are to be agnostic about the particulars of the workings of Providence outside the church, it is unclear what theological warrants exist for sustaining a social project which is based on substantive claims about God's involvement in the world through structures other than the church. A more adequate treatment of these issues would require a greater coherence between claims about what Christians may know of the workings of Providence and proposals for social action which purport to be serving God's purposes in history.

Fourth, Yoder's ecclesiology would be enhanced by a more forthcoming, exacting display of what he means by "church." While Yoder speaks of the church as a community of faith which pursues the discipleship of Jesus as a foretaste of God's reign, it is never clear precisely whom or what Yoder is describing when he discusses the church. While he often points to Christians who lived before Constantine and the early Anabaptists as models of proper ecclesial life, Yoder does not display in exacting historical detail why and how those groups qualify as models of the faithful community. He indicates neither precisely how Christians are to discern what it means to be church in a given historically, socially located situation, nor how communal moral formation, on which his approach to Christian ethics heavily relies, functions materially to sustain the path of discipleship. Yoder's account of the church would be strengthened by a well displayed, exacting portrait of what proper ecclesial life requires in given historical situations, and of how Christians will be able to discern what the church should do and be in various times and places.

Fifth, Yoder's account of the import of eschatology for Christian ethics would be strengthened by a resolution of the tension between his call for an ethic of obedience, which operates without concern for a norm of punctual effectiveness, and his social project of compromising the demands of agape through the use of middle axioms. As noted earlier, Yoder argues that Jesus' resurrection has begun a new age of God's kingdom in which Christians are to imitate their Lord's obedience to God without concern for the consequences of their actions, largely because God's vindication of the crucified Jesus has demonstrated that simple obedience is the proper mode of life "between the times." The coming consummation of the kingdom will bring the ultimate vindication and success of the way of obedience.

It is hardly consistent with these claims, however, for Yoder to suggest that Christians approximate the demands of obedience in addressing society for the sake of effective, though compromised, communication with political leaders. As Yoder demonstrates neither how this social strategy is of a piece with his eschatologically informed call for obedience, nor how it is an implication of "the politics of Jesus" as portrayed in the New Testament, there is a clear point of tension in this aspect of his work. It is especially problematic in light of the fact that Yoder strongly condemns Constantinianism's compromise of the norm of obedience for the sake of effectiveness. In this light, Yoder's account of the Christian life would be improved by a social strategy which is more coherently related to his espoused theological commitments.

Sixth, in order for any method of Christian moral reflection to address substantively questions of social ethics, it will need to give a critical account of its incorporation of non-theological discourses, such as philosophy, medical science, jurisprudence, and the social sciences. As Yoder appears to do little more than suggest that Christians appropriate the best available findings of other disciplines, his method is in need of a more rigorous account of how ethicists will discern among various competing, and often contradictory or perhaps even incommensurable, construals of "the best" sources of secular wisdom. A more adequate approach would provide explicit methodological standards for both discriminating among and appropriating critically the findings of non-theological discourses.

These six areas of criticism are likewise indications of how certain aspects of Yoder's project might be reformulated, and thereby become more adequate for guiding Christian moral reasoning. As it is beyond the scope of this study to expound an alternative to Yoder's method, or to develop in detail a reformulated "Yoderian" approach to Christian ethics, it should suffice to note that the discussion has identified a number of discrete points of difficulty in Yoder's eschatologically informed critique of Constantinianism. While, as argued above, many of our criticisms have cast serious doubt on the adequacy of this aspect of Yoder's work, the conclusions of the study are not intended as an omnibus rejection or denigration of Yoder's entire project. To the contrary, they are the product of critical engagement with a delineated portion of the work of a significant contemporary figure in Christian social ethics who has raised a number of crucial, and often neglected, issues about Christian moral reasoning. As such, the conclusions of the study are an invitation to further, and more adequate, accounts of the import of eschatology for the Christian life.

BIBLIOGRAPHY

I. The Published Works of John Howard Yoder

A. Books and Pamphlets

As You Go: The Old Mission in a New Day. Scottdale, Pennsylvania: Herald Press, 1961.

Balthasar Hubmaier: Theologian of Anabaptism. Translated and edited by John H. Yoder and H. Wayne Pipkin. Scottdale, Pennsylvania: Herald Press, 1989.

Beyond Conformity. Goshen, Indiana: Student Christian   Association, 1963.

Christian Attitudes To War, Peace, and Revolution. Elkhart,   Indiana: Goshen Biblical Seminary, 1982.

The Christian and Capital Punishment. Newton, Kansas: Faith and Life Press, 1961.

The Christian Pacifism of Karl Barth. Washington, D. C.: Church Peace Mission, 1964.

The Christian Witness to the State. Newton, Kansas: Faith and Life Press, 1964.

Documents of the Contemporary German Church Struggle. Translated and Edited by John H. Yoder. New York: Church Peace Mission, 1959.

The Ecumenical Movement and the Faithful Church. Scottdale, Pennsylvania: Mennonite Publishing House, 1958.

The Fullness of Christ. Elgin, Illinois: Brethren Press, 1987. Originally published in Concern Pamphlet #17, 33-93. Scottdale, Pennsylvania: Concern, 1969.

Die Gespraeche zwischen Taeufern und Reformatoren in der Schweiz 1523-1538. Karlsruhe: H. Schneider, 1962. (Th.D. dissertation).

God's Revolution: The Witness of Eberhard Arnold. Edited by the Hutterian Society of Brothers and John Howard Yoder. New York: Paulist Press, 1984.

He Came Preaching Peace. Scottsdale, Pennsylvania: Herald Press, 1985.

Karl Barth and the Problem of War. Nashville: Abingdon Press, 1970.

The Legacy of Michael Sattler. Edited and Translated by John H. Yoder. Scottdale, Pennsylvania: Herald Press, 1973.

Nachfolge Christi: als Gestalt politischer Verantwortung. Basel: Agape-Verlag, 1964.

Nevertheless: The Varieties of Religious Pacifism. Scottdale, Pennsylvania: Herald Press, 1971.

The Original Revolution. Scottdale, Pennsylvania: Herald Press, 1972.

Peace Without Eschatology? Scottdale, Pennsylvania: Concern, 1959. Reprinted as "If Christ is Truly Lord" in The Original Revolution, 52-84.

The Politics of Jesus. Grand Rapids, Michigan: William B. Eerdmans Publishing Company, 1972.

Preface to Theology: Christology and Theological Method. Elkhart, Indiana: Goshen Biblical Seminary, 1981.

The Priestly Kingdom: Social Ethics as Gospel. Notre Dame, Indiana: University of Notre Dame Press, 1984.

Que feriez-vous si?...Response d'un objecteur de conscience. Montbeliard Imprimerie: Metthez Freres, 1950.

Singleness in Ethical and Pastoral Perspective. Elkhart, Indiana: Associated Mennonite Biblical Seminaries, 1974.

Taeufertum und Reformation im Gespraech: Dogmengeschichtlich Untersuchung der fruehen Gespraeche zwischen Schweizerischen Taeufern und Reformatoren. Zurich: Evangelischer Verlag Zurich, 1968.

Taeufertum und Reformation in der Schweiz: Die Gespraeche zwischen Taeufern und Reformatoren 1523-1538. Schriftenreihe des Mennonitischen Geschichtsvereins #6. Karlsruhe: Herausgegeben vom Mennonitischen Geschichtsverein E. V. Weirhof, 1962.

What Would You Do? Scottdale, Pennsylvania: Herald Press, 1983.

When War is Unjust. Minneapolis: Augsberg Press, 1984.

B. Articles in Pamphlets

"The Anabaptist Dissent: The Logic of the Place of the Disciple in Society." In Concern Pamphlet #1, 45-68. Scottdale, Pennsylvania: Concern, 1954.

and David A. Shank. "Biblicism and the Church." In Concern Pamphlet #2, 26-69. Scottdale, Pennsylvania: Concern, 1955.

"Binding and Loosing." In Concern Pamphlet #14, 2-43. Scottdale, Pennsylvania: Concern, 1967. Reprinted in John White and Ken Blue, Healing the Wounded: The Costly Love of Church Discipline, 211-234. Downers Grove, Illinois: InterVarsity Press, 1985.

"The Christian Answer to Communism." In Concern Pamphlet #10, 26-31. Scottdale, Pennsylvania: Concern, 1961. Also published in Gospel Herald 29 (August 1961): 757-758, 766.

"Epistolary: An Exchange By Letter." In Concern Pamphlet #4, 6-9. Scottdale, Pennsylvania: Concern, 1957.

"A Light to the Nations." In Concern Pamphlet #9, 14-18. Scottdale, Pennsylvania: Concern, 1961.

216

"Marginalia." In Concern Pamphlet #5, 89-92. Scottdale, Pennsylvania: Concern, 1958.

"Marginalia." In Concern Pamphlet #6, 46-49. Scottdale, Pennsylvania: Concern, 1958.

"Marginalia." In Concern Pamphlet #7, 56-63. Scottdale,Pennsylvania: Concern, 1959.

"Marginalia." In Concern Pamphlet #8, 44-49. Scottdale, Pennsylvania: Concern, 1960.

"Marginalia." In Concern Pamphlet #9, 44-45, 47-48. Scottdale, Pennsylvania: Concern, 1961.

"Marginalia." In Concern Pamphlet #10, 32-39. Scottdale, Pennsylvania: Concern, 1961.

"Marginalia." In Concern Pamphlet #11, 59. Scottdale, Pennsylvania: Concern, 1963.

"Marginalia." In Concern Pamphlet #12, 51-56. Scottdale, Pennsylvania: Concern, 1966.

"Marginalia." In Concern Pamphlet #15, 77-80. Scottdale, Pennsylvania: Concern, 1967.

"On the Meaning of Christmas." In Concern Pamphlet #16, 14-18. Scottdale, Pennsylvania: Concern, 1968.

and Pierre Widmer. "Principes et Doctrines Mennonites." In Principes et Doctrines Mennonites, 19-47. Montbeliard et Bruxelles: Publications Mennonites, 1955.

"The Recovery of the Anabaptist Vision." In Concern Pamphlet #18, 5-23. Scottdale, Pennsylvania: Concern, 1971.

"What Are Our Concerns?" In Concern Pamphlet #4, 20-32. Scottdale, Pennsylvania: Concern, 1957.

C. Articles in Books

"Anabaptism and History: 'Restitution' and the Possibility of Renewal." In Umstrittenes Taeufertum 1575-1975, 244-258. Edited by H. J. Goerts. Gottingen: Vandenhoeck und Ruprecht, 1975. Reprinted in The Priestly Kingdom, 123-134.

"Anabaptist Origins in Switzerland." In An Introduction to Mennonite History, 37-49. Edited by Cornelius J. Dyck. Scottdale, Pennsylvania: Herald Press, 1967.

"Anabaptist Vision and Mennonite Reality." In Consultation on Anabaptist -Mennonite Theology, 1-46. Edited by A. J. Klassen. Fresno, California: Mennonite Brethren Biblical Seminary for Council of Mennonite Seminaries, 1970.

and Alan Kreider. "The Anabaptists." In The History of Christianity, 24-27. Edited by Tom Dowley. Berkhamsted, Herts, England: Lion Publishing, 1977.

"The Apostle's Apology Revisited." In The New Way of Jesus, 115-134. Edited by William Klassen. Newton, Kansas: Faith and Life Press, 1980.

"The Authority of the Canon." In Essays on Biblical Interpretation: Anabaptist-Mennonite Perspectives, 265-290. Edited by Williard Swartley. Elkhart, Indiana: Institute of Mennonite Studies, 1984. Originally presented at the Council of Mennonite Seminaries Hermeneutics Consultation, 5 April 1977.

"The Authority of Tradition." In The Priestly Kingdom, 63-79. Notre Dame, Indiana: University of Notre Dame Press, 1984. Originally presented as a University of Notre Dame symposium, "Remembering and Reforming: Towards a Constructive Christian Ethics," 25 April 1980.

"The Believer's Church: Global Perspectives." In The Believer's Church in Canada, 3-15. Edited by J. Zeman and W. Klassen. Baptist Federation of Canada and Mennonite Central Committee (Canada), 1979.

"The Biblical Mandate." In The Chicago Declaration, 88-116. Edited by Ron Sider. Carol Stream, Illinois: Creation House, 1974.

218

"'But We Do See Jesus': The Particularity of Incarnation and the Universality of the Good." In Foundations of Ethics, 57-75. Edited by Leroy S. Rounder. Notre Dame, Indiana: University of Notre Dame Press, 1983. Originally a lecture at the Boston University Institute for Philosophy and Religion, 18 March 1981. Reprinted in The Priestly Kingdom, 46-62.

"The Challenge of Peace: A Historical Peace Church Perspective." In Peace in a Nuclear Age: The Bishops' Pastoral Letter in Perspective, 273-90. Edited by Charles J. Reid, Jr. Washington, D. C.: Catholic University of America Press, 1986.

and Gerold Jaspers. "Christen, Krieg, und Kriegsdienst Heute." In Christian im Ost-West Konflikt, 31-47. Hamburg-Bergstedt: H. Reich, 1961.

and Alan Kreider. "Christians and War." In The History of Christianity, 399-403. Edited by Tim Dowley. Berkhamsted, Herts, England: Lion Publishing, 1977.

"Church and State According to a Free Church Tradition." In On Earth Peace, 279-288. Edited by Donald F. Durnbaugh. Elgin, Illinois: Brethren Press, 1978.

"Church Growth Issues in Theological Perspective." In The Challenge of Church Growth. Institute of Mennonite Studies Missionary Studies Series, no. 1. Scottdale, Pennsylvania: Herald Press, 1973.

"Civil Religion in America: A Radical Protestant Perspective." In The Priestly Kingdom, 172-195. Notre Dame, Indiana: University of Notre Dame Press, 1984. Originally presented as a lecture at Wake Forest University, Winston-Salem, North Carolina, 16 March 1981.

"The Contemporary Evangelical Revival and the Peace Churches." In Mission and the Peace Witness, 68-103. Edited by Robert L. Ramseyer. Scottdale, Pennsylvania: Herald Press, 1979. Originally given as an address, "War and Peace and the Evangelical Challenge," at the National Association of Evangelicals, Denver, Colorado, 19 April 1966.

"Dirk Philips." In Mennonite Encyclopedia, Vol. II, 65. Scottdale, Pennsylvania: Mennonite Publishing House, 1956.

"Einfachere Einheit fuer knappere Zeiten" in Oekumene, 107-111. Edited by Karlfred Froehlich. Tuebingen: Mohr/Siebeck, 1982.

"The Enthusiasts and the Reformation." In Concilium 128: Conflicts About the Holy Spirit, 41-47. Edited by Hans Kueng and Juergen Moltmann. New York: The Seabury Press, 1979.

"Epilogue: The Way Ahead." In On Earth Peace, 279-288. Edited by Donald F. Durnbaugh. Elgin, Illinois: Brethren Press, 1978.

"Exodus and Exile: The Two Faces of Liberation." In Readings in Moral Theology #4, 337-353. Edited by C. Curran and R. McCormick. New York: Paulist Press, 1984.

"France." In Mennonite Encyclopedia, Vol. II, 359-362. Scottdale, Pennsylvania: Mennonite Publishing House, 1956.

"Freres Suisses" in Strasbourg au coeur religieux du XVI siecle, 491-499. Edited by G. Livet. Strasbourg: Libraire Istra, 1977.

"Glory in a Tent: Meditation on the Gospel of John, Chapter One." In He Came Preaching Peace, 69-88. Originally presented at Festival of the Word, Goshen College, Goshen, Indiana, 19 April 1974.

"Hans de Ries." In Mennonite Encyclopedia, Vol. IV, 330. Scottdale, Pennsylvania: Mennonite Publishing House, 1959.

Introduction to God's Revolution: The Witness of Eberhard Arnold. Edited by the Hutterian Society of Brothers and John Howard Yoder. New York: Paulist Press, 1984.

Introduction to The Origins and Characteristics of Anabaptism, 3-9. Edited by Marc Lienhand. The Hague: Nijhoff, 1977.

"Is There Historical Development of Theological Thought?" In The Witness of the Holy Spirit: Proceedings of the Eighth Mennonite World Conference, 379-388. Edited by C. J. Dyck. Nappanee, Indiana: Evangel Press, 1967.

"Jesus' Life-Style Sermon and Prayer." In Social Themes of the Christian Year: A Commentary on the Lectionary. Edited by Dieter T. Hessel. Philadelphia: Geneva Press, 1983.

"Karl Barth: How His Mind Kept Changing." How Karl Barth Changed My Mind, 166-171. Edited by Donald McKim. Grand Rapids, Michigan: William B. Eerdmans Publishing Company, 1986.

"Living the Disarmed Life: Christ's Strategy for Peace." In Waging Peace: A Handbook for the Struggle to Abolish Nuclear Weapons, 126-134. Edited by Jim Wallis. San Francisco: Harper & Row Publishers, 1982.

"The Lordship of Christ in the Power Struggle." In The Lordship of Christ: Proceedings of the Seventh Mennonite World Conference, 507-512. Scottdale, Pennsylvania: Mennonite Publishing House, 1963.

"Mennonite Political Conservatism: Paradox or Contradiction." In Mennonite Images, 7-16. Edited by Harry Loewen. Winnipeg, Manitoba: Hyperion Press Limited, 1980.

"Obbe Philips." in Mennonite Encyclopedia, Vol. IV, 10. Scottdale, Pennsylvania: Mennonite Publishing House, 1959.

"On Divine and Human Justice." In On Earth Peace, 197-210. Edited by Donald Durnbaugh. Elgin, Illinois: Brethren Press, 1978.

"A People in the World: Theological Interpretation." In The Concept of the Believer's Church, 250-283. Edited by James Leo Garrett, Jr. Scottdale, Pennsylvania: Herald Press, 1969.

"Persecution and Consolidation." In An Introduction to Mennonite History, 51-61. Edited by Cornelius J. Dyck. Scottdale, Pennsylvania: Herald Press, 1967.

"La pertenencia del concepto biblico del reino para la hermeneutica." In El reino de Dios y Latinoamerica. Edited by C. Renee Padilla. El Paso: Casa Bautista de Publicaciones, 1975.

"The Prophetic Dissent of the Anabaptists." In The Recovery of the Anabaptist Vision, 93-104. Edited by Guy F. Hershberger. Scottdale, Pennsylvania: Herald Press, 1957.

"The Prophetic Task of Pastoral Ministry: The Gospels." In The Pastor as Prophet, 78-98. Edited by Earl E. Shelp and Ronald H. Sunderland. New York: Pilgrim Press, 1985.

"Quelques Anabaptistes Notoires." In Grandes figures de l'humanisme Alsacien, 153-158. Edited by Francis Rapp. Strasbourg: Librairie Istra, 1978.

"Reformation and Missions: A Literature Survey." In Anabaptism and Mission, 40-50. Edited by W. Shenk. Scottdale, Pennsylvania: Herald Press, 1984.

221

"The Social Shape of the Gospel." In Exploring Church Growth. Edited by Wilbert R. Shenk. Grand Rapids, Michigan: William B. Eerdmans Publishing Company, 1983.

"'Spirit' and the Varieties of Reformation Radicalism." In De Geest in het Geding: Opstellen Aangeboden aan J. A. Oosterban, 301-306. Edited by I. B. Horst et. al. Alphen aan den Rijn: H. D. Tjeenk Willink, 1978.

"A Summary of the Anabaptist Vision." In An Introduction to Mennonite History, 136-145. Edited by Cornelius J. Dyck. Scottdale, Pennsylvania: Herald Press, 1967.

"The Theological Basis of the Christian Witness to the State." In On Earth Peace, 136-143. Edited by Donald Durnbaugh. Elgin, Illinois: Brethren Press, 1978.

"Theological Perspectives on Growth with Equity." In Growth with Equity, Strategies for Meeting Human Needs, 9-18. Edited by Mary Evelyn Jegen and Charles Wilber. Paramus, New Jersey: Paulist Press, 1979.

"Three Ways to Respect Life." In The Sanctity of Life: Evangelical Round Table, vol. III, 92-100. Edited by David A. Fraser. Princeton, New Jersey: Princeton University Press, 1987.

"Translator's Preface." In Christ and the Powers by Hendrik Berkhof. Scottdale, Pennsylvania: Herald Press, 1962.

"The Use of the Bible in Theology." In The Use of the Bible in Theology: Evangelical Options, 103-120. Edited by Robert K. Johnston. Atlanta: John Knox Press, 1985.

"The Way of the Peacemaker." In Peacemakers in a Broken World,111-125. Scottdale, Pennsylvania: Herald Press, 1969.

"Zwingli." In Mennonite Encyclopedia, Vol. IV, 1052-1054. Scottdale, Pennsylvania: Mennonite Publishing House, 1959.

D. Articles in Periodicals

"Adventure in Fellowship." Gospel Herald. 19 October 1954, pp. 993, 1005.

"After Foreign Mission-What?" Christianity Today 8 (March 30, 1962): 12-13.

"Alive and Well at Anderson, Indiana." Gospel Herald. 18 November 1980, p. 931.

"Anabaptists and the Sword Revisited: Systematic Historiography and Undogmatic Nonresistants." Zeitschrift fuer Kirchengeschichte 85 (1974): 270-283.

"...And On Earth Peace..." Mennonite Life (July 1965): 108-110.

"Another 'Free Church' Perspective on Baptist Ecumenism." Journal of Ecumenical Studies 17 (Spring 1980): 149-159.

"Armaments and Eschatology." Studies in Christian Ethics 1 (1988): 43-61.

"Balthasar Hubmaier and the Beginnings of Swiss Anabaptism." Mennonite Quarterly Review 33 (1959): 5-17.

"Biblical Roots of Liberation Theology." Grail 1 (September 1985): 55-74.

"Caesar and the Meidung." Mennonite Quarterly Review 23 (1949): 76-98.

"Calling a Council for Peace." Ecumenical Trends 15 (November 1986): 157-160.

"Can There Be a Just War?" Radix 13 (September-October 1981): 3-9.

"Capital Punishment and the Bible." Christianity Today 4 (February 1960): 3-6.

"The Christian Case for Democracy." The Journal of Religious Ethics 5 (Fall 1977): 209-223.

"The Christian's Peace of Mind." Christian Living (November 1955): 32-33, 38, 45.

"The Christian Witness and Current Events." Gospel Herald, 17 August 1954, p. 777.

"Church Discipline." Gospel Herald, 18 August 1964, pp. 709-710.

"Cleansing the Temple." Epiphany 4 (Spring 1984): 16-18.

223

"Conscientious Objection in France." Gospel Herald, 19 April 1960, p. 345.

"A Consistent Alternative View Within the Just War Family." Faith and Philosophy: Journal of the Society of Christian Philosophers 2 (April 1985): 112-120.

"The 'Constantinian' Sources of Western Social Ethics." Missionalia 4 (November 1976): 98-108. Reprinted in The Priestly Kingdom, 135-147.

"Continental Theology and American Social Action." Religion in Life 30 (1961): 225-230.

"Could There Be a Baptist Bishop?" Ecumenical Trends 9 (July/August 1970): 104ff.

"A Critique of North American Evangelical Ethics." Transformation: An International Dialogue on Evangelical Social Ethics 2 (January-March 1985): 28-31.

"Developing a Christian Attitude Toward War." Behold, April 1966, pp. 8-12.

"The Disavowal of Constantine: An Alternative Perspective on Interfaith Dialogue." Annals 1975/76, 47-68. Tantur: Ecumenical Institute for Advanced Theological Studies, 1979.

"Discerning the Kingdom of God in the Struggles of the World." International Review of Mission 68 (October 1979): 366-372.

"Discipleship as a Missionary Strategy." The Christian Ministry (January-March 1955): 26-31.

and Donald E. Miller. "Does Natural Law Provide a Basis for a Christian Witness to the State?" Brethren Life 7 (1972): 8-22.

"Do We Believe in Sharing Our Decisions?" Gospel Herald, 22 May 1973, p. 427.

"Las etapas de la historiographie de la reforma radical del siglo XVI." Cuadernos de teologia 2 (1972): 147-155.

"Evangelicals at Chicago." Christianity and Crisis 34 (1974): 23-25.

224

"Evangelism and Latin-American Politics: A Document." Gospel Herald, 2 January 1973, pp. 4-5.

"Evangelization is the Test of our Ethical Vocation." International Review of Mission 72 (October 1983): 610.

"Exodus and Exile: Two Faces of Liberation." Crosscurrents 23 (Fall 1973): 297-309. Reprinted abridged as "Exodus: Probing the Meaning of Liberation." Sojourners, September 1976, pp. 26-29. Also published in Issues to Discuss, Program Guide 1979-80, pp. 161-169. Edited by Levi Miller. Scottdale, Pennsylvania: Herald Press, 1979.

"Exodus 20:13. Exposition Article." Interpretation 34 (October 1980): 394-399.

"The Experiential Etiology of Evangelical Dualism." Missiology: An International Review 11 (October 1983): 449-459.

"The Free Church Ecumenical Style." Quaker Religious Thought (Summer 1968): 29-38.

"A Free Church Perspective on Baptism, Eucharist, and Ministry." Midstream 23 (July 1984): 270-277.

"Helpful and Deceptive Dualisms." Horizons in Biblical Theology 10 (December 1988): 67-82.

and Nils Dahl. "The Hermeneutic Problem." Subsection Report from the WCC/IMC Study on The Theology of Mission. The Bulletin of the Division of Studies, World Council of Churches, 7 (Autumn 1961): 19-23.

"The Hermeneutics of the Anabaptists." The Mennonite Quarterly Review 41 (1967): 291-308. Reprinted in Essays on Biblical Interpretation/ Anabaptist -Mennonite Perspectives, 11-28. Edited by Willard Swartley. Elkhart, Indiana: Institute of Mennonite Studies, 1984.

"The Hermeneutics of Peoplehood." Journal of Religious Ethics 10 (Spring 1982): 40-67. Reprinted in The Priestly Kingdom, 15-45.

"Historic Multiracial Meeting in South Africa's Capital." The Mennonite, 21 August 1979, p. 503.

"How America Is Different." Katallagete 10 (Fall 1987):76-79.

and Heinhold Fast. "How to Deal with Anabaptists: An Unpublished Letter of Heinrich Bullinger." Mennonite Quarterly Review 33 (1959): 83-95.

"Islam's Challenge to Mennonites." Gospel Herald, 4 February 1958, pp. 110-111.

"Israel's Revenge." Gospel Herald, 11 April 1961, pp. 335, 348.

"Jesus and Power." Ecumenical Review 25 (October 1973): 447-454. Reprinted in On Earth Peace, 365-372.

"Jesus' Kind of Fisherman." Gospel Herald, 1 May 1973, p. 375.

"Der Kristallistationspunkt des Taeufertums." Mennonitische Geschichtsblatter 24 (1972): 35-74.

"La politica de Jesus: su etica pacifista." Cuadernos de teologia 7 (1986): 263-269.

"The Layman's Rule Today." Gospel Herald, 5 October 1965, p. 873.

"Living the Disarmed Life." Sojourners 6 (1977): 16-19.

"Mennonites in a French Almanac." Mennonite Life 9 (October 1954): 154-156.

"A Missionary Church." Gospel Herald. 8 January 1963, p. 38.

"Missions and Material Aid in Algeria." Gospel Herald, 1 April 1958, pp. 306-307.

"The Natural Ritual: Biblical Realism and the Elections." Sojourners 5 (1976): 29-30.

"The Nature of the Unity We Seek: A Historic Free Church View. "Religion in Life (Spring 1957): 215-222. Reprinted in Christian Unity in North America, 89-97. Edited by J. Robert Nelson. St. Louis: Bethany Press, 1958.

"New Life in the German Churches." Gospel Herald, 9 October 1956, pp. 966-967.

"The New Testament View of the Ministry." Gospel Herald, 8 February 1955, pp. 121-122, 124.

"A Non-Baptist View of Southern Baptists." Review and Expositor (Spring 1970): 219-228.

"The Otherness of the Church." The Drew Gateway 30 (Spring 1960): 151-160. Also published in Mennonite Quarterly Review 35 (October 1961): 286-296.

"A 'Peace Church' Perspective on Covenanting." The Ecumenical Review 38 (July 1986): 318-321.

"The Peace Testimony and Conscientious Objection." Gospel Herald, 21 January 1958, pp. 57-58.

"The Place of the Peace Witness in Missions." Gospel Herald, 3 January 1961, pp. 14-15, 19-20.

"Power and the Powerless." Covenant Quarterly 36 (November 1978): 29-35.

"Questions on the Christian Witness to the State." Part A: "Why Should Christians Witness to the State?" Gospel Herald, 30 April and 7, 14, 21 May, 1963, pp. 373, 381-382, 407, 434. Part B: "How Do Christians Witness to the State?" Gospel Herald, 28 May and 4, 11, 25 June 1963, pp. 461, 475, 506, 542. Part C: "What Should Christians Say to the State?" Gospel Herald, 2, 9, 15, 23 July and 13, 20 August, 1963, pp. 560, 572-573, 586, 610, 633, 698-699, 720-721.

"Radical Reformation Ethics in Ecumenical Perspective." Journal of Ecumenical Studies 15 (Fall 1978): 647-661. Reprinted in The Priestly Kingdom, 105-122.

"The Reception of the Just War Tradition by the Magisterial Reformers." History of European Ideas 9 (1988): 1-23.

"A la recherche du Bucer de l'histoire." Bulletin de la societe d'distoire du protestantisme Francaise 122 (1976): 490-506.

"Reformation and Missions: A Literature Review." Occasional Bulletin from the MIssionary Research Library, June 1971, pp. 1-9.

"Reformed Versus Anabaptist Social Strategies: An Inadequate Typology." TSF Bulletin 8 (May-June 1985): 2-7.

"Reinhold Niebuhr and Christian Pacifism." Mennonite Quarterly Review 29 (April 1955): 101-117. Also published as Church Peace Mission Pamphlet #6. Scottdale, Pennsylvania: Herald Press, 1968.

"Response." Theological Education 19 (Autumn 1982): 30-35.

Review of Caesar's or God's? by Peter Meinhold. Mennonite Quarterly Review 38 (1964): 74-76.

Review of Caspar Schwenckfeld, Reluctant Radical: His Life to 1540 by R. Emmet McLaughlin. Horizons: The Journal of the College Theology Society 15 (Spring 1988): 163-164.

Review of Un chretien peut-il etre objecteur de conscience? by Pierre Lorson. Mennonite Quarterly Review 26 (April 1952): 166-167.

Review of Christianity, Diplomacy and War by Herbert Butterfield. Mennonite Quarterly Review 27 (July 1954): 230-232.

Review of Conscience and Compromise by Edward Leroy Long, Jr. Mennonite Quarterly Review 28 (1955): 77-80.

Review of Contemporary Theologies of Mission by Arthur F. Glasser and Donald A. McGabran. Mission Focus 11 (December 1983): 57-58.

Review of The Context of Decision by Gordon Kaufman. Mennonite Quarterly Review 37 (1963): 133-138.

Review of Freedom for Obedience: Evangelical Ethics for Contemporary Times by Donald G. Bloesch. The Journal of Religion 69 (July 1989): 438-439.

Review of Investigationes Historicae: Eglises et Societe au 16 Siecle by Marijn de Kroon and Marc Lienhard. Mennonite Quarterly Review 62 (January 1988): 95.

Review of Krieg, Kriegsdienst und Kriegsdienstverveigerung nach der Botschaft des Neuen Testaments by Walter Bienert. The Mennonite Quarterly Review 27 (October 1953): 356-357.

Review of Land, Piety, Peoplehood: The Establishment of Mennonite Communities in America, 1683-1790 by Richard K. MacMaster. Journal of Church and State (1987): 134-135.

Review of Peace in a Nuclear Age, The Moral Dimensions of Politics, The Catholic Peace Tradition, and Religion and Politics in the United States. America (August 22, 1987), pp. 89-90.

Review of Die religioesen und geistigen Grundlagen der Politik Huldrych Zwinglis: Ein Beitrag zum Problem des christlichen States by Siegfried Rother and Zwinglis Lehre von der goettlichen und menschlichen Gerechtigkeit. Mennonite Quarterly Review 35 (1961): 79-88.

Review of The Responsible Church and the Foreign Mission by Peter Beyerhause and Henry Lefever. Mennonite Quarterly Review 40 (1966): 290.

Review of Tranquillitas Ordinis: The Present Failure and Future Promise of American Catholic Thought on War and Peace by George Weigel. The Conrad Grebel Review 6 (Winter 1988): 95-98.

Review of Unmasking the Powers: The Invisible Forces that Determine Human Existence by Walter Wink. TSF Bulletin 10 (May-June 1987): 34-35.

Review of Le vrai visage de Jeanne d'Arc, heroine de non-violence by Louis Carman. The Mennonite Quarterly Review 16 (January 1952): 94-95.

"The Schleitheim Brotherly Union: Historical Background by John Howard Yoder." Gospel Herald, 22 February 1977, pp. 165-166.

"Sometimes the Truth Surprises." Gospel Herald, 13 September 1983, pp. 633-634.

"The Spirit of God and the Politics of Men." Journal of Theology for Southern Africa 29 (December 1979): 62-71.

"Strategies for Social Change." Radix 13 (September-October 1981): 21-22.

"The Subtle Worldliness." Gospel Herald, 21 December 1954, pp. 1209, 1221.

"Surrender: A Moral Imperative." Review of Politics 48 (Fall 1986): 576-595.

"Symposium on Christianity and Pacifism." Faith and Philosophy: Journal of the Society of Christian Philosophers 2 (April 1985): 97-120.

Symposium Response to "Christianity and Democracy: A Statement of the Institute on Religion and Democracy" by Richard Neuhaus. Center Journal (Summer 1982): 83-88.

"Teaching Mission to Japan." Gospel Herald, 8 May 1960, p. 213.

"The Theology of the Church's Mission." Mennonite Life (January 1966): 30-33.

"To Serve Our God and to Rule the World." The Annual of the Society of Christian Ethics (1988): 3-14.

"The Turning Point in the Zwinglian Reformation." Mennonite Quarterly Review 32 (1958): 128-140.

"The Two Kingdoms." Reply to Anders Nygren's "Luther's Doctrine of the Two Kingdoms." Christus Victor 106 (September 1959): 3-7.

"The Unique Role of the Historic Peace Churches." Brethren Life and Thought 14 (Summer 1969): 132-149.

"Von goettlicher und menschlicher Gerechtigheit." Zeitschrift fuer Evangelische Ethic 6 (May 1962): 166-181.

"The War in Algeria." Gospel Herald, 18 March 1958, pp. 254-256.

"The Way of Peace in a World at War." Gospel Herald, 18, 25 July and 1 August, 1961, pp. 617-618, 637, 645-646, 661-662.

"Das Weib Schweige." Junge Gemeinde (August 1977): 11-12.

"What Do Ye More than They?" Gospel Herald, 22 January 1973, pp. 72-75.

"What Does the Concept of the 'Just War' Mean?" Gospel Herald, 4 June 1968, pp. 496-497.

"'What Would You Do If...?' An Exercise in Situation Ethics." Journal of Religious Ethics 2 (1974): 81-105.

230

"When the State is God." Gospel Herald, 17 February 1954, p. 153.

"Why I Don't Pay All My Income Tax." Gospel Herald, 22 January 1963, pp. 132-134. Reprinted in Sojourners 6 (1977): 11-12.

"Why Speak to Government?" Gospel Herald, 25 January 1966, pp. 73-74.

II. Selected Unpublished Works by Yoder

"The Basis of Barth's Social Ethics."

"Can Modern Armed Conflict Be Conducted Justly?" 5 October 1972.

"Clearing the Decks for Accountability." 10 April 1980.

"How Richard Niebuhr Reasons: A Critique of Christ and Culture." May 1986.

Letter to Stanley Hauerwas. 7 November 1972.

"The Shape of the Debate about the Practicality of Peace." 24 November 1982.

III. Secondary Sources on Yoder

Adams, Bob E. "Christology and Ethics: A Critical and Personal Essay." Southwestern Journal of Theology 21 (Spring 1979), 55-69.

Armour, Rollin. Review of Balthasar Hubmaier: Theologian of Anabaptism. Translated and Edited by John H. Yoder and H. Wayne Pipkin. Perspectives in Religious Studies 17 (Spring 1990): 90-91.

Baasten, Matthew. Review of What Would You Do? by John H. Yoder. Reformed Review 40 (Spring 1987): 263-264.

Barber, C. J. Review of What Would You Do? by John H. Yoder. Journal of Psychology and Theology 12 (Fall 1984): 250.

Basinger, R. Review of What Would You Do? by John H. Yoder. TSF Bulletin 8 (November-December 1984): 32.

Beckley, Harlan. "A Christian Affirmation of Rawls's Idea of Justice as Fairness, Part 1." Journal of Religious Ethics 13 (Fall 1985): 210-242.

_____. "A Christian Affirmation of Rawls's Idea of Justice as Fairness, Part 2." Journal of Religious Ethics 14 (Fall 1986): 229-246.

_____. Review of The Priestly Kingdom by John H. Yoder. Theology Today 42 (October 1985): 371-372.

Bense, Walter F. "The Pacifism of Karl Barth: Some Questions for John H. Yoder." Selected Papers from the 1977 Annual Meeting, American Society of Christian Ethics. Wilfrid Laurier University, Waterloo, Ontario: Council on the Study of Religion, 1977.

Berkhof, Hendrik. Christ and the Powers. Scottdale, Pennsylvania: Herald Press, 1962.

Boers, Arthur. Review of The Fullness of Christ by John H. Yoder. The Other Side 24 (September 1988): 38.

_____. Review of When War Is Unjust by John H. Yoder. The Other Side 21 (October 1985): 21.

Bosch, David J. Review of The Priestly Kingdom by John H. Yoder. Missionalia 13 (November 1985): 141-142.

Brown, Dale W. "Communal Ecclesiology: The Power of the Anabaptist Vision." Theology Today 36 (April 1979): 22-29.

Brown, Ken. Review of What Would You Do? by John H. Yoder. Evangelical Review of Theology 10 (April 1986): 190-191.

Burchard, C. Review of Die Politik Jesus: der Weg des Kreuzes by John H. Yoder. Translated by Wolfgang Krauss. Theologische Zeitschrift 20 (1984): 87-89.

Cartwright, Michael G. "No Peace But Strife Closed in the Sod." Books and Religion: A Monthly Review 14 (November 1986):7, 10-11.

_____. "Practices, Politics, and Performance: Toward a Communal Hermeneutic for Christian Ethics." Unpublished Ph.D. diss., Duke University, 1988.

_____. Review of He Came Preaching Peace by John H. Yoder. Books and Religion 15 (March-April 1987): 14-15.

232

Clapp, Rodney. "Catholics, Anabaptists and the Bomb." The Christian Century 105 (November 2, 1988): 979-981.

Deats, Paul, Jr. "Protestant Social Ethics and Pacifism." In War or Peace? The Search for New Answers, 75-92. Edited by Thomas Shannon. Maryknoll, New York: Orbis Books, 1980.

Dolamo, Ramathate Tseka Hosea. "Religious Pacifism: A Critical Evaluation of John H. Yoder." M. Th. thesis, University of South Africa, 1986.

Eller, Vernard. Review of God's Revolution: The Witness of Eberhard Arnold edited by the Hutterian Society of Brothers and Joh H. Yoder. The Mennonite Quarterly Review 61 (January 1987): 82-83.

_____. Review of The Politics of Jesus by John H. Yoder. Brethren Life and Thought 18 (Spring 1973): 107-108.

Elliott, N. Review of When War Is Unjust by John H. Yoder. The Princeton Seminary Bulletin 5 (1984): 263-266.

Erdahl, L. O. Review of When War Is Unjust by John H. Yoder. Book Newsletter of Augsburg Publishing House 509 (May-June 1984).

Finger, Thomas. "Jesus as Ethical Norm: Anabaptist/Reformed Discussion of The Politics of Jesus." Sojourners 5 (December 1976): 6-8.

Forell, George Wolfgang. "A Christian Rationale for Political Engagement Today." Lutheran Theological Seminary Bulletin 68 (Summer 1988): 7-16.

Friesen, Duane K. Christian Peacemaking and International Conflict. Scottdale, Pennsylvania: Herald Press, 1986.

Greenfield, Guy. Review of The Priestly Kingdom by John H. Yoder. Southwestern Journal of Theology 29 (Fall 1986): 67-68.

Gustafson, James M. Ethics from a Theocentric Perspective. Vol. 1. Chicago: The University of Chicago Press, 1981.

Hardin, Russell. Review of When War Is Unjust by John H. Yoder. Ethics: An International Journal of Social, Political, and Legal Philosophy 95 (April 1985): 763-765.

Hauerwas, Stanley. "Messianic Pacifism." Worldview 16 (June 1973): 29-33.

_____. "The Nonresistant Church: The Theological Ethics of John Howard Yoder." In Vision and Virtue: Essays in Christian Ethical Reflection. Notre Dame, Indiana: Fides Press, Inc., 1974.

_____. The Peaceable Kingdom. Notre Dame, Indiana: University of Notre Dame Press, 1983.

Hays, Richard B. Review of The Priestly Kingdom by John H. Yoder. Quarterly Review: A Scholarly Journal for Reflection on Ministry 6 (Winter 1986): 13-30.

Heffley, Mike. "Biblical Politics: An Evening with John Howard Yoder." Epiphany: A Journal of Faith and Insight 3 (Summer 1983): 84-86.

Herr, Judy Zimmerman. Review of The Priestly Kingdom by John H. Yoder. Journal of Theology for Southern Africa 52 (September 1985): 77-79.

Hill, Michael. Review of The Priestly Kingdom by John H. Yoder. The Reformed Theological Review 44 (Fall 1985): 91-92.

Hoitenga, Dewey. Review of Karl Barth and the Problem of War by John H. Yoder. The Reformed Journal 23 (December 1973): 29-30.

Houser, Gordon. Review of He Came Preaching Peace by John H. Yoder. The Other Side 21 (October 1985): 79-80.

Hughes, David Michael. "The Ethical Use of Power: A Discussion with the Christian Perspectives of Reinhold Niebuhr, John Howard Yoder, and Richard J. Barnet." Unpublished Ph.D. diss., The Southern Baptist Theological Seminary, 1984.

Huetter, Reinhard L. "The Church: Midwife of History or Witness of the Eschaton?" The Journal of Religious Ethics 18 (Spring 1990): 27-54.

Johnson, James T. "Historical Tradition and Moral Judgment: The Case of Just War Tradition." The Journal of Religion 64 (July 1984): 299-317.

Jones, Gregory L. Review of The Priestly Kingdom by John H. Yoder. The Journal of Religion 66 (July 1986): 350-351.

234

Juhnke, James. Review of When War Is Unjust by John H. Yoder. Mennonite Life 40 (September 1985): 28.

King, Robert H. Review of The Priestly Kingdom by John H. Yoder. Christian Century 102 (August 1985): 741.

Kleinheksel, John R. Review of When War Is Unjust by John H. Yoder. Reformed Review 38 (Spring 1985): 295-296.

Koontz, Gayle Louise Gerber. "Bibliography of the Published Writings of John H. Yoder." Unpublished bibliography. January 1988.

_____. "Confessional Theology in a Pluralistic Context: A Study of the Theological Ethics of H. Richard Niebuhr and John H. Yoder." Unpublished Ph.D. diss., Boston University, 1985.

_____. "Confessional Theology in Pluralistic Context: A Study of the Theological Ethics of H. Richard Niebuhr and John H. Yoder." Dissertation Abstract. The Mennonite Quarterly Review 61 (October 1987): 413-418.

_____. Review of He Came Preaching Peace by John H. Yoder. The Mennonite Quarterly Review 61 (April 1987): 239-240.

Kraus, Norman. Review of The Christian Witness to the State by John H. Yoder. The Mennonite Quarterly Review 40 (January 1966): 66-70.

LeMasters, Philip. "Church as the Social Locus of Christian Moral Formation." Proceedings 1990. American Academy of Religion, Southwest Region. Ethics Section. 105-114.

Liao, Timothy. "Luther and the Anabaptists' 'Two Kingdoms' Theory." Taiwan Journal of Theology 6 (March 1984): 15-29.

Long, Edward Leroy, Jr. A Survey of Recent Christian Ethics. New York: Oxford University Press, 1982.

Martin, Dennis D. "Nothing New Under the Sun: Mennonites and History." The Conrad Grebel Review 5 (Winter 1987): 1-27.

McCann, Dennis P. "Hermeneutics and Ethics: The Example of Reinhold Niebuhr." Journal of Religious Ethics 8 (Spring 1980): 27-53.

235

McClendon, James Willam, Jr.   Ethics: Systematic Theology. Vol. 1.
Nashville: Abingdon Press, 1986.

McEntyre, John Erickson.   "The Increasing Significance of Symbolic Resistance
in Selected Fiction from 'War and Peace' to 'Mila 18.'"   Unpublished Ph.D.
diss., Graduate Theological Union, 1981.

Meilaender, Gilbert.   Review of The Priestly Kingdom by John H. Yoder.
Concordia Theological Quarterly 50 (July-October 1986): 275-276.

Miller, John W.   "Schleithem Pacifism and Modernity."   Conrad Grebel Review
3 (Spring 1985): 155-163.

Neuhaus, Richard J.   Review of The Politics of Jesus by John H. Yoder.
Commonweal 99 (22 February 1974): 516-517.

Okholm, Dennis.   "Defending the Cause of the Christian Church: Karl Barth's
Justification of War."   Christian Scholar's Review 16 (1987): 144-162.

Parham, Robert Mereman, III.   "An Ethical Analysis of the Christian Social
Strategies in the Writings of John C. Bennett, Jacques Ellul, and John H. Yoder."
Unpublished Ph.D. diss., Baylor University, 1984.

Parrent, Allan M.   "Christians and the Nuclear Weapons Debate."   Anglican
Theological Review 67 (January 1985): 67-92.

Petzoldt, M.   Review of Die Politik Jesu: der Weg des Kreuzes by John H.
Yoder.   Translated by Wolfgang Krauss. Theologische Literaturzeitung 109
(March 1984): 226-227.

Pinches, Charles.   "Christian Pacifism and Theodicy: The Free Will Defense in
the Thought of John H. Yoder.: Modern Theology 5 (April 1989): 239-255.

Powers, R. S.   Review of What Would You Do? by John H. Yoder.   The
Christian Century 101 (October 17, 1984): 962-964.

Powers, Sheila.   Review of When War Is Unjust by John H. Yoder.   Sojourners
14 (January 1985): 44.

Ramsey, Paul.   Speak Up for Just War or Pacifism.   University Park,
Pennsylvania: The Pennsylvania State University Press, 1988.

Rankin, William. "Six Steps to 'Where We Ought To Be.'" The Witness 71 (March 1988): 10-11, 22.

Redmont, Jane. "Ecumenical, Evangelical, Radical Pacifist: The 'Politics of Jesus' of John Howard Yoder." Harvard Divinity Bulletin 11 (April-May 1981): 6-7.

Rudy, Kathy. "The Politics of Representing Jesus: Jacques Derrida and John Howard Yoder." Critical Theology 1 (1989): 14-22.

Sawatsky, Rodney. "John Howard Yoder." In Non-Violence--Central to Christian Spirituality, 239-269. Edited by Joseph T. Culliton. Toronto Studies in Theology Series, Vol. 8. New York: The Edwin Mellen Press, 1982.

Scriven, Charles Wayne. "The Reformation Radicals Ride Again: After Four Hundred Years of Misrepresentation, Anabaptist Thought Is Not Only Getting A New Hearing But Also Winning Converts." Christianity Today 34 (5 March 1990): 13-25.

_____. "The Transformation of Culture: A Scriptural Perspective." Ph. D. dissertation, Graduate Theological Union, 1985. Published as The Transformation of Culture: Christian Social Ethics After H. Richard Niebuhr. Scottdale, Pennsylvania: Herald Press, 1988.

Shank, David A. Review of The Priestly Kingdom by John H. Yoder. The Mennonite Quarterly Review 60 (April 1986): 215-216.

Skillen, "The Bible, Politics, and Democracy: What Does Biblical Obedience Entail for American Political Thought?" In The Bible, Politics, and Democracy, 55-80. Edited by Richard Neuhaus. Grand Rapids, Michigan: William B.Eerdmans Publishing Company, 1987.

Storrar, William F. "The State and War in Nuclear Age." The Scottish Bulletin of Evangelical Theology 3 (Spring 1985): 53-66.

Sturm, Douglas E. Review of The Priestly Kingdom by John H. Yoder. Journal of the American Academy of Religion 54 (Fall 1986): 622-623.

Tillman, William M., Jr., Review of What Would You Do? by John H. Yoder. Southwestern Journal of Theology 28 (Fall 1985): 70.

Vanelderen, Marlin. "On Studying War--John Howard Yoder." One World 109 (October 1985): 18-19.

Van Gerwen, Jozef M. L. "The Church in the Theological Ethics of Stanley Hauerwas." Unpublished Ph.D. diss., Graduate Theological Union, 1984.

Van Veldhuizen, Milo Dean. "'Philanthropia' in Philo of Alexandria: A Scriptural Perspective." Unpublished Ph.D. diss., University of Notre Dame, 1982.

Verhay, Allen. The Great Reversal: Ethics and the New Testament. Grand Rapids, Michigan: William B. Eerdmans Publishing Company, 1984.

Waters, Brent Phillip. "A Christian Understanding of and Response to Violent Revolution." Unpublished D.Min. diss., School of Theology at Claremont, 1984.

Watson, David L. "Prophetic Evangelism: The Good News of Global Grace." In Wesleyan Theology Today, 219-226. Edited by T. Runyon. Nashville: Kingswood Books, 1985.

Witt, T. W. Review of What Would You Do? by John H. Yoder. Book Newsletter of Augsburg Publishing House 509 (May-June 1984).

Wogaman, J. Philip. A Christian Method of Moral Judgement. Louisville, Kentucky: Westminster/John Knox Press, 1976.

Wood, John A. Review of What Would You Do? by John H. Yoder. Journal of Church and State 27 (Winter 1985): 146-147.

Zimbleman, Joel Andrew. "Theological Ethics and Politics in the Thought of Juan Luis Segundo and John Howard Yoder." Unpublished Ph.D. diss., University of Virginia, 1986.

IV. General Secondary Sources

Arrington, French L. Paul's Aeon Theology in 1 Corinthians. Washington, D.C.: University Press of America, 1978.

Augustine. The City of God. New York: Random House, Inc., 1950.

Barnes, Timothy D. Constantine and Eusebius. Cambridge, Massachusetts: Harvard University Press, 1981.

238

Barth, Markus. Conversation with the Bible. New York: Holt, Rinehart and Winston, 1964.

Bartsch, H. W., ed. Kerygma and Myth. New York: Harper & Row Publishers, 1961.

Beker, J. Christian. Paul the Apostle. Philadelphia: Fortress Press, 1980.

Bultmann, Rudolf. Existence and Faith. New York: Meridan Books, 1960.

_____. Jesus Christ and Mythology. New York: Charles Scribner's Sons, 1951.

_____. Jesus and the Word. New York: Charles Scribner's Sons, 1958.

_____. Theology of the New Testament. Vol. 1. New York: Charles Scriber's Sons, 1951.

Cone, James. God of the Oppressed. New York: Seabury Press, 1975.

Croatto, J. Severino. Biblical Hermeneutics: Toward a Theory of Reading as the Production of Meaning. Maryknoll, New York: Orbis Books, 1987.

Cullmann, Oscar. Christ and Time. Philadelphia: Westminster Press, 1950.

Culpepper, R. Alan. Anatomy of the Fourth Gospel: A Study in Literary Design. Philadelphia: Fortress Press, 1983.

Davis, Harry R. and Robert C. Good, eds. Reinhold Niebuhr on Politics. New York: Charles Scribner's Sons, 1960.

Dodd, C. H. The Apostolic Preaching and Its Developments. London: Hodder and Stoughton, 1936.

_____. Gospel and Law: The Relation of Faith and Ethics in Early Christianity. New York: Columbia University Press, 1951.

_____. The Parables of the Kingdom. New York: Charles Scribner's Sons, 1961.

Doerries, Hermann. Konstantin der Grosse. Stuttgart: W. Kohlhammer, 1958.

Drake, H. A., trans. In Praise of Constantine: A Historical Study and New Translation of Eusebius' Tricennial Orations. Los Angeles: University of California Press, 1975.

Fletcher, Joseph. Situation Ethics: The New Morality. Philadelphia: The Westminster Press, 1966.

Frankena, William K. Ethics. Englewood Cliffs, New Jersey: Prentice-Hall, Inc., 1972.

Frend, W. H. C. The Rise of Christianity. Philadelphia: Fortress Press, 1984.

Gabas Pallas, Raul. Escatologia protestante in la actualidad. Victoriensa: Publicationes del Seminario de Vitoria, 1964.

Gonzalez, Justo L. A History of Christian Thought. Vol. 2 Nashville: Abingdon Press, 1971.

Grant, F. C., ed. Form Criticism. New York: Harper & Row Publishers, 1962.

Gutierrez, Gustavo. The Power of the Poor in History. Maryknoll, New York: Orbis Press, 1983.

Helgeland, John, Robert J. Daly, and J. Patout Burns. Christians and the Military: The Early Experience. Philadelphia: Fortress Press, 1985.

Higgins, A. J. B., ed. The Early Church: Studies in Early Christian History and Theology. Philadelphia: Westminster Press, 1956.

Holsapple, Lloyd B. Constantine the Great. New York: Sheed & Ward, 1942.

Jones, L. Gregory. "Should Christians Affirm Rawls' Justice as Fairness? A Response to Professor Beckley." The Journal of Religious Ethics. 16 (Fall 1988): 251-271.

Kaesemann, Ernst. New Testament Questions of Today. Philadelphia: Fortress Press, 1969.

Kee, Alistair. Constantine Versus Christ. London: SCM Press, Ltd., 1982.

Keresztes, Paul. Constantine: A Great Christian Monarch and Apostle. Amsterdam: J. C. Gieben, 1981.

Kovesi, Julius. Moral Notions. London: Routledge and Kegan Paul, 1967.

Lawlor, H. J. and J. E. L. Oulton, trans. Ecclesiastical History. London: Society for the Promotion of Christian Knowledge, 1927.

Lohfink, Gerhard. Jesus and Community. Philadelphia: Fortress Press, 1984.

MacIntyre, Alasdair. After Virtue. Notre Dame, Indiana: University of Notre Dame Press, 1981.

_____. Whose Justice? Which Rationality? Notre Dame, Indiana: University of Notre Dame Press, 1988.

McCann, Dennis P. Christian Realism and Liberation Theology. Maryknoll, New York: Orbis Books, 1981.

Minear, Paul. Eyes of Faith: A Study in the Biblical Point of View. Philadelphia: Westminster Press, 1946.

Miranda, Jose. Marx and the Bible. Maryknoll, New York: Orbis Press, 1974.

Moltmann, Juergen. The Trinity and the Kingdom. San Francisco: Harper & Row Publishers, 1981.

Niebuhr, H. Richard. Christ and Culture. New York: Harper & Row Publishers, 1951.

Niebuhr, Reinhold. An Interpretation of Christian Ethics. New York: Seabury Press, 1979.

_____. The Nature and Destiny of Man. Vol. 1. New York: Charles Scribner's Sons, 1941.

_____. The Nature and Destiny of Man. Vol. 2. New York: Charles Scribner's Sons, 1943.

O'Donovan, Oliver. Resurrection and Moral Order: An Outline for Evangelical Ethics. Grand Rapids, Michigan: William B. Eerdmans Publishing Company, 1986.

Peachey, Paul, ed. Biblical Realism Confronts the Nation. Scottdale, Pennsylvania: Fellowship of Reconciliation, 1963.

Perrin, Norman. Jesus and the Language of the Kingdom. Philadelphia: Fortress Press, 1976.

_____. The Kingdom of God in the Teaching of Jesus. London: SCM Press, 1963.

Peterson, Erik. Eis Theos: Epigraphische, formgeschichtliche, und religiongeschichtliche Untersuchungen. Goettingen: Dandenhoed & Ruprecht.

_____. Theologische Traktate. Muenchen: Hochland Buecherei, 1951.

Pinches, Charles. "Describing Morally: An Inquiry Concerning the Role of Description in Christian Ethics." Ph. D. diss., University of Notre Dame, 1984.

Rabinow, Paul, ed. The Foucault Reader. New York: Pantheon Books, 1984.

Ramsey, Paul. Basic Christian Ethics. Chicago: The University of Chicago Press, 1950.

_____. Deeds and Rules in Christian Ethics. Lanham, Maryland: University Press of America, 1983.

Rawls, John. A Theory of Justice. Cambridge, Massachusetts: Belknap Press of Harvard University, 1971.

Richardson, E. C., trans. A Select Library of Nicene and Post-Nicene Fathers. (Second Series) Vol. 1. Oxford and New York: 1890.

Roberts, Alexander and James Donaldson, eds. The Ante-Nicene Fathers. Vol. 3. Grand Rapids, Michigan: William B. Eerdmans Publishing Company, 1980.

Schweitzer, Albert. Civilization and Ethics. London: A & C Black Ltd., 1923.

_____. The Quest for the Historical Jesus. New York: The MacMillan Company, 1968.

Sobrino, Jon. Christology at the Cross Roads. Maryknoll, New York: Orbis Books, 1978.

Steinmetz, David D. "The Superiority of Pre-Critical Exegesis." Theology Today 37 (April 1980): 27-38.

Troeltsch, Ernst. The Social Teachings of the Christian Churches. New York: The MacMillan Company, 1931.

Turner, Bryan. Religion and Social Theory: A Materialist Perspective. London: Heinemann Educational Books, 1983.

Wainwright, Geoffrey. "Praying for Kings: The Place of Human Rulers in the Divine Plan of Salvation."Ex Auditu 2 (1986): 117-127.

Walzer, Michael. Spheres of Justice. New York: Basic Books, 1983.

Wilder, Amos. Early Christian Rhetoric: The Language of the Gospel. Cambridge, Massachusetts: Harvard University Press, 1971.

_____. Eschatology and Ethics in the Teaching of Jesus.New York: Harper & Brothers Publishers, 1939.

Willis, Wendell, ed. The Kingdom of God in 20-th Century Interpretation. Peabody, Massachusetts: Hendrickson Publishers, 1987.

INDEX

Adams, B. E., 19-20, 65
Augustine, 114, 122
Barnes, T., 102
Barth, K., 11, 14-17, 152-153
Barth, M., 37
Beckley, H., 21, 26
Bennett, J. C., 5, 154
Berkhof, H., 16, 35, 37, 40-42
Birch, B., 2, 21, 55
Blue, K., 69
Brown, D., 18, 21, 73
Bryan, W. J., 168
Buckley, W. F., 188
Bultmann, R., 48-49, 65
Burchard, C., 21
Burns, J. P., 92, 106
Campbell, A., 168
Cartwright, M., 2-3, 24-25, 37, 50, 53
Celsus, 92
Clapp, R., 21
Colwell, E. C., 5
Cone, J., 76
Croatto, J. S., 67
Culliton, J. T., 8
Cullmann, O., 16-17, 33, 42-44, 49-50, 65
Culpepper, R. A., 54
Daly, R. J., 92, 106
Davis, H. R., 132

Deats, P., 21
Dodd, C. H., 47-49
Doerries, H., 102
Dolamo, R. T. H., 21
Donaldson, J., 113
Drake, H. A., 103
Durnbaugh, D. F., 37
Elliot, N., 21
Epp, E. J., 43
Estep, W. R., 21
Eusebius, 102-105, 107, 109
Fletcher, J., 71
Forell, G. W., 19
Foucault, M., 191-192
Frankena, W., 79
Frend, W. H. C., 102, 195
Friesen, D. K., 21, 73, 133, 187
Gabas Pallas, R., 48
Garrett, J. L., 52
Garrison, W. L., 168
Gonzalez, J. L., 122
Good, R. C., 132
Gustafson, J., 2, 6-7, 19, 189
Gutierrez, G., 159
Hauerwas, S., 2, 8, 20-21, 23, 26, 61, 82, 84, 185-186, 200-201
Helgeland, J., 92, 106
Herberg, W., 15
Hessel, D. T., 46
Hiers, R. H., 47